D0253829

THE DEATH OF COMPETITION

THE DEATH OF COMPETITION

LEADERSHIP AND STRATEGY
IN THE AGE OF
BUSINESS ECOSYSTEMS

James F. Moore

HarperBusiness
A Division of HarperCollins*Publishers*

First paperback edition published 1997.

Designed by Irving Perkins Associates

The Library of Congress has catalogued the hardcover edition as follows:

Moore, James F., 1948–
    The death of competition : leadership and strategy in the age of
business ecosystems / James F. Moore.
      p. cm.
   ISBN 0-88730-809-0
   1. Strategic planning—United States.   2. Strategic alliances
(Business)—United States.   3. Competition—United States.
4. Leadership. I. Title.
HD30.28.M6455   1996
658.4'012—dc20   96-4159

ISBN 0-088730-850-3 (pbk.)

97 98 99 00 01 ❖/RRD 10 9 8 7 6 5 4 3 2 1

To Joanne, Graham, and Arthur

Contents

Acknowledgments

This book benefited immensely from the generosity and able assistance of many fine people. I thank my wife, Joanne Cipolla Moore, for her love, wisdom, patience, and wit through the several years that I devoted to this project. In addition, my two sons Graham and Arthur have asked again and again, "Daddy, when your book is finished, will you have more time to play?" Now I do. I would also like to convey my thanks to the rest of my extended family, including my parents, grandparents, brothers, aunts, uncles, cousins, in-laws, and outlaws.

I am especially grateful to those with whom I have had the opportunity to work closely over the years, and who have become members of my personal ecosystem. Hal Burlingame of AT&T has been a friend for many years, and deserves much of the credit for what I have learned about leadership and organizations. John Petrillo, also of AT&T, taught me a great deal about how to combine intellectual rigor and practical impact, and he has been a true inspiration. Don Schön of MIT has been a trusted mentor and colleague, constantly challenging me to stretch beyond my own limits. Lisa Fitzgibbons and Jane Bouffard have shared in the creation of GeoPartners Research, Inc., from the early days, contributing personal strategy, intellectual partnership, and an ongoing sense of comradeship and adventure. Walter Popper and Fleet Hill have offered steadying, guiding encouragement for many years. Sue

Lowe Franklin has been a reliable friend, a treasured colleague, and an angel of serendipity. Michael Maccoby demonstrated to me that management advisers must be compassionate as well as passionate.

A number of executives helped to make this book happen by sponsoring related research and consulting and by sharing their insights. Jim Henson, creator of the Muppets, illustrated how to dance with change, and how to inspire others to join together to bring visions to life. Bill O'Brien of Starlight Telecommunications is one of the most promising entrepreneurs I know, a man who addresses multiple challenges with continuing creativity. I thank him for sharing his story. Frank Gill, Pat Gelsinger, and Craig Kinney of the Intel Corporation are leaders engaged in one of the most interesting and ambitious future-shaping initiatives in the world of business. All three were vital and valued contributors to the book. Lew Platt, Susan Burnett, Srinivas Sukumar, Claudia Davis, P. J. O'Brien, Kathy Hendrickson, Donna Ritchie, and Byron Anderson of Hewlett-Packard have been key supporters of these ideas. Their many insights are greatly appreciated.

Tom Cummings, Tony Warmsley, and Bob Campany of the Royal Dutch Shell Group provided a rich setting in which I could work with executives to transform scenarios into strategies. These efforts added immensely to the overall approach of this book. On a daily basis, Göran Lindahl, Lennart Haglöf, and Paul Kefalas are engaged in inventing the next ABB Asea Brown Boveri. I thank them for their contribution. Back in 1989, Scott McNealy, Eric Schmidt, Bill Joy, and Nancy Schoendorf of Sun Microsystems opened my eyes wide to the virtues of changing the game.

Much of what I have learned has emerged from working with many fine individuals at AT&T over the years. There are far too many to mention here, and there is too great a risk of omitting someone special to me. Let me then simply express my warm appreciation for all that each of you has contributed. There are two quiet heroes, however, whom I would like to single out and who have been important to my development: Henry "Hoot" Gibson and Tapas Sen. Thanks ever so much.

On the academic front, Gregory Bateson, anthropologist and

cybernetician, put forth seminal concepts that helped me recognize that economic, social, and biological systems have much in common. John Snow of the Episcopal Divinity School challenged me to bring these concepts to action. C. Roland "Chris" Christensen and Harry Lasker, both of Harvard, Richard Pascale of Stanford, Chris and Dianne Argyris, Lee Geltman, Kathy Hearn, and Alan Robinson each taught me in their own special way to understand leadership and strategy as a mental and psychological process—and to work with executives to deepen their capabilities. Bo Ekman underscored the potential for dialogue about business and society. John Rosenblum and Jeane Leidke of the University of Virginia Darden School of Business have been valuable colleagues. They allowed me to see my ideas in the context of others across the field of management, and provided essential encouragement.

Jim Wetterer, a biologist who has done most of his work in affiliation with Harvard's Museum of Comparative Zoology, afforded crucial assistance with ecological and evolutionary concepts, as well as with specific biological examples. My gratitude also to Edward O. Wilson of Harvard for bringing Jim and me together.

A number of management theorists have attempted to unite biology and business, including Bruce Henderson, Michael Rothschild, Richard Nelson, Sidney Winter, Glenn Carroll, Michael Hannan, John Freeman, and Charles Fombrun. However, I owe a special debt to W. Graham Astley, who, during my postdoc work in 1983, pointed out the parallels in ecological and business collapses, and supplied a link in my thinking that I have built on ever since.

Charles Fine of MIT's International Motor Vehicle Program has been important in my understanding of the coevolution of the automobile business. For help in threading my way through the maze of health policy, I would like to thank Sam Levitt, formerly of the Harvard School of Public Health, Alain Entoven and Richard Scott of Stanford, Bo Saxberg of Johnson & Johnson, Norman Weinberg of Emerson Hospital, Don Harrington of AT&T, Kate Wolf formerly of Harvard Community

Health Plan, as well as Ric Marlink of the Harvard AIDS Institute, and the irrepressible David Korkosz. Charles Firestone and the Aspen Institute furnished funding and excellent peer review for a paper on telecommunications and business evolution that proved seminal to this book. Stuart Brotman of Tufts, and Tony Oetinger of Harvard imparted useful insights into telecommunications policy. John Markoff and David Kirkpatrick have been valuable dialogue partners in the world of high technology. Arthur Cipolla Jr. has provided key insights.

My institutional base and second family has been GeoPartners Research, Inc., the strategy consulting and investment firm. Ashton Peery has ably led GeoPartners while I took time away to write this book, keeping our immersion in client challenges vigorously alive. Michelle Crews, as always, kept the community together. Michael Tattersall has taken the ideas and perfected methods to assist managers in developing corresponding strategies. Chris Mines has established business analysis capability to bring our perspective to bear on problems of investment assessment as well as strategic planning. I already mentioned Jane Bouffard and Lisa Fitzgibbons, my longtime collaborators. Abigail Christopher and Tom Hartley supplied vital research, intellectual dialog, and moral support for the book as did Patty Horan, Andrew Kaplan, Ken Bamberger, and Grace Tsai. Other professionals associated with GeoPartners who read and commented on the manuscript include Bob Beitcher and Richard Fishman as well as Ayis Antoniou, Ivar Bazzy, Scott Brady, Abigail Demopulos, Jeff Francer, Ben Goodman, David Halprin, David Hankin, Rebecca Kannam, Linda Levinson, Jim Levitt, and Murray Metcalfe. Nancy Goldberg provided friendship and great graphics. Brenda Jeglinski, Thea Moskat, Maureen Wall, and Mark Anders deserve special mention for their administrative contributions.

Thanks as well to all those others who took the time to convey their thoughts on the manuscript and have not already been mentioned, including Bob Allen, Jim Barksdale, Tom Eisenman, Greg Franklin, Sandy Fraser, Arie DeGeus, John Kelley, David Mellor, Lawrence Miao, Bob Mountain, R. Clay

Mulford, Gil Roeder, Marion Smith, Caroline Vanderlip, Dick Wedemeyer, John Weimeister, Deborah Wolter, Gordon Wu, and our special friend, Amy Thaler.

An author is only as good as his or her editors. I've been blessed with a number of fine ones. They have taught me to write and, in so doing, to think. All of them, without exception, have also become friends. The late Nancy Jackson gave me my first exposure to real editing talent, and I still miss her. Marjorie Williams of Harvard Business School Press worked in my firm for two years, and she taught me a lot about grace in both writing and life. Nan Stone, the stimulating, rigorous, good-humored executive editor of the *Harvard Business Review*, was there for me early and often, all for the price of coffee and good cheer. Esther Dyson has been a wonderful support, demonstrating that character and boldness of both intellect and personal journey matter the most in writing and in life. Joel Kurtzman, executive editor of *Strategy & Business*, has proved a trustworthy guide and ally, not to mention a good friend, as I've grappled with this book and the challenges of big-time publishing. Karen Southwick of *Upside* has been a constant source of ideas and has quelled my panic on several occasions by coming through with emergency editing. Carol Franco of Harvard Business School Press believed in these ideas, and was key in helping me formulate the book in its early stages, and I will always be grateful to her.

Sonny Kleinfield provided editing throughout the book. I thank him for his grace, skill, good humor under pressure, and commitment to the project. Kirsten Sandberg, my editor at HarperBusiness, worked closely with me to bring the manuscript to completion. I appreciate her vast skill, faith, and ability to work around the clock with aplomb. Adrian Zackheim, vice president of HarperBusiness, has been the consummate supporter of the project, its driving conviction and force. Lisa Berkowitz of HarperCollins, and Beth and Leslie Grossman of CMA, did an excellent job in getting the word out about the book. Richard Pine, my agent, has been consistently effective, while also remaining charming and witty. Thanks very much to all of you.

Introduction

Growth, development, and business evolution are on our minds. Entrepreneurship is now the principal concern of businesses large and small. In a fast-moving economy, the status quo is clearly doomed and innovation wins.

Innovation usually requires that other organizations evolve their products and services in concert with yours. You must convince others to dream with you and work at your side. Embracing this challenge changes how you think about your company, your career, your community, and your competition. That's why I chose the title *The Death of Competition*, even though I know that competition is intensifying. In a world of rapid innovation, head-to-head combat is simply not the most useful metaphor for considering your business. It tends to lock you into current patterns of operating and to perpetuate old business models rather than establishing new ones.

Innovation must be the focal point of your vision. In turn, you must enhance collaborations with your customers, suppliers, investors, and other allies. Intel Corporation, for example, is an intensely competitive company that makes microprocessor engines for powering personal computers. Vital to its success are relationships with hundreds of other firms, from giants like Hewlett-Packard and Compaq to tiny makers of electronic games.

Intel *coevolves* with these firms. That is, it seeks ways to work with this web of companies to upgrade everyone's abilities.

To maintain the value of its microprocessor-centered competencies and assets, Intel invests more than $100 million each year to help other companies develop software and hardware that use Intel technology. It encourages video conferencing, multimedia, and other customer applications requiring its most powerful microprocessors. Intel supports advances across the entire computer, communications, and media sector, while assuring the need for its own microprocessors.

Coevolution as a strategic concept is not just for high-tech companies, or for large ones. A magazine must coevolve with its advertisers, readers, contributors, and delivery systems. A restaurant must coevolve with groups of customers, neighboring businesses, and food suppliers. Regardless of your current position, you can unite with others to cultivate and shape the future—of your business, your community, and your life. This book provides ideas to sharpen your vision, engage others, and seize opportunities.

If you want a comprehensive framework for action, then read the first five chapters in sequence. They introduce a practical model for leading business evolution. If you want to focus on specific topics, then look for new ventures in chapter six; struggles for market leadership in chapters seven and eight; alliances among large companies and swarms of smaller ones in chapter nine; the renewal of threatened enterprises, chapter ten; and harmonizing personal and business values, chapter eleven.

The Death of Competition celebrates the birth of many new possibilities. May your enterprises take root and thrive.

1

Why Businesses Fail

Circling the big island of Hawaii in a small plane affords one of the most spectacular visual experiences imaginable. An isolated outcropping in the sea more than 2,000 miles from the nearest continent, Hawaii has as its center Mauna Kea, a magnificent extinct volcano that rises nearly 14,000 feet. Occasionally, its tip is sprinkled with snow. Closer to sea level, along the southeastern shore, glowing red, active volcanoes smolder. These boiling kettles periodically spew lava into the ocean, adding some small contributions to the landmass and generating immense steam clouds. Amid this varied terrain are dozens of distinct and glorious ecosystems, composed of communities of species, and ranging from alpine deserts to teeming rain forests.

For most people, Hawaii brings to mind images of towering hotels and pearl divers, not to mention pineapples and papaya. For me, Hawaii offers a picture of how some communities of businesses behave and evolve.

For most of its thirty-million-year history, Hawaii was a marvelously self-contained biological world. Plants and animals arrived by wind or wave, but few established themselves. The best scientific estimates are that a successful plant immigration occurred only once every 20,000 to 30,000 years. These few colonists gave rise to a wide diversity of new species. From some 270 colonizing flowering plants, more than 1,000 were created. From a few hundred insect settlers, around 10,000 came into being. From no more than 15 bird species, more than 70 developed.[1]

Evolving in protected isolation, Hawaii's flora and fauna are reminiscent of traditional industries: heavily protected by tariffs and regulations, old guard owners, and other well-entrenched interests. Inefficient technologies and business processes abound, similar to the unique life-forms that inhabit the Hawaiian islands.

Unlike Hawaii, however, traditional industries are not scenes of verdant splendor. More often, they exhibit intractable class divisions and crusty resistance to anything that threatens the established order. Yet the pattern of their establishment and the dynamics of their demise are strikingly similar.

Hawaii's prolonged period of ecological equilibrium was snapped by the arrival of Polynesian voyagers more than 1,500 years ago. These settlers brought pigs, dogs, and a variety of new plants. Western influence commenced with James Cook's landing in 1778. Subsequent voyages introduced ants, wasps, cats, rats, mosquitoes, and an immense array of plants. These invaders wrought havoc in paradise. More than 40 percent of the indigenous Hawaiian bird species have become extinct since human settlement began. More recently, golf courses and housing developments have radically transformed many local ecosystems.[2]

In much the same way, new technologies, business processes, and organizational life-forms invade all traditional businesses. They are borne on the winds of global capital flows and managerial migrations. They cross bridges of deregulation. They are encouraged by government policies that foster economic development. A vast tangle of skills and processes is being rendered obsolete.

As a management theorist of sorts, I realize the need and the benefits of these changes. But I also acknowledge the hurt and confusion that innumerable individuals feel as their businesses and livelihoods come under intense pressure. For many people, economic and technological progress constitutes the destruction of their Hawaiian paradise.

The Death of Competition

Shift now from beaches to traffic, from sand to carpet, from bright Hawaiian shirts to gray wool suits. Every day in my work, I observe companies that are drastically affected by the changing ecology of business competition and that seek ways to understand and shape the transformations engulfing them. I tell them about the death of competition.

Not that competition is vanishing. In fact it is intensifying. But competition as most of us have routinely thought of it is dead—and any business manager who doesn't recognize this is threatened. Let me explain. The traditional way to think about competition is in terms of offers and markets. Your product or service goes up against that of your competitor, and one wins. You improve your product by listening to customers, and by investing in the processes that create it.

The problem with this point of view is that it ignores the context—the environment—within which the business lies, and it ignores the need for coevolution with others in that environment, a process that involves cooperation as well as conflict. Even excellent businesses can be destroyed by the conditions around them. They are like species in Hawaii. Through no fault of their own, they find themselves facing extinction because the ecosystem they call home is itself imploding. A good restaurant in a failing neighborhood is likely to die. A first-rate supplier to a collapsing retail chain—a Bradlees, Caldor, or Kmart—had better watch out.

Sometimes the ecosystem as a whole is more or less robust, but the particular niche a business occupies is challenged by newly arriving species. The problem becomes that there are so many similar businesses in a market that none can make a reasonable profit. Airlines, steel companies, long-distance telephone companies, and deregulated electric utilities all face this dilemma. Their contributions have become commodities traded mainly on price. One of the most significant side effects of electronic airline reservation systems has been to enable customers to do comparative shopping. This newly efficient market has been a major factor in driving down prices and margins.

The continued expansion of electronic shopping and the Internet will bring commoditylike trading into markets ranging from groceries to automobiles. While such intense price competition is good for consumers in the short run, the threat of razor-thin margins makes it difficult for companies to justify investing in next generation offers—and can stifle innovation.

Neither of these types of business problems—the collapse of the economic fabric around your business or the invasion of your territory by too many similar contributors—is recognized by the conventional view of competition. In my consulting practice, I have seen instance after instance of well-meaning, thoughtful, hardworking people whose businesses were wrecked by these effects. This despite having good products and services, produced by well-run processes.

By contrast, the executives who lead the world's largest, most sophisticated businesses know a great deal about these issues. In many instances, a large portion of their strategic planning budgets is spent on figuring out how to turn around businesses that are being commoditized by aggressive new competitors, often located in lands halfway around the globe. And in more cases than they care to admit, they know that their products and services face limited lives, because the economic and social conditions to which they contribute are becoming obsolete.

I know a number of executives who find themselves stunningly helpless in the face of these challenges. Their models of management, based on traditional product and service competition and process improvement, are necessary but not sufficient. One executive, who oversees a multibillion-dollar enterprise, told me, "I sometimes dream that I'm driving along in my car, and when I go to make a turn, my steering wheel won't grab. I turn the wheel, but the car just keeps going straight. In this nightmare, I look more closely at the steering wheel, and discover it is one of those plastic wheels for babies. It looks more or less real, but does nothing."

One response is downsizing. With great resolve and a degree of luck, a firm can be cut down to size in advance of collapsing markets. People can be put on the streets. Assets can be written off. Costs can be cut before ruthless price competition causes revenues to fall. This tactic works for a while, but ultimately ruins the business. Morale sinks. Economies of scale are lost. Costs cannot drop forever. Margins suffer. Investors and other stakeholders withdraw. The last person out shuts off the lights.

Another response is market creation. Many executives rightly recognize that innovation is the only way to move forward. They search out growing economic sectors and promising new approaches—the Internet, biotechnology and health care, new markets like those in Asia. Here they face a different concern, one also not foreseen by the traditional concept of competition: Market creation is actually a form of applied economic development. It requires intensive cooperation among diverse contributors to realize a workable economic future. It takes generating shared visions, forming alliances, negotiating deals, and managing complex relationships. Few have been schooled in these arts, nor are they anticipated by most corporate planning and budgeting systems or supported by conventional organizational structures and job descriptions. So, in many cases, the new market creation initiative stumbles along. The originating executives should be commended for aiming at new business development, but their success rate is likely to be disappointing.

A Perspective from Which to Lead Business Evolution

The rate of economic change is going to continue to be high. Obsolescence and commoditization will not abate. What we need are better tools for business development and market creation. This book provides a start. Its intended audience includes entrepreneurs and corporate managers, as well as interested citizens who are concerned about the economic well-being of our society. It is intended to be a book of hope, despite its title. Beyond the death of competition lies the advent of something new and better. There are managers and companies who are figuring out how to prosper in the new economy, and who have much to teach us.

In the new world, product and service competition remains an important aspect of what we do, as does process improvement. But the new paradigm is about market creation. It is about envisioning and helping to shape networks of contributions and processes in order to weave rich new economic tapestries.

Let me illustrate what I mean. ABB Asea Brown Boveri is a worldwide electrical engineering company that provides power generation technology, electricity transmission and distribution systems, and a wide variety of electrically powered industrial equipment.[3] Headquartered in Zurich, it is jointly held by Swedish and Swiss owners and does business in 140 countries. For many years, it has been widely recognized as a source of innovative strategy-making and leadership.

In 1994, Paul Kefalas became CEO of ABB Canada, a region suffering from stagnant sales. The classic approach to reinvigorating the region would have been to concentrate on improving products and processes—that is, to ask what new offers might really catch on and what could be done to produce them efficiently and effectively? These questions direct attention to the present, and to oneself. Kefalas did the opposite. He asked his organization to look outward to the business environment it hoped to serve, and forward to the future. What he wondered was, Who are the major shapers of the future in this region? What visions and strategies do they have? By gleaning insights into the influences and interests shaping industry in Canada, he was able to set up learning teams to work with the movers and shakers to find ways that ABB could contribute to their success.

Leading companies were approached and asked to share their strategies with ABB. Prospects were selected because of their importance in influencing the future, regardless of whether they happened to be ABB customers. When a company was willing, ABB assembled a small group of experts from across ABB's units and had them work with the company's representatives to conceive creative ways to help the company realize its dreams. In one case, a large mining concern was struggling to reduce production costs and create safer working conditions. ABB is now collaborating with this firm to produce a system of mining robots, controlled by technicians stationed in comfortable offices remote from the mine, that can handle many of the most perilous and unpleasant tasks. This firm had not been an ABB client, nor was it being targeted by conventional product-oriented sales efforts.

Doing business this way has produced dramatic results for ABB Canada. More than a dozen major customer-partnering arrangements, including several joint ventures, were established by the end of 1995. Sales have turned strongly upward. Because most of the new sales are in the context of long-term partnering agreements, revenues can be expected to continue to increase.

As we will see throughout this book, close attention to one's economic environment, and to those influencing its evolution, is essential to prosperity in the new economy. Indeed, the corporate strategy for ABB Canada reads, "ABB contributes to the success of its customers by developing mutually beneficial long-term relationships." Not a word about specific technologies or offers or markets. This strategy stresses that, in an economy of constant change, what you do is not as important as how your capabilities relate to what others are doing. Strategy-making involves having an awareness of the big picture and finding ways to play a role in it.

Successful business strategy helps us coevolve with others to create more attractive futures. Along this line, Kefalas tells an interesting story. In 1995, ABB moved its Canadian headquarters to a new building on the outskirts of Montreal, near the airport. Down this stretch of highway lie other similar buildings, housing multinational firms like Canon, Motorola, and Sun Microsystems. In early 1995, an entrepreneur bought a flagging fast-food restaurant on this same strip. After carefully studying the area, the new owner concluded that what this microeconomy of corporate headquarters really needed was not more fast food but a high quality restaurant catering to executives. Within months, the resulting restaurant was a runaway success, largely because it filled a need. Put another way, it nicely complemented the other components of the local economic system—the real estate development activities, the office buildings, the airport, and the executives working in the area.

For ABB Canada and the restaurant, competitive advantage stems principally from their cooperative, coevolving relationships with a network of other contributors to the overall economic scene. This is the new paradigm in strategy-making, and it means the end of competition as we know it. The basic idea is simple: Understand the economic systems evolving around you and find ways to contribute. Start with an understanding of the big picture rather than of products and services. Of course, there are many subtle matters of leadership and strategy that must be addressed in order to succeed. In the new economic environment, many otherwise great businesses fail, because the context around them changes, rendering them unimportant or obsolete. The rest of this book will be devoted to exploring these issues.

The new paradigm requires thinking in terms of whole systems—that is, seeing your business as part of a wider economic ecosystem and environment. Systems thinking is a mental capability that can be strengthened and improved. There are a number of ways to do so. My personal favorite is to study biology, and especially ecology. Nature is endlessly inventive and fascinating. This book includes a fair amount of biology. The biology may sometimes seem excessive to a business reader, but it serves an indispensable purpose. Biological examples are quite simply the most direct way to explain difficult systems concepts. Each time you master a biological example, you learn a systems concept that will be valuable for comprehending the dynamics of business in the new economy.

Frameworks for Understanding Change

During the past decade, a great deal of insight has been gleaned about complex biological communities—illuminated by biologists poking around in Central American jungles, collecting insects in Asia, and observing birds in the Arctic. Much of this work has focused on the intricate and far-reaching relationships among species: predator and prey, pollinator and plant, protector and herd. What has become clear is that some ecosystems, notably those besieged by wave after wave of potential settlers, develop a special resiliency, flexibility, and resistance to catastrophes. In contrast, those that develop in isolation like Hawaii can become highly vulnerable to ecological disasters, and may even face mass extinctions.

Recent work in community ecology has dwelled on topics like "keystone" species, the most critical of the species in an ecosystem. When they disappear from an ecosystem, life within the system itself changes radically. One example is the sea otter. Sea otters on the California coast prey on sea urchins. The urchins feast on kelp beds and other seaweeds along the ocean floor. When the otters were hunted almost to extinction during the nineteenth century, urchin populations grew exponentially and consumed much of the kelp beds, diminishing the biodiversity of the ecosystem. The ocean floor became almost barren. Through aggressive efforts, conservationists reintroduced the sea otter to the area. The urchins have now been harvested and the rich complexity along the coast restored.

Biologists have also concentrated on highly aggressive "exotic" species that can have a particularly disruptive effect when injected into an ecosystem. The hydrilla plant, for instance, was introduced into Florida from Asia in the 1950s. Today hydrilla infests over 40 percent of the waterways in the state—choking lakes and rivers, killing native fish and other wildlife. The hydrilla is almost impossible to control and seems destined to have a permanently damaging effect on biological diversity and robustness in the region.

An excellent chronicle of the enormous progress in ecological studies is found in Edward O. Wilson's masterly *The Diversity of Life*, a rich source of inspiration to anyone wishing to understand the majesty of complex systems.[4]

Unfortunately, the study of business communities lags well behind the biological. Yet close examination of the history of business innovation and the creation of wealth shows that there are important parallels between these two seemingly dissimilar worlds.

While biological analogies are often applied to the study of business, they are frequently applied much too narrowly. Almost invariably, the recurring focus is on the evolution of species. For example, some argue that in a market economy a Darwinian selection occurs in which the fittest products and companies survive. More recently, as businesses have been dissected into processes through the quality and reengineering movements, some now maintain that the fittest processes and systems of processes drive out the weak. In either instance, the "species" are seen to be subject to genetic mutation and selection that gradually transforms them.

In my own work, I have become convinced that the world is more complicated than that, and that we must think in grander terms. Species-level improvement of business processes is unquestionably crucial for keeping companies successful, and creates unmistakable value for society. But there are complementary forms of evolution that play vital but grossly underrated roles in both biology and business. They encompass the ecological and evolutionary interactions that occur across an entire ecosystem, comprising all the organisms of a particular habitat as well as the physical environment itself. Leaders who learn to understand these dimensions of ecology and evolution will find themselves equipped with a new model for devising strategy, and critical new options for shaping the future of their companies.

In biological ecosystems, changes take place over different time scales: many ecological changes occur within the lifetime of the individual organism, whereas evolutionary changes transpire over numerous generations. In business ecosystems,[5] these two time scales collapse into one, because, unlike biological species, a business can guide its own evolution and effect dramatic evolutionary changes during its lifetime. A leader in a business ecosystem has an important edge over the species in a biological ecosystem: the ability to see the big picture and understand the dynamics of the ecosystem as a whole. This enables a business to alter its traits to better fit its ecosystem. What is more, a business can anticipate future changes in its ecosystem and evolve now so that it is well prepared to face future challenges.

This book is meant to be a field guide to the complexities of biological and business ecosystems, those vast webs of intricate relationships. I will examine how biological and business ecosystems pass through distinct stages of development, and how different approaches are best suited to different stages. Understanding the intricacies of ecological and evolutionary relationships will help you turn them to your advantage. By applying principles borrowed from biology, you can help your business both thrive and grow.

Coevolution: Working Together to Create the Future

The late anthropologist Gregory Bateson, who had a lifelong obsession with the workings of complex systems, greatly influenced my thinking. His thought-provoking theories of coevolution, culture, and addiction as they applied to natural and social systems are very intriguing, and I was struck by how he often studied systems in biological terms and then tried to understand how consciousness played its part in those systems.[6]

In his thinking, Bateson focused on patterns. One of his observations was that behaviors within systems—companies, societies, species, families—coevolve. What does "coevolve" mean in this context? In his book *Mind and Nature*, Bateson describes coevolution as a process in which interdependent species evolve in an endless reciprocal cycle—"changes in species A set the stage for the natural selection of changes in species B," and vice versa. Take the caribou and the wolf. The wolf culls the weaker caribou, which strengthens the herd. But with a stronger herd, it is imperative for wolves to evolve and become stronger themselves to succeed. And so the pattern is not simply competition or cooperation, but coevolution. Over time, as coevolution proceeds, the whole system becomes more hardy.

From Bateson's standpoint, coevolution is more important a concept than simply competition or cooperation. The same holds true in business. Too many executives focus their time primarily on day-to-day product and service-level struggles with direct competitors. Over the past few years, more managers have also emphasized cooperation: strengthening key customer and supplier relationships, and in some cases working with direct competitors on initiatives like technical standards and shared research to improve conditions for everyone.[7]

A small number of the most effective firms in the world develop new business advantages by learning to lead economic coevolution. These companies—such as Intel, Hewlett-Packard, Shell, Wal-Mart, Creative Artists Agency, and others discussed in this book—recognize that they live in a rich and dynamic environment of opportunities. The job of their top management is to seek out potential centers of innovation where, by orchestrating the contributions of a network of players, they can bring powerful benefits to bear for customers and producers alike. Their executives must not only lead their current competitors and industries—whether by competition or cooperation—but hasten the coming together of disparate business elements into new economic wholes from which new businesses, new rules of competition and cooperation, and new industries can emerge. The rest of this book gives you an inside look at how these companies are working consciously to shape business evolution itself.

The New Approach Is Spreading, Obliterating Industry Boundaries

There are certain spots on the earth—Amazon rain forests, for instance—where biological evolution proceeds at madcap speed. In these hyperdomains, nature brazenly experiments with new evolutionary loops and wrinkles, as well as new strategies for genetic invention. As a consequence, new organisms are spawned that, in due course, crawl out and populate the rest of the world.

Similar and unprecedented upheaval is astir in the world of business. There are certain identifiable hot spots of rapidly accelerating evolutionary activity in the global economy, places where the speed of business is exceedingly fast and loose. New technologies, deregulation, and changes in customer behavior are the metaphorical equivalent of floods and fires, opening up new competitive landscapes. On such newly cleared and fertile grounds, embryonic or transformed businesses are sprouting.

These new renditions are businesses with an edge. In a sense, they are renegades. In their marauding ways, they do not respect traditional industry paradigms and partitions. Indeed, what they share is a tendency to upend business and industry models and to redraw increasingly porous boundaries.

What we are seeing, in fact, is the end of industry.

That's not to say that we now need to mourn the dissolution of the airline industry or the cement industry. Rather, it means the end of industry as a useful concept in contemplating business. The notion of "industry" is really an artifact of the slowly paced business evolution during the middle of this century. The presumption that there are distinct, immutable businesses within which players scramble for supremacy is a tired idea whose time is past. It has little to do with what is shaping the world. The designation itself is simplistic, describing certain players better than others. But, in truth, the label is not much more than a crude grid used to compare and contrast businesses, a fiction conjured up by policymakers and regulators, investment analysts, and even academic students of business strategy.

There has been a profound change in management thinking of senior executives over the last two or three years. Earlier, many senior managers could rightfully be accused of living in denial about the structural transformations of the world economy and its impact on their businesses. Today, nearly no senior management team can really be charged with living in such a state. There is no need to argue that the economic times have shifted—there is widespread agreement that this is true. The traditional industry boundaries that we've all taken for granted throughout our careers are blurring—and in many cases crumbling.

Michael Ovitz is one potent catalyst for such change. Ovitz, former chairman of Creative Artists Agency and current president of Disney, has broken from conventional business approaches to invent whole new business ecosystems. In 1991, with characteristic adventurousness, Ovitz extended CAA's territory well beyond packaging talent to advertising product by successfully stealing a big chunk of the Coca-Cola account from McCann Erickson. Today, Ovitz is masterminding yet another unprecedented business ecosystem, a new advertising agency in which both Coke and Disney have stakes. As president of Disney's ever evolving empire, Ovitz has identified and pieced together matchless resources to create a whole system. Who would have thought that Disney would leverage its branding expertise and codevelop a business with Coke? And yet, who better than Ovitz and his team at Disney to advise Coke on how to retain and strengthen its brand? Ovitz has orchestrated a highly innovative whole economic system that will likely engender hundreds of co-branding and merchandising ventures.

Disney, under the Ovitz leadership, is not the only one broaching its boundaries. Along with its tuners and amplifiers, Circuit City is now selling used cars. Shell Oil, to my surprise, ranks as the largest seller of packaged sausages in the Scandinavian countries. A good many of its gasoline stations have been converted into discount convenience stores that quench the appetites of motorists as well as cars.

Enter a New Logic to Guide Action

The important question for management today is not whether such changes are upon us but how to make strategy in this new world. Few management teams have been able to put together systematic approaches for dealing with the new business reality. Most find themselves struggling with varying degrees of effectiveness, but with no clear way to think about and communicate, let alone confront, the new strategic issues.

What is most needed is a new language, a logic for strategy, and new methods for implementation. Many of the old ideas simply don't work anymore. For instance, diversification strategies that emphasize finding "attractive" industries often assume the fixedness of industry structure, yet our experience tells us that industry structures evolve very rapidly. Our traditional notions of vertical and horizontal integration fail us in the new world of cooperating communities. Competitive advantage no longer accrues necessarily from economies of scale and scope. Many firms can attain the volume of production to be efficient. Flexible systems are widely available that enable firms to customize their offers, proliferate variety, and do so at little additional cost. In the new world, scale and scope matter, but only as they contribute to a continuing innovation trajectory so that a company continually lowers its costs while increasing its performance.

Companies agitating to be leaders in the volatile new world order must transform themselves profoundly and perpetually so as to defy categorization. Is Wal-Mart a retailer, a wholesaler, or an information services and logistics company? Is Intel governed by the economic realities of the semiconductor industry, or does it lead one of several coevolving, competing personal computer–centered ecosystems? Are its competitors Texas Instruments and NEC or Microsoft and Compaq?

In place of "industry," I suggest an alternative, more appropriate term: *business ecosystem*. The term circumscribes the microeconomies of intense coevolution coalescing around innovative ideas. Business ecosystems span a variety of industries. The companies within them coevolve capabilities around the innovation and work cooperatively and competitively to support new products, satisfy customer needs, and incorporate the next round of innovation. Microsoft, for example, anchors an ecosystem that traverses at least four major industries: personal computers, consumer electronics, information, and communications. Centered on innovation in microprocessing, the Microsoft ecosystem encompasses an extended web of suppliers including Intel and Hewlett-Packard and myriad customers across market segments.

A second new term is "opportunity environment," a space of business possibility characterized by unmet customer needs, unharnessed technologies, potential regulatory openings, prominent investors, and many other untapped resources. Just as biological ecosystems thrive within a larger environment, so do business ecosystems. As traditional industry boundaries erode around us, companies often unexpectedly find themselves in fierce competition with the most unlikely of rivals. At the same time, the most creative and aggressive companies exploit these wider territories, transforming the landscape with new ecosystems. Thus, shaping cohesive strategy in the new order starts by defining an opportunity environment. Within such an environment, strategy-making revolves around devising novel ways to seize opportunities and create viable networks with other business ecosystems.

Unfortunately, most prevailing ideas on strategy today begin with the wrongheaded assumption that competition is bounded by clearly defined industries. As a result, these ideas are nearly useless in the current business climate and are sure to be even less valid in the future. Can one understand the economic events of tomorrow relying on these ideas? I very much doubt it. It is more important to see a company within its food web than in competition with superficially similar firms bundled together in an industry.

We compete in a bifurcated world. Executives today really must view strategy from two perspectives: They must pay attention to the wider opportunity environment and strive to lead in establishing the business ecosystems that will best utilize it. The dominant new ecosystems will likely consist of networks of organizations stretching across several different industries, and they will joust with similar networks, spread across still other industries.

At the same time, executives must continue to see their

companies in the traditional sense, as members of homogenous industries clawing away at rivals for market share and growth. In terms of strategy, it no longer matters if the industries are old and venerable like banking and automobiles, or frisky new ones like cable television and personal computers. So understanding one's industry will be only the first step to pursuing customers, innovation, and the creation of wealth.

Learn from Companies Investing in the New Approach

A word about structure and intent: In this book, I put on my naturalist's outfit and report from the field some observations on leading businesses in the new and fluid environment. This book combines scholarship with on-the-ground accounts to inspire lasting change in the way that corporate leaders formulate strategy and purpose—thinking as biologists and cognitive scientists—so that they can triumph in this marvelous new world. I believe that this change in conceptualizing is vitally important for three reasons.

First, the conditions and challenges prevalent in the fastest-moving sectors of the global economy are spreading inexorably to all the others. The dynamics of these centers, and the challenges confronting their feistiest companies and leaders, are now relevant to us all.

Second, some of the hottest centers of economic competition—computers, communications, media, retailing, health care—are now devising fresh approaches to strategy and leadership. These approaches are not very well understood, even by many of their creators, and they surely are not appreciated by the wider public. Nevertheless, the scope of the strategic ambitions are truly breathtaking. If their creators succeed in their endeavors, their initiatives will have profound implications in our daily lives. What it already means, as the title of this book emphasizes, is the end of competition as we know it.

Third, these ideas are already propagating across the general business landscape and thus are guaranteed to have a dramatic and irreversible impact on how we do business from now on.

Because of these reasons, business people, no matter what business they conduct, must comprehend at least the broad outlines of what is afoot.

The Special Task of Business Leadership: Creating Communities of Shared Imagination

In one significant respect, a strictly biological metaphor does not apply to business. Unlike biological communities of coevolving organisms, business communities are social systems. And social systems are composed of real people who make decisions. A powerful shared imagination, focused on envisioning the future, evolves in a business ecosystem that is unlike anything in biology. Conscious choice does play an important role in ecology. Animals often choose their habitats, their mates, and their behavior. In the economic world, however, strategists and policymakers and investors spend a great deal of time trying to understand the overall game and find fruitful ways to play it or change it. This consciousness is central to economic relationships.

Even more, shared imagination is what holds together economies, societies, and companies. Therefore, a great deal of leadership and business strategy relies on creating shared meaning, which in turn shapes the future. For example, during 1995 millions of people from diverse backgrounds became convinced that the Internet would become a major locus for commerce, entertainment, and personal communication. They rushed to become involved and, in the act of so doing, established a foundation for the very reality they believed was coming about. While many other factors encouraged the exponential growth of interest in the Internet, Sun Microsystems played a powerful role by introducing a software language called Java. Java made it possible to create appealing animated experiences across the Internet.

Sun makes a wide range of computers. Java was the result of a small research project, outside the company mainstream. Nonetheless, Sun executives saw Java's potential to enliven the community. Sun executives chose not to treat Java as just another product. Instead, they essentially gave away Java to the rest of the world in order to feed the Internet frenzy and reinforce Sun's image as a leader of the movement. What mattered was Java the campaign—not Java the product. A widespread perception formed that Sun was prescient and well positioned for the future. Sun's sales rose, its stock appreciated, and it became more able to get other stakeholders to follow its lead.

It is the mind that imparts the harmony and the sense and the syncopation to the business ecosystem. The larger patterns of business coevolution are maintained by a complex network of choices, which depend, at least in part, on what participants are aware of. As Gregory Bateson stressed, if you change the ideas in a social system, you change the system itself. We are seeing the birth of ideas. The very fact that new ideas are coming into existence is changing the conditions. If you don't follow these new ideas, you will be totally lost.

As companies get more sophisticated in creating new ecosystems, become more like the guiding hand of a forester or gardener in an ecological environment, the more this new level of consciousness will become the dominant reality of business strategy. The game of leadership will evolve to new levels. There is a wonderful book of business history by Alfred Chandler called *The Visible Hand.* It chronicles the rise of the multidivisional organization between 1900 and 1930 and the consciousness of people like Alfred Sloane who made the development of this then new organization possible.[8] We are witnessing the next revolution beyond multidivisional organizations and beyond the visible hand. It is the ability in an environment of immense resources, immense plasticity, and powerful information systems to make and break microeconomic relationships with enormous subtlety and velocity. We are entering an age of imagination.

In an age of imagination, the ultimate struggle among companies is for the souls of customers and the hearts of vast communities of suppliers and other associated companies. Strange things can happen in the new world of virtual organizations.

In the new world, strategy based on conventional competition and cooperation gives way to strategy based on coevolution—which in turn defines a new level of competition. At this higher level, competition defines attractive futures and galvanizes concerted action. We can vividly see the tremendous power of a company like Microsoft, which leads and shapes the collective behavior of thousands of associated suppliers, even though during most of the years of its most powerful influence, Microsoft never had more than $6 billion in sales.

But heightened consciousness of the benefits of ecosystem power and influence can also make prospective partners wary of committing to a leader. Competition to lead coevolution can bring its own peculiar paranoia—and fragment a community of companies. We already see this sort of effect within the PC business, where the heightened consciousness of Microsoft's role in overturning IBM's dominion has put all participants in the computer, communications, and even the entertainment business on notice.

Now prospective allies and partners of Microsoft appreciate the costs as well as the benefits of allegiance to the company from Redmond. Many of them have become reluctant coadventurers. In the summer of 1993, for example, the "Cablesoft" new media discussions among Microsoft, cable giants TCI and Time Warner, and other companies broke down because the partners' worries over Microsoft's motives and leadership outweighed the genuine benefits that appeared to be achievable by working together. Such worries also helped Sun Microsystems and Java. Java appealed to some stakeholders in part because it did not orignate from Micosoft. The success of Sun and Java was welcomed as a limiter of Microsoft's influence on the future.

The New Ecology of Business

In the chapters that follow, we will look at how business ecosystems develop like biological ecosystems. The heart of strategy is understanding these evolutionary patterns. We will tour the four distinct stages of business ecosystems: Pioneering, Expansion, Authority, and Renewal. In reality, the stages blur, and the managerial challenges of one stage often recur in another. Still, we can observe each of the four stages in many companies over time, across businesses as disparate as retailing, entertainment, and pharmaceuticals. What is consistent from business to business is the process of coevolution, the complex interplay between competitive and cooperative business strategies.

This book serves to fill in the blanks, so to speak, of a new ecological road map of business evolution and competition. For it is this road map that may well guide us to the future of economic systems.

The immense changes that have taken place in business are minor compared to what is yet to come. When an ecological approach to management becomes more common, and when an increasing number of executives become conscious of coevolution, the pace of business change will accelerate at an exponential rate. Executives whose horizons are bounded by traditional industry perspectives will miss the real challenges and opportunities facing their companies. Shareholders and directors, who perceive the new reality, will eventually oust them. For companies caught up in dynamic business ecosystems, the stakes are considerable, but the rewards are commensurate and the challenges exhilarating as never before.

2

An Ecological Metaphor

A quarter of the way around the globe from our Hawaiian paradise lies Costa Rica, a land that while physically very similar is biologically profoundly different.[1] Like Hawaii, Costa Rica is a tropical land of erupting volcanoes and ecological diversity. The difference is location: Costa Rica sits squarely on the land bridge between North and South America, not isolated in the vast Pacific Ocean. For nearly three million years, Costa Rica has been continually invaded by innumerable species journeying from the north and the south. The term "exotic species" scarcely has meaning in a place so accessible to new entrants.

The survivors in this caldron of competition are vigorous and tenacious defenders of their niches. Needing to constantly ward off invaders, the species acquire layers of protection. Plants, for example, develop an elaborate array of booby traps against their predators, including hairlike appendages that make it treacherous for insects to walk across the stems, glue-like substances that entrap enemies, and substances that block digestion. The combined result of millions of such defenses in millions of species is that very few exotics manage to establish themselves, and even those only to a limited extent. Overall, the ecosystems of Costa Rica are much more robust and resilient than their Hawaiian counterparts. Unlike Hawaii's fragile ecosystems, Costa Rica's are notably resistant to disturbances by Johnny-come-lately exotics. Moreover, the Costa Rican ecosystems are generally better able to restore themselves after an attack. This latter capability is clearly evident in the remarkable story of the restoration of the dry forest.

The Costa Rican dry forest has long proved alluring to farmers and cattle ranchers looking for land. By the middle of this century, nearly all of the forest had been cleared of native species. Recently, however, a major campaign began to restore the forest. Starting in 1971, through the assistance of the Costa Rican government and with funds raised by environmental organizations around the world, land was purchased and incorporated into Costa Rica's national park system. Ecological regeneration of the pasture and farmlands was seeded by the few remaining stands of primary forest. Almost immediately, native dry forest species have begun to reestablish themselves throughout the new park areas. Park biologists estimate that within another fifty years or so the replenished areas will be virtually indistinguishable ecologically from undisturbed native forest.

What we see, then, is that natural ecosystems vary widely in their robustness and ability to repel challenges. While they still develop quite intricate relationships, ecosystems like Hawaii that coevolve in comparative isolation and protection from intruders don't acquire effective defenses. These ecosystems are extremely vulnerable to exotic species, and find it difficult to rebound after catastrophes. On the other hand, ecosystems that evolve under a constant flood of new entrants develop a nearly impenetrable toughness.

Similarly, businesses protected by high tariffs, traditional industry boundaries, or government regulations also tend to lack the arsenal of defenses of more openly rivalrous ecosystems. Consider the electric utilities, telephone service, transportation companies, banks and other financial service companies in the years before deregulation; medicine prior to the 1980s with the imposition of cost controls on public and private health care expenditures and the rise of managed care programs. All evolved in heavily protected preserves. Essentially, they developed in Hawaiian conditions. They had an excessively inward focus and lacked effective institutional defenses against attack.

On the other hand, there are many other business sectors with the traits of Costa Rica—more open boundaries and environments accessible to new ideas, people, and organizations. Some of the examples that come to mind are retail and whole-sale distribution of goods, manufacturing, electronics, computer hardware and software, and many aspects of entertainment. These sectors generally seem to have hardier competitors. Companies become dominant despite and even contrary to government and regulatory influence, rather than because of it.

Probably the most openly competitive Costa Rica–like environment in business is the one arising from the convergence of computers, communications, entertainment, and financial services. The leading companies boast very high and continuing rates of product and process innovation. It is an environment of unmistakable winners and losers. Companies that can't keep up drop out—or at least they drop very far down. The businesses that play in this environment are increasingly built around one or more specialized contributions, having outsourced everything but what they consider necessary to maintain a steep trajectory of value improvements and cost reductions. Yet these organizations know they need to work together, and they use information and communications technologies to assemble networks and virtual teams. They also have become adept at finding ways to coordinate their visions of the future so that their research and development, product plans, and market creation activities are aligned with others, and thus are more efficient at getting results.

I recently had a conversation with a manager at a merger and acquisitions firm that works with computer and communications companies. She talked about their work as focusing on the "information space." I had to laugh—the term was perfect, albeit unexpected for this business Costa Rica. In a dynamic world, we need to be able to discuss not only established, bounded markets, but potential markets. We need language that reflects the sweep of our imagination as we scan for opportunities. That is why "information space" is far more apt than "computers and communications" or some similarly narrow expression.

It is within this Costa Rica–type "information space" that many of the ideas in this book have reached their highest and most widespread form. A pitched struggle for territory is erupting. Out of this chaos, it is difficult to say who the winners will be—or what form the ecosystems that ultimately become dominant will take. But I'm convinced that participants can gain a significant edge by more clearly understanding the dynamics of ecosystem transformation. More important, these same issues are developing in most other business sectors—and thus are critically relevant for all managers. One of the best ways to clarify these issues is by using biology as a metaphor.

A New Perspective—Business and Ecosystems

To understand the premise of this book, you need to adopt a different vocabulary and see yourself and your environment in what might strike you as an unusual way. It may not be easy for everyone to make this shift—most executives don't naturally think of themselves as gardeners or foresters or wildlife managers working to shape the futures of ecosystems—but it can mean the difference between success and failure.

Right now, managers think of themselves as managers, companies as companies, the environment in which they compete as their markets or industry. It is my view that executives need to think of themselves as part of organisms participating in an ecosystem in much the same way that biological organisms participate in a biological ecosystem.

Instead of thinking of your "company," think in terms of species or organisms. In today's sophisticated world, an organism can be a process, department, business unit, or an entire company. Instead of thinking of your "customer-supplier network," or your "extended enterprise," think of your ecosystem, which can be far larger and richer than your immediate network. The press of daily exigencies has tended to force executives to dwell only on their core businesses, or on what they perceive to be their extended enterprise. I feel that their focus should be on their entire business ecosystem. Before going further, let's consider some definitions.

Biological ecosystem. Community of organisms, interacting with one another, plus the environment in which they live and with which they also interact; for example, a lake, a forest, a grassland, tundra. Such a system includes all abiotic components such as mineral ions, organic compounds, and the climatic regime (temperature, rainfall, and other physical factors). The biotic components generally include representatives from several trophic levels; primary producers (mainly green plants); macroconsumers (mainly animals), which ingest other organisms or particulate organic matter; microconsumers (mainly bacteria and fungi), which break down complex organic compounds upon the death of the above organisms.[2]

There is no dictionary as yet that includes the term business ecosystem, so let me take a stab at what it means to me:

Business ecosystem. An economic community supported by a foundation of interacting organizations and individuals—the organisms of the business world. This economic community produces goods and services of value to customers, who are themselves members of the ecosystem. The member organisms also include suppliers, lead producers, competitors, and other stakeholders. Over time, they coevolve their capabilities and roles, and tend to align themselves with the directions set by one or more central companies. Those companies holding leadership roles may change over time, but the function of ecosystem leader is valued by the community because it enables members to move toward shared visions to align their investments, and to find mutually supportive roles.

When I talk to executives about business ecosystems, they find the concept intriguing, but they are also a little fuzzy at first. What exactly are a business ecosystem's components?

What are the boundaries of a business ecosystem? I tell them that the simple answer is that a business ecosystem is made up of customers, market intermediaries (including agents and channels, and those who sell complementary products and services), suppliers, and, of course, oneself. These might be thought of as the primary species of the ecosystem.

But a business ecosystem also includes the owners and other stakeholders of these primary species, as well as power-ful species who may be relevant in a given situation, including government agencies and regulators, and associations and standards bodies representing customers or suppliers. To one extent or another, an ecosystem includes your direct competi-tors, along with companies that might be able to compete with you or with any other important members of the community. This rich mix of species can be seen as the flora and fauna that make up a particular ecosystem.

To help you visualize it, Figure 2.1 depicts a more or less typical business ecosystem. Notice how much broader it is than the core businesses and even the extended enterprise.

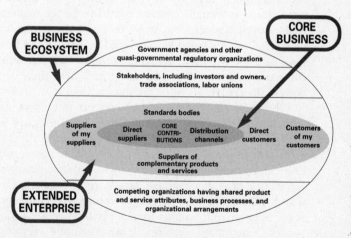

Figure 2.1

When you think in terms of ecosystems, don't get too hung up on size. "Business ecosystem" can refer to small business initiatives or to vast collections of enterprises. A neighborhood restaurant often becomes entwined with nearby institutions and populations: the senior citizens home on the corner, the insurance company that needs takeout every weekday, the Little League team in search of a sponsor. The restaurant's centrality to the community enables it to both give and receive. Those are the sort of reciprocal, mutually beneficial relationships that can define a business ecosystem. More important, cultivating that network of relationships could and should become a conscious strategy for the restaurant manager.

Keep in mind that the concept of an ecosystem is mutable in biology. Sometimes it is used to describe focused ecological communities (a "marsh ecosystem") and sometimes to describe the earth's biosphere (the "ecosystem"), as well as systems of mutually beneficial relationships between these extremes.[3] Similarly, the value of the concept for business is to use it to identify and nurture nested, intertwined relationships that have the potential for dramatic benefits, regardless of whether the systems are big or small. What matters is that they embody novel ideas to benefit customers and to better organize and lead a business enterprise. As we shall see, the key to how the new AT&T pieces are able to succeed depends upon how well they can put together dramatically valuable information and communications solutions for customers with their contributions at the center.

A business ecosystem does not respect traditional industry boundaries. It can thrive within conventional industry lines or straddle them. Indeed, the manner in which the business ecosystem relates to traditional industry boundaries is similar to how the boundaries of natural biological ecosystems often cross geopolitical lines. For example, an electronic commerce solution that AT&T might create for a large commercial customer could easily require contributions from several industries: computers, systems integration services, local telephone service, long-distance telephone service, retail banking, and credit and transaction services. This relationship is illustrated in Figure 2.2.

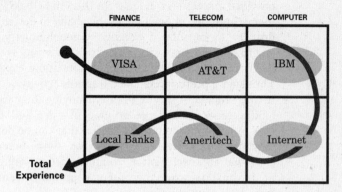

Figure 2.2

In the old world, the companies listed above would primarily see themselves as competing with similar businesses within their respective boxes. In the new world, companies compete to unite disparate contributors to create powerful total solutions or experiences—and then to establish thriving business ecosystems dedicated to providing these solutions to customers.

Strategy-Making in a World of Ecosystems

At the heart of a successful business ecosystem is the following economic model:

- There are one or more core capabilities that can become the basis for providing great value to end customers. Within the information market, for example, the capability to create microprocessors enabled the widespread use of electronic computation; the Internet may similarly liberate global telecommunications. In manufacturing, a revolutionary capability might be reflected in a new way to organize production or to engage the talents of people. For instance, the work of W. Edwards Deming and others

provided a crucial set of ideas for the Total Quality movement. Similarly, in health care the ability to design a new
drug or to organize a potentially revolutionary public
health program may supply the basis for business ecosystems. The immense potential value of these capabilities
stimulates a profusion of allied business activity.

- A core product or service offer embodying the new capabilities generates a large volume of sales and realizes
powerful economies of scale. Offers that can be delivered
in chips and software, in particular, have incremental
costs that approach zero as volumes become large. Thus,
in information space the potential economic returns to
large-scale businesses are vast.

- A total experience is ultimately provided to customers.
The total experience depends not only on the core product or service but on a variety of complementary offers
that enhance the customer experience. The Internet
reflects a collection of capabilities having to do with computer networking; Netscape and others are providing core
software products and services to enable electronic commerce on the Internet. But it is millions of users and
thousands of suppliers of content that make the experience come alive.

- Profits from the core products and services (those having
strong economies of scale) are reinvested in further addi-
tions to capabilities and in developing future generations
of offers. A continuing "innovation trajectory" of decreas-
ing prices and expanding performance is established. End
customers and allies become convinced that this core
business will bring them the future—in addition to being
there for them in the present.

- Returns from the core business are also invested in
leadership and support for the ecosystem itself: for
"alliance community development" activities like evangelism, standard setting, and oversight and dispute resolution across the community of associated firms. End
customers and community members come to feel that
the alliances that make up the ecosystem are well led.

- The above factors are joined together in what I call a "virtuous cycle" of investment and return. The cycle is double-looped to achieve continuous improvement in both the core offer and in the community of allies.

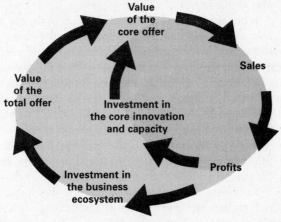

Figure 2.3

Similarly, in biological succession the initial colonists convert sunlight and minerals into biological structure. This activity in turn provides a foundation—food, soil, and shelter from the elements—to nourish later species.

In the classical paradigm of industry-based competition, products and even product leadership have become comparatively easy to dislodge. Newcomers simply clone the required technologies, make the requisite investments in equipment and people, and have at it. By contrast, the environment-shaping leader of a business ecosystem is difficult to dislodge. Once established, the virtuous cycles are hard to attack. Microsoft and Intel have found myriad ways to dig in during repeated sieges on their positions. Even Novell, the networking software company that was distracted by difficult internal questions of who should succeed founder Ray Noorda, and when, still managed to stave off insurgents for many years.

There are many reasons why ecologically savvy incumbents remain in power. Naturally, they have paid their start-up costs and are realizing the economies of scale inherent in their business models. This gives them an edge over new entrants—but not a decisive one, in a day of global markets and ample capital.

What sustains these particular incumbents is that their role as ecosystem leaders tends to make other members of the ecosystem reluctant to switch to a new entrant. They ask: Will the new entrant last? Can it supply adequate volumes? Can it protect me from retaliation from the ecology-influencing incumbent? Will it provide constructive and insightful leadership to the community? Will it be able to adjudicate disputes and keep rogues in line? Will it be fair to those who support it? In general, the members will answer in the negative, even if they are positively disposed to a change.

To be sure, it is not easy to become this sort of ecologically entrenched incumbent. This is certainly the lesson of a number of ecological wannabes who have failed to establish themselves in information space. For an ecological initiative even to begin to make sense, it must promise that dramatic value will be realized by the combination of players and contributions involved. In general, an architectural alliance must be seen as the only practical way to bring forward something of very real value to large numbers of end customers.

Innumerable products and services seem much more valuable to their creators and promoters than to anyone else. Lack of interest, due to lack of compelling new value, has killed many offers that progenitors thought would take off. The EO communicator, the GO palmtop computer, the 3DO video game box, and General Magic's operating software for personal digital assistants are all notable examples of products that did not give customers a convincing reason to buy them—and volume sales never developed. The lesson of the business ecosystem is that you must have value, economies of scale, and continuing innovation, and you must invest in an expanding community of allies.

An Expanding Landscape, Home to Many Ecosystems

The many opportunity environments of the new world continue to grow in size and capability. This means that there is constantly room for more and more ecosystems, and that more centers of coevolution are possible. This is especially evident in the world of information space. Specialty contributions that were once trapped in small niches—such as financial applications software—now have sufficient sales volume to fund intense reinvestment in product and community development. What once was a business environment of a few centers of coevolution and a few leaders is now hospitable to many more.

All of this suggests that competition in information space has a new flavor—companies are working hard to establish new centers of innovation—new business ecosystems—rather than attack incumbent positions of others. Companies are increasingly adopting the Hewlett-Packard motto—"Attack the undefended hill." Many are shying away from fighting to capture established centers of business ecosystems, recognizing that those territories are thickly settled and usually quite inhospitable to new colonists. Instead, strategists are appropriately focusing on trying to accomplish the following options:

1. Rediscover and reinforce your own strongholds—and strive to establish business "subecosystems" around them. Identify contributions for which you already possess economies of scale and the competencies to continue to innovate. Find ways to better embed your contributions into the products and processes of adjacent companies, as well as to shape architectural standards and customer preferences to align with your strengths. AT&T is doing this with its communications services, finding ways to work with partners like Lotus and Novell to create new offerings that revolve around its networks and software.

2. Tie together your stronghold subecosystems and/or use them to help create new positions in adjacent territories.

Microsoft is a master at this. By grouping its leading applications together into Office, Microsoft found it controlled more than 90 percent of the $700 million market for application suites by 1995. Sometimes you can "lend" economies of scale from one position to another. Microsoft Network takes advantage of the distribution scale Microsoft has achieved in operating systems, hitching a ride with Windows 95.

3. Invest in identifying and capturing undefended hills. Hewlett-Packard did this with printers. Several years ago, HP rightly observed that there were many potential innovations—in design, manufacturing, and distribution—that had not been exploited with printers that worked with personal computers. From an innovation standpoint, printers as a category of functionality were underdeveloped. The company put its mind to the problem—sourcing technology from Canon in Japan, adding high-quality software (with powerful economies of scale), developing low-cost manufacturing, and establishing a dominant, preferred position with distributors and retailers.

The key to pursuing undefended hills is to:

- Find some aspect of value creation where the niche is becoming important and no player has made a really strong stand.
- Commit yourself to putting together the required competencies.
- Make the investment and effort required to dominate the niche.
- Work with many partners to create a defendable position.

One of the most fascinating versions of this option is that pursued by Netscape Communications. In 1995, Netscape put itself on the map by aggressively pursuing the undefended hill of Internet software. What is notable here is that Netscape made the commitment to take the hill prior to establishing conclusively whether the hill, once captured, could support a profitable business. Netscape chairman Jim Clark rightly recognized that the graphics-rich World Wide Web was ripe to take off. He found a recent college graduate named Marc Andreesen who understood the technology and the subculture of the Net. He added Jim Barksdale, a seasoned and well-known operating manager to whom Wall Street investors would relate. Netscape then invested heavily in product development, gave away free entry-level desktop "browser" software, and allied itself with dozens of other software companies to bring combined offerings to market. Finally, Netscape went to the public financial markets with such a strong story—and such a tiny quantity of available shares—that its price rose meteorically.

Within a year, Netscape stood atop the Internet software hill. However, Netscape's initial core business did not have sufficient scale and gross margins to support its massive campaign over the long term. Only time will tell whether Netscape can grow the core business and turn its initial position into a sustainable, profitable business ecosystem.

4. Consider acquiring key franchises—that is, positions of ecosystem leadership. IBM chose to purchase Lotus for its Notes franchise rather than try to build its own. Most observers think that IBM overpaid for Notes, but if IBM can turn it into a franchise that lives in the experiential space between the end user and the Windows interface, IBM might be able to use Notes to recoup desktop leadership. Interestingly, both IBM and Netscape are seeking similar roles in the personal computer world—both are striving to surpass Microsoft by lodging themselves at the center of Internet-based ecosystems. IBM bought its position by acquiring Lotus, and Netscape is buying a position by giving away software. It will be interesting to see whether either is successful in turning its position into a profitable, self-sustaining business.

More recently, the move to acquire dominant positions has died down. The widespread recognition that ecosystem-leading incumbencies are difficult to dislodge has driven market capitalizations of companies that control defended hills way up. This in turn has made it exceedingly difficult to afford to buy one.

AT&T and Business Ecosystems

AT&T's decision to split itself up is a milestone in one firm's journey from vertically integrated company to ecosystem creator and leader. It reflects AT&T's view of how best to emerge from behind collapsing industry and market boundaries to embrace the wider opportunity environment. As a case study, it reveals a great deal about the changes going on in "information space"—and what it takes to succeed in this chaotic environment.

Until 1984, AT&T was mostly kept out of the broader information space by the terms of consent decrees it had signed with the U.S. government. It stuck to its role as communications service provider, as well as designer and manufacturer of related equipment. To AT&T's great frustration, Bell Labs was the source of many of the revolutionary technologies that transformed the wider environment during this time—yet the company was seldom able to profit from these contributions.

When AT&T finally entered the computer business, it was as if a gentle Hawaiian palila, an endangered bird found only on the volcano Mauna Kea, tried to establish itself in the frenzy of the Costa Rican jungles. AT&T had the wrong business model for the times. In addition, the swirling complexities of the 1984 breakup made implementing anything difficult. AT&T entered the market as a vertically integrated systems manufacturer at just the historic moment that aggressive networks of smaller companies, joined together in the ecosystem governed by the IBM standard, were sweeping the world. The computer effort bled money. Vicious cycles were the order of the day—not virtuous ones.

AT&T then became an early participant in a second wave of strategy-making. Its alliance with hip, aggressive Sun Microsystems was a tacit recognition that it needed help in understanding the more aggressive ecology of the emerging information space. The two companies hoped to create a new business ecosystem (they didn't call it that yet, but the idea was the same) by combining powerful new chips with software that both companies already controlled.

More radically, they hoped to get such widespread adoption of their software by other manufacturers that a new "open standard" would come about. This standard, the reasoning went, would be irresistible to customers because it would allow them to mix and match computers from several vendors—and to use this interchangeability to drive down prices.

As important, this new ecosystem was intended to siphon business from the current leaders of the computer business—IBM, Digital Equipment Company, and Hewlett-Packard—by making their ecosystems look closed, expensive, and rigid. In computer industry terms, AT&T and Sun hoped to unify the two major UNIX software camps, establish a new RISC microprocessor standard (SPARC), promote open systems, and loosen the hold that traditional mainframe and minicomputer companies had on the computer market.

The result was not as AT&T and Sun had hoped—although their efforts provided a key boost to the open systems movement. The AT&T/Sun ecosystem had trouble taking off. Systems companies would not adopt SPARC until a volume fabricator of microprocessors could be established. The major semiconductor manufacturers, including Texas Instruments and Fujitsu, refused to invest in capacity without commitments from systems companies. The alliance was trapped in a Catch-22—unable to establish a virtuous cycle of volume, profits, and reinvestment.[4]

Meanwhile IBM, DEC, and Hewlett-Packard—three companies that together accounted for three-quarters of all sales in the computer business—did something unheard of. They banded together into a counteralliance to found the Open Software Foundation, as a way to blunt interest in the AT&T/Sun offers. This defense required that these companies make their offerings somewhat more "open" and interchangeable—and this in turn helped drive down their prices over time. The result was that their ecosystems were shored up—their hills defended, but their margins reduced.

Sun managed to maintain its own incumbency—selling

workstations—but AT&T was thwarted in its broader ambitions. AT&T eventually bought NCR—acquiring small incumbencies in financial services and retail—but at a steep price. It invested in the architectural efforts of EO, GO, and General Magic—which, as noted, failed to take off.

In the early 1990s, AT&T's senior executives concluded that they needed a better strategic logic. John Petrillo, then strategist for the services business (and now head of strategy for the corporation), led several initiatives to rethink the business, starting with a broad look at the overall opportunity environment and how other players were succeeding within it. John's work demonstrated the value of AT&T's voice and data services, particularly when they served as central elements in total solutions merging communications, computing, and media.

This services-centric view argued the following: In the new world, customers will be served by a variety of communications and computing-based services. Customers will buy complementary products and services to work together. Sometimes they will buy in pieces; other times they will desire bundles. In either case, AT&T cannot possibly provide all of the components of value to these solutions. The company will need to learn to participate in multiple ecosystems, some not even controlled by the firm.

The fundamental organizational logic of the new information businesses, AT&T recognized, is that of continually innovating specialists at the center of business ecosystems. Companies specialize in one or more contributions that they do best—and work flexibly with others to make total solutions happen. AT&T needed to identify those few things in which it had a differential advantage and specialize in those, creating business ecosystems around each major offer. To do this, it would need to become much more agile in partnering with other specialists—ranging from chip companies to systems integrators to consumer electronics marketers.[5]

The most important kind of differential advantage for AT&T, the thinking went, would link economies of scale with continuing innovation. Economies of scale—that is, where each new increment of service costs less than the previous one—were something AT&T knew plenty about. Its core network handled more than 150 billion circuit minutes of traffic each year. Its marketing and sales organizations reached out and touched more than 80 million customers. Continuing innovation would provide ongoing cost reduction. Equally important, it would help keep AT&T service features ahead of the commodity "clone company" offers, and would make AT&T's contributions more valuable to its customers.

Alex Mandl (now incoming president of the entire firm) accelerated this work when he became operating head of AT&T Communications Services. According to the view he advocated, the Communications Services business had two obvious areas of strength. First, AT&T had in place the world's leading high-reliability, high-capacity communications services—and the work force to sell them, service them, and continue to evolve them. Second, AT&T was one of the world's premier marketing firms—with a trusted brand, global reach, and insights into millions of customers. Thus strategic questions began to turn on how to create new total systems of value—business ecosystems, if you will—with AT&T network-based services and/or AT&T marketing at the core. Relationships with Intel, Lotus, Novell, and others grew out of this strategy, as well as the acquisition of McCaw Cellular and various entries into providing local telephone services in the United States and globally.

A services-centric strategy raised a number of corporate questions for AT&T. For example, what should be done with AT&T's equipment businesses? The most important equipment unit, AT&T Network Systems, provides switching hardware and software, as well as complementary equipment and services, to large-scale communications services businesses. While AT&T communications services is a big customer, Network Systems also supplied the regional Bell operating companies, the so-called Baby Bells, and other carriers worldwide. Network Systems also had important interests in the advanced networks being created by entertainment companies. For example, Network Systems was a partner with Time Warner in the Orlando interactive-TV trial. All of these companies could see that at least one aspect of the future—declining regulatory boundaries and expanding global networks—would mean that they would be increasingly creating total solutions and business ecosystems in direct conflict with one another.

Some of the non-AT&T customers of Network Systems were more and more reluctant to purchase gear from the company. They regarded these purchases as ultimately subsidizing AT&T's attempts to establish its own business ecosystems—ecosystems that would eventually seek to invade their geographies and businesses. As the dates for regional and national boundaries to decline drew closer, their fears mounted.

At the same time, some executives of AT&T worried that Network Systems was providing "arms to the enemy"—or rather, genetically engineered species to opposing ecosystems—when it sold advanced equipment to the Baby Bells and foreign telcos. The fact was that all the carriers felt dependent upon their equipment providers. In a world of carrier-to-carrier ecosystem-based competition, each worried about buying and selling to the other.

In early 1995, CEO Robert Allen and a small group of trusted associates tackled the organizational challenge. In the end, the answer was unmistakable. Focus AT&T on the Communications Services business, and work with partners to create a variety of new applications and services-centric ecosystems. The era of conventional vertical integration was over. Network Systems and the other equipment businesses should be spun off into an independent firm. That way they would be free to supply any and every potential customer on the same basis—and to support any services-centric business ecosystems that arose. Competing issues among carriers could be handled with internal "Chinese walls" within Network Systems, and no carrier would need to worry much about subsidizing its competitors' ecosystems.

AT&T's computer business would also be spun off. Having failed to establish itself as a manufacturer or marketer of mainstream personal computer-based systems, it would exit this business. It would focus on creating three major subecosystem targets—financial services, retailing, and communications—

where it had expertise, market presence, and credibility. It would take its cues from leading customers, understanding the business ecosystems they were creating. It would offer itself as "their computer company" in a manner not unlike Silicon Graphics' relationship to the entertainment business.

At the announcement of the breakup of AT&T in September 1995, Bob Allen was asked whether he still believed that a "convergence" of computers and communications was occurring. He answered strongly that he did. He emphasized, however, that the manner in which convergence was happening, and the ways in which the market environment was evolving, required a new form for AT&T. Just because computers, communications, media, and other businesses are coming together does not justify vertical integration. Rather, along with convergence, AT&T is grappling with the deintegration and specialization of the companies in the information space. The logic of business ecosystems is what makes all the difference. More than anything, it is the strategic issues—and not the companies—that are converging across the new landscape.

It is important to realize that just because AT&T is getting itself structurally organized for the new world doesn't assure it of an easy time in its ecosystem-to-ecosystem struggles. Getting organized is only the beginning step for a company— necessary, sometimes very difficult, but not sufficient. It still must master the strategic challenge of creating and shaping business ecosystems. Moreover, there is no forgetting that the environmental conditions that prompted the company to dismantle itself become more threatening every day. To mention just two: The Baby Bells are spreading rapidly across the wider landscape; the Internet and other forms of computer-based ecosystems provide increasingly viable substitutes for AT&T's core long-distance service. Without question, AT&T faces a tremendous challenge, and its chances of success depend on far more than strategy and structure.

It is worth pointing out that companies participating in information space have a variety of ways to organize. Interestingly, many of the leading firms are moving to be able to pursue ecosystem-centered strategies—and most are seeking to do so in a way that respects their own heritage and culture, and builds on their core assets and capabilities. It is instructive to compare how different firms are approaching the challenge. We have seen how AT&T is gravitating from vertical integration to a service-specialized structure. Hewlett-Packard has followed a contrasting journey—starting from specialization and learning to think in terms of whole ecosystems.

Hewlett-Packard has a history of decentralization—of making components, test equipment, and computers that play in total solutions, and business ecosystems, that more often than not were defined by others. Its great strengths are in technology and implementation—in being a strong member of an ecosystem, rather than a leader and definer of the overall vision for the community. While the company is continuing to emphasize being a vital contributor, under CEO Lew Platt it is also trying to focus on defining business ecosystems and is consciously seeking critical roles and leadership positions. In many instances these new ecosystem leadership roles will require executives of the company's units to work closely together—amending the tradition of staunch independence and product-focused decentralization.

Electronic Data Systems provides yet another approach. As a systems integrator, its historical task has been to take responsibility for business systems from beginning to end. Now it is looking for broader business ecosystems—in fields such as health care and telecommunications—to become the overseer of the information that links the ecosystem together.

Some of the entertainment and media companies have embraced what they call "vertical integration," which may sound quite conventional. However, what they are actually doing is a far cry from traditional vertical integration—where a company sought to be its own exclusive supplier, in order to put the total process of value creation under tight hierarchical control. In the new version, companies are using their presence in several critical contributions to jump-start new ecosystems—to which they will not be the sole contributors. For example, News Corporation used its ownership of a few U.S.

television stations, together with its television content production capabilities, to establish the Fox Television Network. Similarly, News Corporation has established satellite-based television services in Europe and Asia, again seeded with its own content, but open to other contributors as well.

None of these companies is doing it "right" or "wrong." Rather, they are making adjustments to their historic ways of understanding and organizing their businesses to play more effectively in a world where business ecosystems are of increasing importance.

To What Ecosystem or Ecosystems Do You Contribute?

Before reading further, it is probably worthwhile to pause a moment to consider your own situation. What is the nature of the ecosystem or ecosystems that your business inhabits? You may play primarily in one, or in several, fast-moving camps. Microsoft plays in the personal computer ecosystem it helps to define, and by being the largest seller of packaged applications like spreadsheets and word processors for Macintosh computers, it also plays in Apple's ecosystem. Senior executives at Microsoft spend vast amounts of time managing their relationships with key members of both communities.

You may discover that some ecosystems are very important to your current success. Others may hold promise for the future, even though they are in the early stages of their formation.

For example, until about 1990 the world's major pharmaceutical companies used the American prescription drug market as a rich environment in which to build ecosystems that they dominated. Companies like Merck and Hoffmann–La Roche ruled over powerful ecosystems specializing in the discovery and testing of new treatments, which were ultimately sold through extensive—and expensive—sales forces to individual physicians.

After 1990, however, drug companies found the center of influence in health care shifting to a new set of ecosystems that were shaped largely by others. The most important were the managed care ecosystems, centered around a heady combination of provider networks, cost control, and health insurance, all bundled together and encouraged by government and business. The drug companies were forced to reassess their roles and seek leadership beyond their narrow industry. They became active players in reshaping new end-to-end ecosystems across the broader landscape of health care, insurance and benefits, and government.

Consider an ecosystem in which you participate: Who are the main organizational members? Who are the leaders? Are you a leader? Are you shaping the future of this ecosystem, or mainly responding to the initiatives of others? It can be very revealing to list the key members and consider to what extent they have similar and diverging visions of the future. You will find that some ecosystems have members who are well aligned; others are full of strife. While the leadership challenges and opportunities are tactically different, it is critical in both cases that the ecosystem as a whole develop a comprehensive understanding of its condition. There is a need for forums—informal as well as formal—where leading members of an ecosystem can talk.

What are the most important threats to this business ecosystem, now and in the future? What are the most promising ways to continue to coevolve across the community to bring richer benefits to customers and create new wealth for the members? These are pressing questions for any ecosystem, and you may find that you can raise your own profile in your business community by finding ways to put these issues on the table.[6]

3

Leading Business Ecosystems

One of the more memorable sights in the lush forests of Costa Rica is a congregation of the ubiquitous leaf-cutting ants at work.[1] Great hordes of these ants, each carrying a leaf fragment, stream down trees throughout the forest. The patches of slowly moving green coalesce into broad trails that lead back to the ants' nest, which can be more than a hundred yards away. The ants seem to devour the forest. In fact, the leaf-cutting ants are the leading consumers of vegetation in Costa Rica.

Why are they so successful? Part of the reason is the stunning efficiency of their organization. The ants have established a rigid division of labor so that various-sized workers perform the tasks at which they are most efficient. The largest workers serve as soldiers that guard the nest. A broad assortment of medium-sized workers forage for leaves, with the largest foragers tackling the thickest and toughest leaves. The smallest workers spend most of their time in the nest, processing the leaf material.

Curiously, the leaf-cutting ants do not feed on the leaves they harvest. Instead, they use them as a fertile mulch for growing gardens of fungus that they then eat. This is the ingenious secret to the leaf-cutters' success. By using the mutualist fungus, the ants can feed indirectly upon the leaves of trees—a tremendously abundant resource largely unexploited by other ants. Leaf-cutting ants, though, do not pursue leaves indiscriminantly. Instead, they prefer to cut young, sappy leaves that promote fungal growth and avoid leaves with coevolved chemical defenses that poison the ants or kill their fungus. It turns out that these chemical defenses against herbivory are of enormous value to humans. Most of the drugs that we get from plants, both legal and illegal varieties, result from the coevolutionary "arms race" between plants and herbivores.

Biologists have suggested that most mutualisms in nature evolve from antagonistic relationships.[2] Pollinators evolve from pollen feeders. Seed dispersers evolve from seed predators. The mutualism between leaf-cutting ants and their fungi probably arose from the ants opportunistically harvesting fungus they found in the forest. Similarly, our early ancestors opportunistically fed upon the wild plants and animals that they found. Later, humans learned to cultivate favored plants and domesticate favored animals. These mutualisms have undoubtedly contributed to the tremendous ecological success of our species. An important lesson, then, is to create and promote mutualisms. You could even go so far as to try to convert your antagonistic relationships into mutualistic ones.

The complex social organization and ecological dominance of the leaf-cutting ant is impressive for an animal with a brain the size of a speck. But what no animal has is a consciousness of the entire system. And that is the pivotal difference in business ecosystems. Managers can and should have what I call an "ecological consciousness."

Unfortunately, it seems to me, most don't. Even investment analysts tend to look at the world in industry terms or in terms of company fundamentals. The consciousness of most managers is, how do I sell the next widget? Or, at most, how do I make the process of manufacturing widgets better? The danger of this tunnel consciousness is that you can be selling a lot of widgets with a very effective process, but if the whole system is on the brink of dissolution you won't know it until it is too late.

Sadly, the way most managers do their strategic planning today is by searching for investment and expansion opportunities within the same old paradigms of business, and within the same old definition of their industry. Inevitably, this leads to utter futility. As one hapless search gives way to another, the strategist finds himself helplessly trapped on a treadmill. This compulsion simply fuels the overall rate of industry commoditization. The predictable result is continued disappointment, as the following diagram illustrates.

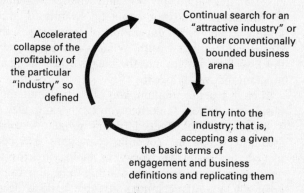

Figure 3.1

As more and more of the currently defined industries descend into ruinously intense competition, the prospects for discovering an attractive industry worsen. The mood is neither triumph nor euphoria. With so many powerful global players in the game, excessive assets are being sunk into replicating what already exists. The energy and vitality of corporations is being channeled into the abyss of worn-out paradigms, where it atrophies. Meanwhile, new approaches that might be organized into innovative systems languish without attention. Customer needs that might be addressed if only there were fresh thinking remain unmet.

Strategy-Making Should Aim to Create New Microeconomies and New Wealth

Continued strategy-making in the context of existing industries and paradigms has left many of the world's most resource-rich companies stumped about how to grow their businesses and create new wealth for society. Yet, by assuming a broader vantage, it is painfully obvious that real wealth comes from finding better ways of doing business. The spaces between the status quo and its alternatives are the breeding grounds of primary wealth, for consumers and producers alike. As the old powers wait and wonder, vast new fortunes are rising on foundations built by swarms of entrepreneurs jostling to apply the integration of technologies and market creation that brings wealth. What is missing, therefore, is not this high-level insight, but the means of designing a workable program that will bridge it.

There is a better solution. You can actually attempt to shape business evolution—and then you can begin to play the part of a grand gardener. Indeed, doing so allows companies to assume the role in economic ecosystems that people have played, for better or worse, in biological ecosystems. Put another way, companies are starting to be able to play with a greater hand. Adam Smith's invisible hand is becoming the visible hand. Managers now have an opportunity to do more than construct companies. They can work at constructing entire economies.

There is a new cycle to replace the fruitless search inspired by narrow-minded, industry-based strategy-making. In this new cycle, the focus is on forming whole ecosystems with innovative power—ecosystems whose purpose is to absorb more customers and more good ideas into their orbit. Ultimately, you want your efforts to be at the center of a rich range of innovative contributions. You want to serve the world by applying the abundant human creativity available to solve prominent problems. You want to provide the architecture for large-scale cooperation. In a sense, what you are doing is a form of community organizing. You are forging new economic relationships. Starting business ecosystems, unlike the search for attractive industries, is in fact a highly evolved form of economic development.

The new cycle of ecosystem-based paradigm development appears as:

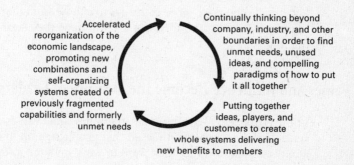

Figure 3.2

To be sure, there is a risk of hubris and self-delusion in all this, a risk of thinking you can control far more than you can. Moreover, because people and companies can read one another's intentions, a devilish game can be unleashed with people trying to top each other in terms of integrative visions. Thus, you must do your gardening with care.

What is exciting and inspiring is that the ecosystem cycle is inherently expansive, a fundamental process for producing order. There is no denying, as you will see, that it is also inherently unpredictable—the behavior of the system will not be reducible to that of any of its parts. Most interesting, the cycle shows how new centers of industrial organization and coevolution can be created. A new ecosystem and its paradigm have the power to bring about a fresh consensus in a heaving market about what are desirable goods and services, and how to buy them. Gordon Wu of Hopewell Holdings combines road building, power generation, and real-estate development to establish new economic infrastructures in Asia. The Internet is bringing together visual artists, commercial businesses of all kinds, and individual computer users to create a worldwide communication medium of unprecedented variety and reach. The whole approach represented in the ecosystem cycle is relentlessly proactive and creative, rather than, as in the case of the industry cycle, reactive and restrained. Those who follow it will soon have more pathways to choose from than they have ever known. Those who don't will have the certainty of nothing.

Values and Influence Become the Measure of Leadership

In the ecosystem cycle, personal and professional values play a central role. An important reason that people sign up to create a new ecosystem is that they want to work on a program both meaningful and important. The excitement of participating in the new, the thrill of forming history, the satisfaction of collaborating to make a difference—these are real pleasures. Many of us will take financial and career risks, work unbelievably long hours, and tolerate unending ambiguity when what we do matters.

Sadly, for many people such pleasures are rare. As individuals, many of us work for organizations trapped in the narrow industry-based cycle and, as a result, find ourselves pushing the wheel for outdated values and tired ideas. In an expanding world of opportunities, playing an established game is not only bad strategy but also deadly dull. In contrast, shaping business ecosystems stirs up inner passions and lights fires. In a corporation, it requires true leadership.

As a consultant, I learn much from my clients. I probably learned most about leadership from Jim Henson. Jim is best remembered and loved as the creator of the Muppets. He was also the CEO of a vibrant community of talent, known collectively for many years simply as Henson Associates (the business cards read "HA!"), and today as Jim Henson Productions.

Jim had three special leadership skills. First, he was keenly attuned to the social and business ecology within which he lived. An avid student of culture—pop, high, and folk—he went to the movies constantly and loved to discuss them. His office was a jumble of Muppet memorabilia and American folk art, while his apartment leaned toward African art, a strong personal interest and a major influence on his puppet designs.

Jim avidly studied business models and the larger adaptations and emerging patterns of organization across the entertainment business. A creative catalyst, he joined in the early pioneering of television, public broadcasting, feature-length fantasy films, and digital and multimedia production. He continually contemplated the evolving economics and organizational dynamics that related him and other independent producers to the TV networks, movie studios, writers, actors, directors—and to the increasingly powerful global media empires like Disney. In short, he thought about ecosystems.

Second, Jim contributed by nestling in and becoming a vital member of various ecosystems—such as that anchored by the Public Broadcasting System and the Children's Television Workshop, which resulted in *Sesame Street*. He linked talent and opportunities, and invested in what we will later examine as an "innovation trajectory." An innovation trajectory is a line of contribution that is invested in over time with singular commitment to attain deep and unique practical capabilities. Jim's overriding interest—the innovation trajectory to which he was most committed—was to establish "classic characters," entertainment personalities such as Kermit the Frog, Miss Piggy, or Oscar the Grouch who built enduring relationships with audience members.

Jim and his team mastered this ability across several distinct media—television, film, music, and books. At the center of his innovation trajectory were a number of specialized skills, brought together on each project. For example, there were the puppeteers. Few actors, whether working live or through puppets, have the special qualities of personal chemistry that enable them to touch an audience through film and television.

Some "have it" and can make almost any character take off. Others do not. For many years Jim held regular auditions and training programs to discover and promote people who might blossom into successful puppeteers. Similarly, art and stage direction were a high priority, specialized to each medium. Michael Frith, a visual artist who began as an illustrator working with Dr. Seuss, became among the world's best at making a tiny television screen seem like a whole universe—inviting, deep, and jumping with dazzle and color.

Third, Jim used these capabilities to explore and express the personal values important to him. One was respect for individual differences, even for grouchiness (Oscar), naïveté (Big Bird), obsessiveness (The Count), and self-centeredness (Bert), all in the higher service of a diverse, creative community that benefited from the positive contributions of each. These values, as a play within a play, animated Jim's wider ecosystem. Reinforced by the production capabilities and personal chemistry of the puppeteers, these values resonated with a broad audience and had a marked effect on the world. Jim showed me how the ecosystem cycle works: A leader expresses a set of values through a strategic combination of core capabilities, complemented holistically by a wider ecosystem of individuals and organizations.

We Must Change How We Manage Day-to-Day

To be sure, the ecosystem cycle demands managing in a sharply different way. For more than a decade, companies have been learning how to move beyond traditional product-focused customer/supplier transactions. The first developments dwelled on preferred supplier and preferred customer agreements, and more recently managers have positioned themselves at the helm of so-called extended enterprises or networked organizations.

From the standpoint of day-to-day leadership, executives are dealing with coevolving coalitions of diverse economic players. Companies and their executives are reconceptualizing the business world as a place bristling with coalitions, camps, and communities—allied interests working together on shared visions with powerful potential for innovation.

The day-to-day implications of this expansion in the scope of leadership are summarized in the following chart. As you read the chart, you might reflect upon how your own business life—even your phone calls and meetings—has changed over the past few years. Many managers are spending much more time on tasks toward the right-hand side of the chart below than on the left, clear evidence that the new world is hard upon us.

SCOPE OF STRATEGIC MANAGEMENT	CORE PRODUCTS AND SERVICES	+ EXTENDED ENTERPRISE	+ COEVOLVING ECOSYSTEM
Concept of business relationships	A portfolio of transactional and long-term preferred customer and supplier relationships	Managed system of relationships	Coevolving, symbiotic, self-reinforcing system of strategic contributions
Focus of continual improvement	Products and processes	Organizational interactions, extended processes	Investments in innovation by members of the community
Measure of improvement	Reduction in product defects; reduction in product deviations from standard	Rate of progress on improving products and processes	Rate of progress on creating end-to-end total experiences of dramatic value to customers
Most important contracts governing the relationship	Product specifications, process specifications, and TQM standards	Letters of agreement among key organizations	Community governance systems, quasi-democratic mechanisms
Alignment of the intentions of key parties	Alignment on the importance of consistency of customer/supplier satisfaction and performance on benchmarks	Alignment of the parties' strategic direction and investments	Alignment of the community around a shared vision of a desired future, and the road map and key contributions required

Table 3.1. The increasing scope of strategic management.

To accomplish the tasks that are further toward the right-hand side of the table, you need to devote your attention to the contributions of all the key members of the business ecosystem. You need to understand these contributions, their sources of innovative potential, and how well they are being realized. You need to design business relationships to bring in the most powerful players and contributions, and they must be choreographed into a dance that provides dramatic new benefits for customers.

Premises of the Ecosystem Strategy

It may seem a little tricky at first, but this new, ecosystem-centered approach to leadership and strategy-making gains strength from four avowedly simple premises:

1. With the collapse of traditional industries, the only sensible way to compete is by being better than your rivals at molding new ecosystems, not just products. In fact, once you get the hang of ecosystem creation you can never again be pigeonholed in an "industry." As Bill Joy of Sun Microsystems said so aptly, "The goal is not to win at someone else's game, but rather to change the game to one that you can win." Translated for our purposes, the goal is not to become an industry leader, but to be a destroyer of old industries and a creator of new ones.

2. The reason these new communities exist is to bring bold innovations to customers. By innovation, I do not mean simply product or process improvements, or whatever gets pumped out of the research and development engines. That is not enough. I mean an entirely original outcome. I am talking about a new set of benefits available to customers, demonstrably better than what it supplants. Otherwise there is no way to justify the costs of creating the ecosystem. These costs include the expense of developing new processes and dedicating new assets, patching together networks of collaborators, and coaxing customers to switch to the new way.

3. The scope of what is considered "contained" in the ecosystem is a central strategic decision. You can create a comprehensive, end-to-end economic community involving dozens or, in the case of the personal computer business, hundreds of thousands of individuals and organizations. On the other hand, you can also confine business ecosystems to a narrow purpose and yet still meet the essential test of solving important problems and rewarding its organizers. Norand makes hand-held digital assistants for blue-collar workers who perform tasks like inventory control and equipment maintenance. The business is wonderfully successful, and for good reason: It solves problems and furnishes solutions of real value. As a result, Norand's ecosystem has thrived even though the first generation of technically similar, albeit more general, digital assistants failed. The most spectacular flop, of course, was Apple's Newton.

The scope and boundary of a business ecosystem are not dictated by traditional practices but must be managed in a determinedly hands-on fashion. Otherwise, the fruits of innovation will never be tasted. When the new strategist decides to treat a set of activities as part of a business ecosystem, the strategist is wagering that the benefits of doing so will far outweigh the costs, at least over the life of the venture.

4. Competitive advantage in the new world stems from knowing when and how to build ecosystems, and from being able to steer them to lasting growth and continuous improvement. It is as if the eagle or the fox can sense its ecosystem coming under threat and can act to invigorate and enlarge it.

Granted, these principles seem straightforward, but their execution is anything but. It calls for rapt attention to the demands of both cooperation and competition. New ecosystems require leaders who can work across traditional organizational and cultural lines to form a compelling vision that transcends company, industry, and, often, national lines.

We can summarize these points as follows:

From COMPANY & INDUSTRY	to ECOSYSTEM
Business boundaries—such as industry or nation—as a given	Business boundaries as an issue and to some extent a matter of choice
Industry or the company is the primary unit of strategy-making	The business ecosystem, or community of coevolving, innovating participants, is the primary unit of strategy-making
Economic performance is a function of how well the company is managed internally—and how profitable, on average, is its industry	Economic performance is very much a function of how the company manages its alliances and relationships within the network that constitutes its business ecosystem
Individual company growth is the central concern	Development of the economic network as a whole is the central concern, as well as the position of the company within the network
Cooperation among players is largely limited to direct suppliers and customers to improve traditional customer/supplier relationships and/or to maintain existing industry or national boundaries	Cooperation is expanded to include all players relevant to the search for ideas and unmet needs that can be innovatively combined into new communities of coevolving participants
Competition seen as primarily between product and product or company and company	Competition is also understood to be among business ecosystems—as well as for leadership and centrality within particular ecosystems

Table 3.2

Strength and Competitiveness Come from the Community

This new approach to strategy makes so much sense today because of a certain truism: The strength that a company derives from its ecosystem can be as much as, or more important than, the competitiveness it derives from its own virtues. Just look at Apple Computer. Why was it successful for so long? Because it had won the favor of aggressively loyal customers and third-party software developers. What triggered its dramatic stumble in 1995? Namely, the cumulative effects of widespread defections from the community over the previous few years, as the Microsoft/Intel-led computer community outstripped Apple's in so many ways, especially in the number and aggregate resources of the companies in its community, and in the corresponding price and performance improvement trajectory. This shows that the visible assets of a company (for example, machinery, facilities, and inventory) are often far outweighed by the innovation-driving power of its invisible assets—community goodwill, shared vision, enthusiasm of customers. All these invisible assets translate into hordes of creative people and organizations, innovating, coevolving, and extending the influence of the company.

Along these same lines, Ford and Chrysler do not compete head to head only in cars and trucks. Both are trying to establish communities of suppliers, linked to market intermediaries and customers, that can collectively produce better results. As we will see later, Ford and Chrysler have distinct theories of how to lead their respective ecosystems. Ford banks on global economies of scale, whereas Chrysler embraces a radical outsourcing concept.

All of these examples suggest that the central game of strategic management is moving from managing oneself to leading a community of allies. Having a business model for your own firm is not enough. Executives must become ultra-sophisticated at developing business models for their respective communities.

Even in the rough and tumble world of American presidential politics, competition shifts from candidates and concepts to alternative ways to construct political ecosystems. Bill Clinton and Al Gore benefit mightily from the networks and relationships seeded and nurtured by the Democratic Leadership Committee—and from the permanent campaign that Clinton began while governor of Arkansas. Over time, they have established a mutualistic community of activists, think tanks, and contributors that helps them stay true to their values, evolve their ideas, and find ways of exerting influence. At the opposite end of the political spectrum, but quite close in his approach, is Newt Gingrich. His Progress and Freedom Foundation is just the most visible part of a highly adaptive political ecosystem that has taken many years to grow. In some ways, Gingrich is the Johnny Appleseed of politics; unique is his multiyear investment in recruiting, training, and supporting candidates for office, many of whom today make up his band of loyalists in the House of Representatives.

Last but not least, Ross Perot's United We Stand is transforming itself from a social movement into a viable, continuing national third party. This transformation has required investing time and energy in electoral reform in states across the entire union, to remove the barriers that now make forming such a party virtually impossible. Regardless of your political convictions, you can gain insight into leadership and strategy by observing how information technology, a willingness to assume risk, and an investment in long-term ecosystem gardening are all vital ingredients of influence in politics, just as in business. With such a base, ideas and values can move society—without it, they are likely to do little.

Consider the ecosystem or ecosystems in which you play a role. Are they growing or declining? How effectively are these economic communities being led? Are they innovating and improving their performance with customers? How secure are their futures? How are they faring against competing communities? These questions are vital, for many executives and companies have focused entirely on their own virtues and altogether missed the decline in the ecosystems upon which they were dependent.

Competitive Advantage in a World of Business Ecosystems

Remember that not all ecosystems, and not all roles, are equally lucrative. IBM made possible the PC ecosystem, but has struggled mightily to make any money from it. It's not enough just to create ecosystems. If you want to succeed financially, you must generate a new kind of dynamic competitive advantage within and through your participation in business ecosystems.

The way I see it, competitive advantage in the new world requires having a leadership position embedded in a successful business ecosystem. To take a conspicuous case, the competitive edge of Wal-Mart derives from its place in the larger system of which it is member and master. Wal-Mart the company does so well because it is the leader of Wal-Mart the network—in other words, the web of business processes, the community that runs those processes, and the resulting business ecosystem. By no means does Wal-Mart wallow in a protected position within an industry. Retailing in North America has to be one of the least protected and most bitterly competitive industries on the face of the earth.

Wal-Mart, however, does enjoy a protected position. It is the sole supplier of leadership, retail stores, wholesale distribution, information services, purchasing, marketing expertise, human resources planning, and much else to its own broader network. And because the Wal-Mart network is so customer-focused and innovative, flocks of customers are almost religiously faithful to it, especially in the somewhat isolated small towns where it is mightiest. Needless to say, quite a nice position to be in.

Intel provides another rather dramatic example of competitive advantage. From 1991 to 1995, Intel was one of the most profitable companies in the world, ranking with the DeBeers diamond monopoly, the Malaysian oil and gas monopoly, and leading drug companies. In this same period, the average profitability of the semiconductor industry was less than a quarter of Intel's. How do we explain this? Was Intel that much more efficient than its competitors? Hardly. Personal computer buyers in those days were ravenous for more microprocessor power. Year after year, they hungered to add power to drive their new software. Only Intel specialized in delivering this. Clone semiconductor makers like Advanced Micro Devices could supply microprocessors that would run customers' software, but the clones always lagged behind Intel in offering more power. Intel was selling something in ferocious demand that only it could supply.

What is more, the personal computer ecosystem ruled by Intel and Microsoft was furnishing enormous value to myriad other ecosystems. So Intel's great success during this period was largely due to its position as the locked-in, sole supplier to a larger ecosystem that was providing critical productivity gains to virtually every business sector in the world. As we will see later in this book, it was when this role came under siege from alliances of companies hungering to get into the ecosystem that Intel had to fight tenaciously to cling to its position.

The new source of competitive advantage comes from establishing a protected position within an innovative ecosystem, an ecosystem so superior at capitalizing and organizing the resources in the opportunity environment that customers prefer it to competing ecosystems. Protection means that it is extremely difficult to dislodge the company from its role in the community, and that the role bestows enough bargaining power—over others in the ecosystem—for the company to realize attractive margins. Thus at least one truth holds up from the conventional strategy canon: Everything else being equal, the bargaining power that comes from having something that others really need, and for which you are the only or one of the few practical sources, improves profitability. But remember, bargaining power in the new world seldom follows industry lines. It stems from dynamic contributions, not static barriers. Security does not come from regulation or heritage, but from leadership and innovative contributions to an ecosystem's customers.

You Can't Do It Alone

This shift in leadership scope that I've been talking about is neither discretionary nor a fad. It is necessitated by powerful, specific changes in the underlying economic and technical realities of business life. In virtually all businesses, the potential for innovation is increasing dramatically. This potential is being stimulated by concrete factors such as technological advances, diffusion of knowledge, globalization of capital markets, the widespread availability of risk capital, deregulation, and increasing managerial skill in leading innovation.

Players can therefore achieve significant economic rewards if they are able to bring potential innovations into actuality more efficiently and effectively than others. But any given innovation requires customer and supplier partners to be implemented. And the more radical the innovation, the more deeply and broadly must other players, especially customers, be involved. This places a premium on learning to manage a very wide community or network of organizations, in which all the players share a vision about how to make the innovation happen. Indeed, the major factor today limiting the spread of realized innovation is not a lack of good ideas, technology, or capital. It is the inability to command cooperation across broad, diverse communities of players who must become intimate parts of a far-reaching process of coevolution.

If you could look into the minds of all the executives in all the companies listed in your ecosystem, you would discover something that they probably all share: a recognition that many aspects in their businesses are changing and that they will have to offer new benefits to customers—or provide the old benefits remarkably well—to stay in business. They will have to invest in new skills, new assets, new directions. But they cannot make these decisions unilaterally, because they are interdependent with at least some of the other members of the community. They must seek out shared visions to coordinate their investments; they cannot afford to invest in all possible futures and in all possible scenarios of partner investments.

While any company probably wants to maintain as much autonomy as it can, and wants to be secretive about its own future plans, it must balance this desire with the need to work with others. There can be a tremendous economic advantage in coordination when it comes to shaping the future—in terms of focusing investment, avoiding dead-ends, and finding a role in the center of a powerful community. It is this tension, between the desire for autonomy and the recognition of a collective destiny, that makes strategy-making for business ecosystems so important. In many cases, a company can have it both ways, by becoming not just a member of the community but a leader and director of the future.

If you want to start to test this idea in your own business, ask yourself the following questions: What innovative idea could I bring to my customers, if I could orchestrate a wider community of players to endorse it, that would be profoundly more effective than what I offer? Where are my own innovative contributions hampered by lack of wider cooperation, coinvestment, and adoption of my ideas?

The answers to these questions will begin to give you some ideas for the leadership agenda that you might want to run at the ecosystem level.

Multidimensional Campaigns Create Competitive Advantage

The old ways of defending your turf just don't work anymore. With metronomic regularity, established businesses competing in standard ways will continue to be gnawed at by potent new rivals. Some of these competitors will set up new ventures to clone current business practices, and others will use advanced technologies or other ideas not only to steal business but to render the assets of established companies obsolete. In many cases, the new rivals will violate industry or geographic boundaries. In some cases, these trespassers will strike from largely similar businesses, and in other instances they will arrive from surprisingly different businesses that happen to share some core capabilities.

Stated simply, the end result will often be a rapid plunge of market share and revenues for the established companies, accompanied by the obsolescence of assets and even the diminution of skills and human resources. Initially, the best defense is usually downsizing and reengineering existing processes to be more efficient at doing what one has always done. This enables established companies to shore up their margins and muster some fighting strength. In the short term, price cuts, promotions, and incremental product and service improvements, funded by downsizing and reengineering, can stave off the challengers and buy time.

Over the longer term, that approach will get nowhere fast. A meat-ax will help for a while, but eventually there will be nothing more to chop. An established company will have to pay a lot more attention to growth and fundamental innovation—to innovation both in its core processes and its overall business model—for it to regain its leadership and develop competitive advantages suitable to its new reality.

Companies that do not do so will become mired in a vicious cycle of decline—sweeping away people and assets in an increasingly desperate attempt to cut costs ahead of declines in revenue, all in the almost certainly futile hope of sustaining margins. Meanwhile, these companies will fail to realize that it is their fundamental business ideas that have become worthless, not their execution. We have seen this sort of tragic decline and collapse, or near collapse, in any number of seemingly permanent fixtures of world business. In every case, the companies plunged into free fall until they could manage to reorient their approach to strategy-making. Then—if they were fortunate—they were able to regenerate their businesses through a firm understanding of their new customers, new marketplace, and new technologies and business models.

The secret to avoiding all this agony is to mount a multidimensional campaign aimed at the two levels at which one must create the new: the protected direct contribution and the preferred ecosystem itself. This campaign must span the seven dimensions of competitive advantage, which I will come back to again and again:

- customers
- markets
- products
- processes
- organizations
- stakeholders
- government and society

It will be the mission of the rest of this book to explore the nature of these campaigns and to see how they vary over the life of an ecosystem. But first, we need to learn a little more about how ecosystems evolve.

4

The Stages of a Business Ecosystem

Biological communities do not spring full blown upon the earth, but rather develop over time. Life arrives only through spectacular stamina, patience, and luck. This intricate and heroic process is called biological colonization. Community development is most basic when it involves the colonization of barren land: mountainsides denuded by landslides, silt-covered fields left behind when floodwaters recede, or lava flows in Hawaii. Biologists refer to this as primary colonization, the establishment of an ecosystem literally from the ground up.

In Hawaii, new lava comes in two textures—solid *pahoehoe* and rough-hewn *'A'a*. *'A'a* lava is the best base for colonization, because its innumerable small cracks collect moisture and provide some precious shade to shield early settlers. Microorganisms, lichen, and ferns are among the first to establish themselves, creating microscopic quantities of humus and primitive soil, as well as extending the awning of shade.

Over time, the resilient *'ōhi'a-lehua* trees sprout within these small zones of habitable microclimate. The trees in turn shelter other species. Much of the initial activity is around the roots of the *'ōhi'a-lehua* trees, which tunnel through the air pockets in the hardened lava, carving out miniature underground caves where spiders, crickets, and other insects can live.

As years and then decades pass, vegetation clothes the once-barren tract of land and the assembly of life inevitably diversifies. The local ecosystem becomes more densely structured and able to nourish a cornucopia of species. Herbivores pour in, followed by successive levels of carnivores. All these strangers rapidly make themselves at home, and a sort of communion of dependence takes hold. Given the right conditions, a richly canopied forest can establish itself within a single human lifetime. The desolate territory becomes transformed into a full-fledged forest ecosystem with a rather complex soul and destiny.

Establish New Value by Creatively Linking Business Elements

In recent years, ecologists have sought to understand the specific ways in which biological communities establish themselves and to distinguish the results of chance and historical accident from biological necessity. They have come up with what they call "assembly rules." These rules tell which species can coexist in a community, as well as the sequences in which species are likely to colonize an ecosystem. Not until a plant establishes itself can the grasshopper that feeds off it arrive. Not until the grasshopper is there can the dragonfly that dines on it enter. Other assembly rules describe how much competition can exist in an ecosystem. A songbird species may arrive and multiply, consuming so much of the food supply that when additional songbird species come along, only one or perhaps two can squeeze into the ecosystem. The others are rebuffed and must settle elsewhere.

The parallel to business ecosystems is strong. In both cases, a system and a sequence of symbiotic relationships are established. Early business ideas galvanize a small number of supporters, who inject additional ideas, capital, and, if the ideas can demonstrate benefits, cultivate still more support. Over time, the continuing cycle of new contributions and expanding benefits may result in a rich business ecosystem of interrelated customers and suppliers, products and services, processes and organizations.

If we look at any business ecosystem over time, we can see that specific capabilities and relationships were established in complex sequences. For example, Fidelity Investments now makes about 15 percent of all the trades on the New York Stock Exchange. It anchors a vast and powerful financial services ecosystem. But none of this happened overnight. When Ned Johnson took control of his family's small mutual fund company in the 1960s, he concluded that the brokers that had hitherto made the funds available to consumers did not add enough value to justify their cost. Hence he began to assemble the telemarketing capabilities to make his products available directly to end users. The cost savings were partly passed on to consumers to encourage participation, and partly poured into national advertising that established Fidelity as a leading brand in investment services.

Embrace Your Executive Role: Creating Sequences of Synergistic Competencies

Increasingly managers must anticipate what needs to be done to take their ecosystem to the next level. As innovation becomes more important, and as companies realize they can't go it alone, the explicit study of business assembly rules is becoming a high priority. The notion of the "whole product" or "whole offer" has emerged in Silicon Valley to help managers sketch out the full scope of what the customer must experience to exploit a particular technology. Managers are learning to ask: If I want my customers to take maximum advantage of the potential in my products and services, what other capabilities besides those I am directly supplying will be needed by the customer? What can be supplied by third parties? What must the customer provide? A technical product will often require complementary goods and services to become a viable offer for all but the most advanced customers. Similarly, suppliers must be able to make available key components or services. Finally, the customers themselves must build capabilities and demands for the innovation.

As a manager, you must not only have a plan for your own product or service, but a plan to help out the entire ecosystem. Some leading companies are now introducing what they call "precursor products," which are specifically designed to draw customers into a cocreating, coevolving relationship with the company. Then they can concurrently create supply chains, complementary products and services, and customer and lead supplier competencies. Computer software companies are particularly attuned to this way of doing business. Quicken, from Intuit, is an inexpensive program that allows users to write checks and keep financial records using their personal computers. But Intuit has more in mind. It wants to link its customers with financial institutions, becoming the center of a universe of offers and relationships.

It is the identification of capabilities and relationships and the choices about how and when to establish them that are central to strategy-making in our new economy.[1] Later on, when we look at specific cases—from a telephone company in Africa to Wal-Mart—we will see how an initial set of starting elements were elaborated upon, ultimately creating a rich community of interdependent organizations.

The close study of these sequences is the key to answering a number of difficult strategic questions. For example, it has become a truism that companies often fail by being "too early" with particular innovative contributions. But there is little systematic guidance on how to get the timing right. Study of business ecosystems reveals that often the problem is better seen not as a matter of being early or late, but of not being sensitive to the current state of capability building within an ecosystem. In some cases, the necessary precursors to a product are not likely to become available soon, whether in technology, organizational capabilities, or customer and market readiness. In the early 1990s, computers without keyboards failed because voice and handwriting recognition technologies were not ready.

On the other hand, sometimes a business will fail because its offer has already been superseded by that of an emerging ecosystem. Federal Express's Zap Mail assumed people would pay for expensive fax service from FedEx, office to office, delivered to businesses and homes by local couriers. Zap Mail was a flop because FedEx executives misread the importance of, and timing of, developments in telecommunications, semiconductors, and consumer electronics that were spawning business ecosystems that made affordable business and personal fax machines.

Think in Terms of Eras and Stages of Coevolution

Ecologists sometimes speak of the changes undergone by biological ecosystems in terms of stages of succession. My preferred definition of ecological succession is: Progressive change in composition of a community of organisms, e.g., from initial colonization of a bare area (primary succession) or of an already established community (secondary succession), toward a largely stable climax.[2] Not only does the biomass of the community increase during this succession, but the very structure and organization of the community goes through changes. Grasslands and weedy plants give way to alder trees, which in turn convert enough nitrogen in the soil to a nutrient that enables conifers to thrive.

Business leaders often sensitize themselves to such changes in their business ecosystems by thinking in terms of what I call "eras." They try to define the eras that describe their ecosystem. They try to determine what era they are currently in, how long it is likely to last, and what will herald the next era. By doing this, they find that they can better anticipate important potential changes and take precautionary action. In some cases, companies can prepare themselves to supply the next key contribution to the community. In other cases, they may be able to determine how valuable their current contribution will be in the next era and take the appropriate action.

An ecological analysis shows that the sequence and nature of the great eras in the development of a business ecosystem are to some extent predictable. In my work with companies, I have found it extremely helpful to think of the succession that occurs in a business ecosystem in terms of a series of four roughly sequential stages: *pioneering*, when the basic paradigm of the ecosystem is being worked out; *expansion*, when the community broadens its scope and consumes resources of all types; *authority*, when the community architecture becomes stable and competition for leadership and profits within the ecosystem gets brutal; and either *renewal*, when continuing innovation must take place for the community to thrive, or *death*.

Each stage presents particular developmental challenges for the business ecosystem. Moreover, it presents predictable issues for the managers of companies that are already part of the ecosystem as well as those eyeing entry. By identifying the stage that characterizes a given business ecosystem, you can better anticipate the challenges, and better focus executive action. Most large firms have multiple business units and subsidiaries, each of which is apt to be playing in several different business ecosystems. By understanding the complete landscape of positions across multiple ecosystems, executives can better funnel the right talent and resources to each opportunity.

I will devote separate chapters to a detailed examination of each of the four stages, but it is worth delineating them briefly here. To appreciate the stages, it helps to consider what must be accomplished in each one, and how cooperation and competition are redefined as an ecosystem wends its way through each stage.

Stage I: Pioneering an Ecosystem

LINK CAPABILITIES TO CREATE CORE OFFERS ON WHICH
TO BUILD

During this stage, the search for a viable new business ecosystem takes place. It is a brainstorming stage, a time when visionaries aflame with zeal and armed with stiff-backed reserve focus on identifying the particular seed innovations, whether technologies or concepts, that will create radically better products and services than those already available. During this period, entrepreneurs struggle to form embryonic ecosystems that, while hardly mature, are at least complete enough to fulfill the needs of initial customers. In this stage, they attempt to establish "proof of concept"—in other words, unmistakable evidence that here is a viable and exciting alternative to the status quo.

It is also critical during this period to integrate resources and define the nature of value for the customer. You need to invest in coevolutionary sequences of building capability that establish the elusive trait known as *value*. Or, more properly, you need to establish the capabilities for creating value more effectively than any other approach. Most of us know the term "value chain," which refers to the set of activities required to produce a product or service and get it to market. For most of us, this concept is a static one. We try to understand the value chain of our particular business, benchmark our capabilities, and find opportunities for improvement.

In the new world, we need to go from identifying and improving value chains to the active generation of new value chains. I prefer to call this "value chaining" to emphasize its active quality. You should ask yourself what opportunities there are for dramatic performance improvements in your business if all the direct and complementary capabilities were reorganized and new technologies, customers, markets, and regulatory regimes were in place.

Once you become attuned to how business ecosystems function, you can play the game of value chaining with more consciousness and felicity. You can do creative value chaining, mixing and matching capabilities and intentions to invent new offers, capabilities networks, and ecosystems. Ned Johnson's combining of old-line mutual funds with telemarketing and national advertising illustrates such creativity.

CREATE VALUE THAT IS MUCH SUPERIOR TO THE STATUS QUO

In the first stage, you must in your imagination string together capabilities to make new end-to-end systems of value creation that are far more effective than the status quo. In some cases, only certain elements will be available initially. Some may be just potentials. But the notion is that you want to design and create working value chains, usually with partners, that are built around new opportunities and new paradigms of integration.

Without a doubt, this can be a daunting undertaking. In retailing, it took several turbulent years, starting in the late 1960s, to iron out the concept of discounting. The original insight was that customers would willingly drive to stores offering many types of goods at consistently low prices. The early discount stores basically evolved from the old five-and-dime idea. Pioneers like S.S. Kresge (later Kmart) took that notion and expanded it to include a broader range of goods. Still, it took several years and much trial and error before companies began to understand the keys to success—the right product mix, store location, behavior of sales clerks, logistics, and purchasing practices. These concepts evolved dramatically yet again over the next two decades, as Kmart and Wal-Mart, among others, explored the outer limits of the concepts and sculpted systems of truly impressive scale and scope.

The means to victory in this stage is in part being better than others at defining and implementing an offering that customers will desire. Moreover, you must be protective of your ideas, while at the same time learning everything you can from others. The fabled success stories of Stage I are tales of "idea thieves." Sam Walton, Bill Gates, and David Sarnoff were all master bandits willing to swipe ideas from wherever they could find them, just as long as they advanced the products that obsessed them. To succeed, you need to get integration "right enough" to keep the business and the learning going. Failure results if you miss what the customer wants and needs, or are not able to provide it. When that happens, not enough interest is generated to fund further growth of the business ecosystem.

Of the four fundamental challenges facing a business ecosystem, value is the most critical in Stage I. Doing something of dramatic value, compared to what is already available to customers, is the sine qua non of the early days of a business ecosystem. Only the hope—and ultimately the reality—of significant gains and the anticipation of benefits to both customers and suppliers are going to rouse the enthusiasm and commitments of funds, talent, and other resources essential to starting a new ecosystem. In the beginning, the ecosystem bears an extra burden in its struggle against the establishment, for its gains must compensate for the costs of switching over to it. Later in its life, the situation will reverse itself, and the ecosystem will actually be able to weather a slight performance disadvantage against newcomers, because it will be costly for customers to desert it. The test of relative value, while always a matter of importance to an ecosystem, is utterly critical in the first stage.

Stage II: Expansion of an Ecosystem

START WITH A CORE SET OF SYNERGISTIC RELATIONSHIPS AND INVEST IN INCREASING THEIR SCALE AND SCOPE

As it becomes fully structured, the biological community typically spreads across a wide available range, conquering all appropriate territory. The community itself now behaves like a complex, territorial organism, swallowing up sources of nutrients and enlarging its surface area to maximize exposure to the light.

Effective business ecosystems must also expand to fill their available range. This can involve sopping up demand, or it can mean tying up the available supply of key components or related products and services and making sure that they support your position and your conception of the overall ecosystem. Some of the most bruising strategic conflicts occur when similar business ecosystems seek to infiltrate the same market or geographic space. In high technology, these are often experienced as standards battles. In consumer markets, events like the "cola wars" are often not only about immediate market share, but about the underlying battles of ecosystems to spread across territories.

For many managers, the great marketplace battles may seem remote—interesting, perhaps even spectacular, but not particularly relevant to day-to-day business life. To the contrary, most of you are involved in constant ecological struggles. It is in your interest to understand the reach of your products and services and those that are deeply entwined and complementary with yours. More important, it is crucial to assess how much demand exists within what you consider to be your natural market, and how well you are doing at absorbing all of it, and thus precluding entry by competing ecosystems.

All in all, Stage II is the period when the successful paradigm must be more broadly applied and made more reliable and replicable. Additional waves of customers and other stakeholders must be recruited. The focus here is in identifying and rounding up the most desirable potential allies available: the best customers, the strongest suppliers, the most important channels. Moreover, one must be able to accomplish this while keeping reasonable control over the direction of the whole enterprise.

It is crucial that the cooperative network be able to address whatever problems arise, and you can be sure that many will. In product businesses, a major issue is balancing surging demand with a supply capability that is still being refined. Logistics, production, purchasing, and financing can all present withering problems for the growing ecosystem. The community must discover ways to work together to respond to unexpected setbacks. Sometimes if the early players do not have the resources to handle the challenges, they will force the restructuring of the ecosystem. For example, the early biotechnology companies tried to do too much. They thought they could do their own research and development, testing and certification, and sales and support. However, most of them failed to foresee how costly and time-consuming it would be to gain FDA approval for their first products. As a result, many companies began to falter. In the end, the biotechnology companies were not able to create a stand-alone ecosystem and have become more limited research and development houses grafted on to the ecosystems of the established and traditional pharmaceutical companies.

ESTABLISH CRITICAL MASS WITHIN WHATEVER MARKET BOUNDARIES YOU WISH TO RESPECT AND EXPLOIT

From a competitive standpoint, a Stage II ecosystem must prevail in any inter-ecosystem struggles for potential customers, partners, and suppliers. Often two or more camps will arise with strikingly similar core ideas and a similar organizing paradigm. The battle between them is likely to become ugly, as each side tries to pressure key actors to join it and each side tries to sunder its opponent's coalition at every opportunity. In consumer electronics businesses, these inter-ecosystem competitions have manifested themselves in some legendary standards wars: the VHS versus Betamax, and digital compact cassettes versus recordable compact discs. Inter-ecosystem struggles may also surface as fights for consumer share and the best software, as in the quite visible Nintendo versus Sega showdown. In the entertainment world, international conglomerates like MCA, Matsushita, Sony, Walt Disney, Time Warner, and Paramount are all furiously vying for market power in the diversified entertainment industry that now spans theme parks, movies, videos, and retail stores. Each has its own architecture for how to exploit synergies between multiple media and multiple sources of software.

Of the four fundamental challenges facing a business ecosystem, critical mass matters the most in Stage II. The measure of success in this stage is how well one enlists sufficient early support. Once you have this critical mass, more conservative potential allies will join forces, which in turn will have the effect of generating business volume and welcome economies of scale and scope. These economies can then be used to amass profits for partners and to fund further expansion of the marketplace, either through discounts or direct investments in areas like advertising and customer education. Those unable to achieve a critical mass will surely fail, and will helplessly watch their ecosystem expire from lack of customer and supplier interest.

Stage III: Authority in an Established Ecosystem

CONCENTRATE ON EMBEDDING YOUR OWN CONTRIBUTIONS
WITHIN THE HEART OF THE ECOLOGICAL COMMUNITY

In business and in biology, you want to become a part of the establishment if you can. A rather curious facet of the colonization process is how some species can become central to the community, remaining firmly entrenched once the ecosystem is fully formed. While the community is developing, which of the multitude of species that actually appear in the ecosystem often is determined by caprice and historical accident. Some species are specialized to pioneering and are fast to establish themselves on disturbed ground but are pushed to the fringes as the ecosystem matures. But once the community has reached a high level of complexity and fullness, those species that have successfully established themselves tend to persist. The architecture of the community—the basic species that make it up and the special relationships among them—becomes quite fixed.

Similarly, business ecosystems evolve toward stability, and players who happen along at the right time and in the right place sometimes become snugly ensconced in some of the best roles in the community. The agreements and relationships among the participants that compose the business ecosystem become fixed reference points around which the community organizes its work. These relationships are seen by members as guarding their interests. Any attempt to alter a relationship will therefore be highly disruptive to everyone who depends on it. All these relationships often boast indirect links to one another as well. An agreement between company A and company B may provide the specifications and funding for the activities of company C, a supplier to B. In many cases, particular agreements are seen by certain members as favoring and protecting their interests. This therefore increases the number of natural constituencies militating for stability whenever change is contemplated.

In time, this structure of conventions takes on some permanence. In essence, it becomes the operating logic of the business ecosystem. The logic will typically persist unless toppled by cataclysm. This event could be anything from regulatory shifts to lessened customer interest to competition from a more powerful ecosystem.

If you can't be an original member of the establishment, consider becoming a clone—for there is a notable opportunity in biological and business ecosystems that manifests itself after architectural maturity. In biology, there is often some species turnover as new organisms enter the ecosystem and triumph over others. In business, insightful outsiders can often clone the products and processes that are central to the business ecosystem and then find ways to vie for membership. Maturity leaves the business community far more vulnerable to entry and attack by such clones.

Let me explain why. During the formation and expansion period, it is nearly impossible for players to breach the borders of the ecosystem unless they are already strong enough to play a leading role. All of the roles in a system are, in effect, moving targets. Companies that set their sights on one of those roles flirt with disaster. They face the staggering and implausible risk that by the time they are suited to fulfill the role, it will have changed into something else. Once the community becomes set in its ways, however, the once indeterminate roles are fairly fixed. Pillaging outsiders can more safely venture into the ecosystem and find happiness.

MAINTAIN YOUR AUTHORITY WITHIN THE BUSINESS ECOSYSTEM

In the third stage, therefore, new entrants may begin to force their way into the ecological community. The existing players begin to quarrel over the spoils of victory and the continued leadership of the coalition. It is easy for the established leader to be blind-sided by another ecosystem member. In short, competition at this stage turns inward as well as outward. To stay successful, a lead company must maintain and fortify its ability to shape the future direction and investments of the ecosystem's key customers and suppliers. It must fend off rivals within the ecosystem. And it must exceed the attractions of other ecosystems. It must look pretty and stand tough.

Since competition within the ecosystem is for a share of the spoils, any company that craves healthy margins must maintain its bargaining power over other members of the ecosystem. In Stage III, a failed lead company is one that loses its ability to control the ecosystem's future. A failed member is one that loses its bargaining power and then sacrifices some of its profit margins.

A central challenge facing business strategists in maturing ecosystems is how to maintain their authority and the uniqueness of their contribution to the community while also encouraging communitywide innovation and coevolution. We can see this dynamic most vividly in the now ancient history of the personal computer business, circa 1983 to 1985. When IBM entered the business, it made two moves that profoundly stabilized the ecosystem as well as opened it to internal competition. First, it bet on a single, rather slow-changing technical architecture. Second, it bought key components from third parties and diffidently allowed those suppliers to sell to others. In effect, IBM established explicit relationships and made it possible for others to participate in them. This had the very positive effect of triggering explosive growth in the ecosystem, because billions of dollars of risk capital and enormous talent were drawn in. For IBM, however, it had the distinctly unfortunate drawback of eventually causing dire declines in profit margins across the entire community and undermining its stewardship of the very ecosystem it created.

Business ecosystems are also vulnerable to outsiders, who

conclude that they can create alternative ecosystems and take business from the entire industrial community. The stability of an ecosystem can increase the probability that such initiatives will succeed. There are two reasons for this. You may be able to reverse-engineer a well-defined architecture and then go it one better, building an alternative around more advanced underlying technologies or paradigms. Moreover, the mass of the existing ecosystem can make the ecosystem's leaders conservative and render them unwilling or unable to counterattack a competitor with a new paradigm. Barriers to entry become barriers to retaliation. For example, massive amounts of capital invested in plant and equipment, vast proliferation of business processes, and deeply honed skills and technologies tend to cause members of an existing ecosystem to become extremely unwilling to admit their obsolescence.

Accordingly, authority is the critical fundamental challenge facing a business ecosystem in Stage III. Maintaining authoritative leadership, of course, is always vital in a business ecosystem, but it poses a special challenge once a level of success has been realized. Some of the leadership struggles will be internal. Partners and allies may tussle over their portions of the profits of the overall ecosystem. They may also fight over the direction of the ecosystem, as well as their desire to play a key part in driving the performance gains of the whole system.

In later stages of the ecosystem, its nature and composition are increasingly evident for all to see, and competitors may find it attractive to compete against those who helped build the ecosystem. This process tends to be accelerated by customers, who, content with the products and services of the ecosystem and increasingly savvy about how the value is accomplished, may prove surprisingly fickle and willing to switch their business to alternative providers, as long as those providers adhere to the architecture of the larger system.

The Hawaii versus Costa Rica issue of isolation versus access to new entrants plays an important role in Stage III. In the increasingly rare instances that an ecosystem is isolated from new entrants—for example, by regulation or by lack of other key resources—the business ecosystem may evolve a much more stable version of Stage III than if it is highly open to new entrants. A number of the classic academic studies of innovation take their cases from situations that should be considered Hawaiian. It is often argued that so-called "dominant designs"—such as that of the mechanical typewriter—enable companies that popularize the given design to establish almost impenetrable impediments to new entrants. This hypothesized linkage of dominant design and dominant company does often occur in environments with little competition. However, the connection is so tenuous as to be misleading when conditions move toward the wild and chaotic economic environments I have been calling Costa Rican.

Dominant designs are product and process designs that become the industry standards and are widely accepted and built upon by others. In terms of this book, dominant designs are one of the potential outcomes in architecturally stable business ecosystems. The IBM PC shone as a dominant design for the personal computer business. According to the conventional argument, those companies that control a dominant design enjoy vast economies of scale that make them virtually invincible.

There is just enough truth in this story to be dangerous. Being an incumbent in a stable ecosystem, including controlling a dominant design, is unquestionably a nice advantage, but it is not necessarily a permanent one. In the new world, there are many factors that favor those agitating to get in. One need look no further than the dethroning of IBM and the entry of thousands of clone companies into the IBM-created ecosystem to prove the point. Incumbency, as we will see throughout this book, must be continually reinforced and restored. Even Intel and Microsoft, the current sovereigns of the personal computer ecosystem, must be on their guard, for they are constantly being challenged.

Stage IV: Renewal or Death

FIND WAYS TO INSERT NEW IDEAS INTO THE OLD ORDER

I have spoken of trends like deregulation and diffusion of technology that are increasing the rate of improvement and transformation in business. In addition, the consciousness of management of the dynamics of creating ecosystems—and the increasing capabilities of managements to understand one another's paradigms of future ecosystems—is touching off battles over ecosystem leadership.

Such circumstances can lead to round after round of what might be called "paradigm-based competition," an escalating game of dueling paradigms. What was formerly a safe haven becomes a hot spot of rivals crawling over every inch of territory. The automobile industry, for instance, is playing this game rigorously today. Each of the participants wants to outsmart the other by devising ever better business models. The challenge for any ecosystem competitor is never to take for granted its existing ecosystem and role, but to continue to strive for maximum performance improvements, either within an existing ecosystem or through the creation of new ones.

Stage IV is the geriatric stage, when the ecosystem must win the struggle against obsolescence. It is important to remember that a dominant ecosystem is never free from potential obsolescence at the hands of ecosystems built around superior approaches. Even the sturdiest ecosystem will eventually be attacked—and perhaps replaced—by a new ecology that offers greater customer value. Put another way, all business ecosystems depend for their survival on a certain range of conditions in their environment and on their superior ability to exploit those conditions vis-à-vis competing ecosystems. If environmental conditions change—for example, through new regulations or consumer buying patterns—the ecosystem must also change or be seriously damaged. Similarly, if new ecosystems develop that are more effective at capitalizing on environmental opportunities, they can seize territory from existing ecosystems. The cycle of opportunity-hungry competition never ceases. For every successful, established business ecosystem, there are dozens if not hundreds of entrepreneurs plotting to create new alternative ecosystems that will blow it away.

STAY COMPETITIVE WITH OTHER ALTERNATIVES

In terms of the four fundamental challenges facing a business ecosystem, continuous performance improvement is uppermost for Stage IV. For those companies that are established leaders of a prospering ecosystem, prolonging life must at some point become a top priority. Otherwise, they will get done in by their own conservatism. Longevity comes from finding ways to inject new ideas into the existing ecosystem. In its most typical form, it is sometimes talked about as "technology insertion," because new ideas are grafted on to the ecosystem, like a turbocharger added to a car engine. In more radical cases, people talk about "asset reuse," in which the assets of the ecosystem are carved up and recombined. This would be akin to using the chassis of an old Chevy as the convenient starting point for building a dragster.

Sometimes the leaders of ecosystems try to retard customer appetite for change by conditioning the customer to expect some definable range of progress, but not to demand overly disruptive advances. Car companies have been canny in this way. Over the years, they have taught buyers to pay rapt attention to the yearly cosmetic changes in sheet metal but to pay little heed to fundamental advances in the underlying platform of engine, drive train, and chassis. Such managed conservatism is a risky strategy in the new world, because it leaves the ecosystem ripe for exploitation by those organizing new ecosystems. The U.S. auto companies' short-sighted focus on sheet metal changes may have contributed to their blindness to the advances that were being perfected by Toyota and other Japanese firms, advances that were for the most part only apparent if one looked deep into the production process that was turning out the cars.

Challenge Yourself and Your Colleagues to Meet the Four Tests

As a business ecosystem matures, it must surmount four fundamental tests. These can be used by managers to help focus thinking—both their own and that of their associates across their organizations and ecosystems. Indeed, one of the central tasks of management may be seen as focusing attention and investment to create networks of competencies and relationships that will meet the four tests:

1. Establishing a system and sequence of symbiotic relationships that result in the creation of something of real *value* relative to what else is available
2. Establishing *critical mass* as the ecosystem expands across the available customers, markets, allies, and suppliers
3. Lead *innovation* and *coevolution* across what one has wrought
4. Ensuring that the business sustains *continuous performance improvement* rather than becomes obsolete

Considering these tests is an excellent way to evaluate the robustness of a business ecosystem as well as the leadership contributions of a particular member. Ecosystem-savvy strategies should be designed to address these tests. Finally, these tests help us to anticipate challenges that will emerge during the life cycle of a business ecosystem. The specific tests tend to come forth in a sequence that corresponds to the four stages of development.

There is an ongoing discussion in business circles about the primacy of cooperation or competition. Which is more important? The study of business ecosystems suggests that both are important in each of the stages of development, but in differing ways. What a holistic approach to leadership requires is the shaping of coevolution. Coevolution—in biology and in business—proceeds by both competition and cooperation. In the pioneering stage, you must cooperate with others to create something of real value, while also protecting your ideas. In the expansion stage, you must work with others to achieve market coverage, while also blocking alternative ecosystems. In the authority stage, you must provide a galvanizing vision to motivate the community to keep working together, while also ensuring that your leadership position and margins are not weakened. Finally, in the renewal stage, you need to look beyond the community for innovative contributions, while also attempting to prevent customers and partners from defecting to more recently established ecosystems.

The challenges of leadership, cooperation, and competition across the stages of ecosystem development can be summarized as follows:

Stage of development of the business ecosystem	Overall leadership challenges	COOPERATIVE CHALLENGES	COMPETITIVE CHALLENGES
Pioneering	Value	Work with customers and suppliers to define the new value proposition and a paradigm for providing it that is dramatically more effective than what is available	Protect your ideas from others who might be working toward defining similar offers
Expansion	Critical mass	Bring the new offer to a large market by working with suppliers and partners to increase supply, and to achieve maximum market coverage and critical mass	Defeat alternative implementations of similar ideas; ensure that your approach is the market standard in its class through dominating key market segments; tie up critical lead customers, key suppliers, and important channels
Authority	Lead coevolution	Provide a compelling vision for the future that encourages suppliers and customers to work together to continue to improve the ecosystem	Maintain strong bargaining power in relation to other players in the ecosystem—including key customers and valued suppliers
Renewal	Continuous performance improvment	Work with innovators to bring new ideas to the existing ecosystem	Maintain high barriers to entry to prevent innovators from building alternative ecosystems. Maintain high customer switching costs in order to buy time to incorporate new ideas in your own products and services

Table 4.1

In the next chapter we will explore in detail how the auto industry has evolved and show how the distinctive contribution of leadership, from Ford to Sloan to Iacocca, creatively addressed these four tests.

5

Coevolution and Cars: Stages in Action

What would happen if somehow the tectonic plates under the earth shifted so radically that Hawaii and Costa Rica were thrust together? Ecosystems would meet ecosystems, species would commingle across the land. The probable result would be the wholesale transformation of the Hawaiian ecosystems—and the continuance and expansion of the Costa Rican communities—albeit with a few new introductions. Actually, with the collapse of industry and other similar boundaries, such experiments are going on all the time in business ecosystems.

For example, most of the large business ecosystems that grew up behind industry walls had middle years of Hawaiian isolation, even if their early formation was often tumultuous. This was the case for big oil, big steel, railroads, autos—and utilities from electricity to telephony. In each of these domains fierce initial competition eventually gave way to a few dominant players and roles—and long periods of relative stasis. In some cases regulation kept the environment simple; in others it was the lack of capital, a lock on expertise, and a firm grip on key markets. But today land bridges are being erected, and species are on the move. Globalization of capital and markets, and the challenge of substitute technologies and offers has made life substantially more complicated. It is as if the isolation of the Hawaiian paradise has been breached. Costa Rica, here we come.

The Varieties of Coevolutionary Time

The large traditional industries—including steel, oil, and autos—all took many decades to go through the four stages. Most of the initial slowness is probably explained by the fact that these were the first generation of industrial ecosystems on earth—and a vast array of capabilities had to evolve from scratch. But isolation no doubt played a major role, particularly in extending the reign of established business paradigms.

On the other hand, since their isolation has been breached, business evolution is now speeding up dramatically. What once took decades may now take a few years. Moreover, many business arenas are becoming so deintegrated, so modular, and so competitive that we are experiencing the almost constant emergence of multiple, concurrent ecosystems.

What I will do in this chapter is examine the development of the great auto-making ecosystems.[1] My purpose is to give you a rich feeling for the stages of development, including the challenges at each stage to executives. The stages of business evolution have existed since the beginnings of commerce; therefore an ecological approach can be used to analyze the emergence of any major business, illustrating both cooperative and competitive challenges and the approaches necessary to master them. I will also contrast the long, slow development of a traditional industry with the hypercompetitive, paradigm-breaking competition engendered once its boundaries are breached.

Engage History to Gain Insights for Strategy-Making

The problem with most business analysis is that it focuses mainly on the current performance of a company or business ecosystem and tends to gloss over the events that produced it. The result is that managers get little help in trying to create leading performance over time. Long-term case histories, on the other hand, can provide much more insight into the situations facing managers, the choices made, and the consequences.

For many years, Richard Neustadt and Ernest May have taught a course at Harvard to midcareer and senior political and government leaders. The ideas in the course are summarized in the excellent *Thinking in Time: The Uses of History for Decision Makers* (Free Press, 1986),[2] where they point out that it is important not only to read historical cases, but to bring certain questions to the stories: "Of each illustration, we ask whether the decision makers, within the limits of their circumstances, could have done a bit better. If so, how? And what generalizations could practitioners extract for their own—or anyone else's—workaday use?"

These sorts of questions can serve as a kind of special nutrient to develop your personal capacity for strategic thinking. By wrestling with these questions, you can sharpen your ability to see patterns in change, and to position yourself more effectively to take advantage of emerging conditions. This book will tell a set of stories of business growth and coevolution. We will examine the choices that were made by key executives and record the consequences. We will explore alternative actions that might have been available if decision makers had been better able to read the dynamics of business evolution around them.

I find many executives intrigued by business history—as well as by their own role in history-in-the-making. As the rate of business evolution increases, the relevant historical timetables are shortening. In many sectors, individual managers have lived through several major periods, with distinct conditions, in the past several years. In almost all instances, managers looking into the future can anticipate tremendous dislocations and transformations in business conditions. The radically compressed timetable of change is making a historical perspective both relevant and necessary.

The histories of Ford Motor Company and General Motors are fascinating in their own right.[3] But more important, automobile companies have had a monumental impact on world society. In their heyday, these large-scale industrial ecosystems were among the most technologically advanced of their time. Many of the organizational and leadership ideas that we have come to associate with large integrated firms were invented in auto companies—from the concept of business units and the multidivisional firm to market forecasting and production planning. For all of these reasons, we can learn much by following them briefly through the three-quarters of a century it took them to evolve and by looking at how leadership challenges vary with each stage.

Cars are certainly familiar to us. They trigger fond memories. A special appeal of car-making ecosystems as subjects is that they demonstrate the whole range of business evolutionary timelines. Their early formation was central to the original machine age. Their reinvention, at the hands of Toyota and the Japanese, happened in about twenty years. As we come to the end of the twentieth century, the large American auto companies—Ford, General Motors, and Chrysler—belong to the global economic environment, and are pursuing three distinct strategies for creating and managing ecosystems.[4]

A Case Study of Business Coevolution

Above all else, business evolution is a story of alternative visions for organizing and leading ecosystems. And indeed, Ford and General Motors started with models that were vastly different. Ford was oriented toward product simplification and a single great business process architecture as the means to growth. General Motors was formed by acquiring a host of beginning ecosystems and trying to forge a coherent, synergistic enterprise out of them. As such, Ford taught the world much about large-scale production. General Motors taught it about how to manage multidivisional firms. Let's watch them from the beginning.

Stage I: From Horseless Carriages to Motor Cars

Stage I for a host of potential automobile-centered ecosystems began around the turn of the last century. The late 1800s were a time of experimentation, as the first pioneers struggled to grasp the potential of individualized, motorized transportation. Ransom E. Olds and a handful of others were the ones who established the first viable automobile business ecosystems. Essentially, they took the rolling technologies of horse-drawn buggies and wagons and added engines to them. The critical technology turned out to be small gasoline engines, which provided locomotion without the enormous weight required for steam-powered alternatives. Their machines worked reasonably well, were accepted by a small but dedicated number of customers, and could be profitably produced in limited quantities.

Few of these pioneering ecosystems, however, became the basis for expanding industrial communities. A partial reason is that their founders lacked systemic vision. Henry Ford was almost unique in this respect. From the beginning of his career, he was interested not just in cars but in the overall business process architecture for producing and distributing cars on a mass scale. His organizational learning was fixed on the creation of a large-scale system. Indeed, he envisioned what we would now call a multidimensional campaign, encompassing the creation of customer interest and development of the market, including not only dealer networks but the construction of supporting infrastructure, ranging from roads to service stations. Ford, of course, founded the Ford Motor Company, and in 1908 introduced his mass-produced, mass-marketed Model T.

William C. Durant was another pioneer who shared Ford's desire to create an expansive ecosystem. In 1904, Durant began building what would become General Motors. Durant was less systematic than Ford, but just as ambitious. His approach centered on buying up other firms, creating an expanding if disorganized collection of car companies.

Stage II: Vast, Expanding Industrial Ecosystems

Ford and Durant rapidly became the two major forces in the nascent auto business. Over the next twenty years, near-legendary battles between Ford and General Motors would erupt, struggles as much for the soul and future definition of the business as for simple market share.

Ford's approach was based on vertical integration, carefully engineered production, and product simplicity. Ford's ecosystem had what we would now call "scalability"; by 1914, his company had produced more than 267,000 cars and held 48 percent of the market. Moreover, the company had achieved dramatic economies of scale. In 1914, Ford factories produced 20.6 cars for every worker employed, while the average for the rest of the industry was just 4.3 cars per worker.[5]

Durant, as we have noted, had a different idea. His strategy for GM was based on acquisitions of early companies, marketing might, sales coverage, and product variety. In a sense, Durant's innovative paradigm was one of corporate strategy and structure, not of production logic. Durant created an ecosystem that captured market share by pooling the markets and the production facilities of a variety of smaller companies. However, the elements of the General Motors ecosystem could not work together to achieve sufficient economies of scale and consequently GM was stuck with high-cost structures and increasingly uncompetitive products. Moreover, while Durant had a corporate structure paradigm that resembled the modern multidivisional firm, he had none of the systems and expertise required to oversee such an octopus. By 1920, the General Motors ecosystem had nearly collapsed because of these shortcomings. Durant was ousted by his investors.

From about 1910 to 1930, industry leaders directed the large-scale, Stage II expansions of their ecosystems. Ford simply scaled up his mass production system in the United States, while licensing others in nations around the world to clone its major features. In this manner, Ford was able to meet the explosive demand for low-cost, simple motorcars. On the other hand, he left unaddressed the market for more sophisticated cars, as well as those adapted to particular lifestyles.

Alfred P. Sloan's design for General Motors, initiated after the firing of Durant, was more notable. Sloan's design specifically allowed for the management of a complex business ecosystem by splintering the diverse company into product lines, which, in turn, could be focused like Ford's mass-produced lines. Sloan also centralized financial oversight of decentralized product lines, and GM became the very prototype of the modern multidivisional company. General Motors combined mass production with financial and administrative controls that allowed it, in essence, to oversee several systems like Ford's.

Even more interesting, Sloan came to realize that not all customers wanted to be treated alike. More affluent customers would willingly pay for distinctive vehicles. So Sloan set out to create customer segments, by aiming his various car lines at customers at particular economic and social levels. In the status-conscious, conformist America of the mid-century, Sloan was able to help customers forge identities centered around his car brands. Chevy people saw themselves differently from Cadillac people, and both were proud to be associated with their chosen brands.

Sloan's General Motors became dominant in the U.S. market, vastly outstripping Ford. Moreover, GM's organizational design became the shared business model for all of the major auto-centered ecosystems when it was adopted by Henry Ford's successors, and it would last beyond the middle decades of the century. In a sense, the two companies converged on one overall business model, encompassing product, process, and organizational ideas. This business model is most commonly known today by the term "mass production," even though the model goes beyond production techniques to include approaches to customer segmentation as well as enterprise and supplier management.[6]

Stage III and the Long Stasis

The third stage of business ecosystems, authority, involves struggle over the rewards and profits generated by the ecosystem. In automobiles, this stage was in full force in both the Ford and General Motors ecosystems starting in 1930. For the auto company executives, success largely consisted of managing relationships with the other major members of each ecosystem—big steel, big labor, and big government. Some of the most important battles revolved around the principal supplier to the auto industry: labor. In the late 1920s, around 500,000 people worked in the Detroit area car factories. No one was organized. Working conditions were dangerous; one auto body plant was eerily known as "the slaughterhouse." But by the mid-1930s, the United Auto Workers union had formed. In 1937, the UAW achieved a landmark victory when GM recognized the union as an official representative of its employees.

Over time, organized labor brought workers crucial bargaining power, which the union used to force the companies to share the spoils of victory. The tug-of-war between workers and companies continued for decades, mediated with varying effectiveness by the U.S. government. While it protected workers, this Stage III struggle also carried with it high costs: work-rule rigidity and the polarization of workers and management. These costs would come back to haunt the U.S. automobile business in the next stage of ecosystem development.

Besides the major direct species, many other organizations had important roles in supporting the auto ecosystems. Automobile liability insurance grew from its roots in rural co-ops to become an international business. Gasoline production and distribution systems generated huge fortunes for their owners. Road construction and maintenance became constant on the landscape, supported primarily by taxes, which in turn were authorized by various local, state, and national government bodies. None of these species challenged the fundamentals of how the major auto ecosystems were organized and conducted their business. Instead, they extended and completed the value proposition, enriching but not fundamentally changing the experiences of customers.

During the long Stage III stasis, the government itself

became increasingly involved in what it now saw as a full-fledged "industry." Government regulation and intervention emerged as a major factor in both dividing the spoils of the system and further reinforcing its deeply ingrained modes of thought and action.

Labor-management struggles, mediated by government, continued into the 1970s, until all sides were drawn together by a much deeper crisis: the obsolescence of the management approaches, business practices, and systems of production that had been only incrementally improved since the 1920s. The near collapse of the U.S. automobile business came, of course, at the hands of the Japanese.[7]

THE EMERGENCE OF AN ALTERNATIVE ECOSYSTEM IN JAPAN

In biology, a set of individuals may become separated from the main population of a species. This subpopulation, as well as the ecosystem of which it is part, proceeds to live its own separate history and to evolve unique adaptations to its environment. Its members may, over time, develop such distinct characteristics that the group becomes a separate species.

Auto making in Japan had evolved after World War II in a manner not unlike an isolated subpopulation: separated from the mainstream during its formative years, it benefited from parallel evolution. Prior to the war, the Japanese had begun building auto-making ecosystems modeled after those in the United States. These nascent efforts were destroyed by the fighting and the subsequent occupation of Japan.

The new postwar Japanese ecosystems began with very different assumptions about their opportunity environment and were stimulated to create original visions of how to make cars. As the Japanese rebuilt, Toyota and others started with the challenge of building cars in limited quantities with minimal capital investment and extremely dedicated and meticulous employees. These, of course, were the conditions of a Japan that had lost the war. What emerged, beginning in the early 1950s, was a production system built around careful, continuous coordination of efforts and optimization of resources.

In addition, American ideas about organizational learning were transferred to Japan by Edward Deming, among others, in a movement that became the Quality Revolution. These ideas helped teach Toyota and others how to measure performance and engage their dedicated workers in continuous process improvement and continued individual and team learning.

By the 1970s, these ideas had coevolved into a sophisticated new business ecosystem based on a combination of customer-focused design, concurrent engineering, flexible manufacturing, learning-oriented workers, and networks of suppliers, all tied together through statistically refined management practices. This ecosystem was profoundly innovative, as reflected in the dramatic price/performance gains it realized compared with alternative systems. Higher-quality vehicles were built with half the development time and engineering costs, half the manufacturing capital investment, and half the labor.

By the 1970s, the Toyota ecosystem, for one, was capable of unheard-of levels of product variety, product quality, and efficiency.[8] Its overseers had also spent a decade exploring the opportunities in the American market. They decided that the time had come to launch a major campaign of entry and colonization. A figurative land bridge between Japanese and American environments had been established, and species started pouring across. Hawaii was about to be invaded.

Stage IV Comes to the American Auto Ecosystems

The lead ecosystems of the American automobile industry, as traditionally defined, now found themselves in a full-fledged Stage IV war, defending against a new influx of business ecosystems. Self-renewal proved difficult, and companies like Chrysler and Ford had nearly collapsed by the late 1970s, along with numerous closely associated suppliers.

The superiority of Japanese approaches ultimately forced the transformation of the world automobile industry into what we see today. By the mid–1990s, key elements of the Toyota ecosystem had been adopted by other auto-making ecosystems around the world. Like the combination of Ford's "Fordism" and GM's multidivisional organization, which came to be known as "mass production," the Toyota system is now known as "lean manufacturing," and it was clearly the benchmark used by industry leaders, analysts, academics, and consultants who work at ushering in change.[9]

Naturally, the degree to which it was adopted varied because of the challenges of converting vast Stage IV ecosystems. In a sense, what was required was to establish new Stage I thinking, acting, systems, and organization within the shell of the old. In biology, this process is known as "secondary colonization," when species of one ecosystem penetrate the territory of another and ultimately change its composition and structure.

In the case of GM, new paradigm plants were built—NUMI in California, and Saturn in Tennessee—but their revolutionary results were ignored by the rest of the company for many years. Instead, GM spent billions of dollars attempting to automate its version of the mass production paradigm, going so far as to buy Electronic Data Systems to accelerate this initiative. Unfortunately, the results were dismal, and in the early 1990s GM was forced to intensify efforts to adopt lean manufacturing.

Ford was a more promising student. Starting in about 1980, it made a heroic effort, renegotiating its labor contracts to gain job flexibility, and investing in Total Quality programs throughout Ford. Finally, Ford tackled its most daunting challenge: transforming its suppliers and supply networks, which involve literally thousands of suppliers intertwined in a complex web. While Ford was not able to match the Japanese, it dramatically improved its own performance and cost position, advancing decisively beyond General Motors on the most important benchmarks.[10]

In a later chapter, we will return to the challenges of transforming Stage IV ecosystems. For just as there is a need to understand the creation of new ecosystems, there is a profound value in being able to convert existing ones. In our celebration of technology and newness, we sometimes miss the recognition that fast-paced business evolution leaves in its wake many obsolete but still functioning capabilities. The conversion of these capabilities to new purposes may turn out to be one of the most important businesses of the next century.

A New and Faster Timeline

The four stages of mass production took about three-quarters of a century to develop within the original auto-centered business ecosystems. Many Ford and General Motors managers spent their entire careers in just one of the stages—or at most two. Given that lengthy historical trajectory, one wonders how long the new pattern established by the Japanese will remain valid. The answer, I believe, is not long. There are two reasons. First, the hot conditions of business evolution today mean that any new paradigm gets replicated and transcended very quickly. Second, the resource intensity of automobiles— whether mass produced or lean—probably is not sustainable over long time horizons because of the decline in the world's fossil fuels.

The new lean production paradigms of automobile design, manufacturing, distribution, and consumer consensus are now deeply embedded in business ecosystems throughout the world. Already, American companies have cloned and extended critical technologies, processes, and organizational ideas—the business equivalents of species—derived from the Japanese system. In about twenty-five years, we have witnessed what might be best thought of as a secondary colonization of the major auto-centered ecosystems, as species from one center of industrial organizations have migrated into and partially transformed other ecosystems.

Currently, the worldwide auto ecosystems are going through a new round of change, as the lean production concept reaches Stage III maturity in most of the ecosystems in which it is lodged. With architectural stasis coming to lean production, the modularization, outsourcing, and deintegration characteristic of modern Stage III ecosystems are bursting full force upon the world.

Like the personal computer business, autos are becoming products that to some extent can be put together in a plug-and-play manner, at least by the major assemblers. As the leading lean manufacturing ecosystems move deeply into Stage III, fast-paced moves are taking place toward both flexible manufacturing and platform cars, as well as toward radical deintegration, unbundling, and outsourcing across the industry. Astonishingly, in less than twenty-five years, the world of car manufacturing—an extraordinarily capital-intensive business—has not only completely adopted the lean manufacturing innovation, it has begun to rip it apart.

Stage III in an Open, Modular Economy

Most observers of the auto business remain chiefly interested in the spread of lean manufacturing across the several major ecosystems. But this may not be the most arresting story. The world automobile business is coming to be dominated by a few great Stage III ecosystems led by companies that all essentially subscribe to the tenets of lean manufacturing. What is interesting is that the new Stage III—the Stage III of lean manufacturing—is very different from the Stage III of mass production that preceded it. Evolutionarily, it is as different as the jungles of Hawaii and Costa Rica.

In the new economy, as we have emphasized, industry and national boundaries are declining, technological know-how is widely distributed, and capital and management talent are plentiful. Moreover, information technology and new management thinking have allowed virtual organizations and networked companies to proliferate. In this environment, the stability of product and process paradigms that is the hallmark of Stage III produces, paradoxically, a raft of new organizational species and designs. In the new economy, stable ecosystems are open ecosystems, ripe for new entrants. The very stability of the basic

business model makes it a sitting target for enterprising companies that are willing to work a little harder, or accept smaller
returns, than the members of the establishment.

Thus in the auto business, as in personal computers, cloners
and new entrants are banging away at the established players.
Cars are now made in Taiwan and Korea and myriad other
nations; suppliers are evolving at a very fast clip. For example,
Ryder, the trucking company, is now a major provider of integrated logistics services for auto companies.

What is most interesting is how three major auto companies—Ford, General Motors, and Chrysler—have decided to
orchestrate their respective ecosystems. They have each taken
a distinctive approach, demonstrating three ways in which
large companies can play within the highly modular, deintegrated, highly rivalrous environments that emerge when business ecosystems do not become isolated.

Three Strategies for Leading Open Ecosystems

Chrysler has focused on what might be called "lean orchestration"; that is, on becoming a systems engineer and systems
integrator of the contributions of a number of players.[11]
Chrysler goes quite far in getting these players to assume
responsibilities for engineering, production, assembly of major
auto subsystems, quality assurance, and just-in-time delivery.
Chrysler is exploiting the vast collective resources not only of
its ecosystem, but of all the great automobile ecosystems.
There is immense variety and vitality in the worldwide supplier communities that serve these ecosystems. Chrysler's theory is that it can learn to ride atop this community as a shrewd
and powerful hitchhiker, becoming the best selector, shaper,
and integrator of its capabilities. So far, the strategy is paying
off. Chrysler is realizing lower costs and shorter development
time. Combined with some true design "hits," this approach
has led to quite a resurgence for the Iacocca-less company. On
the other hand, some observers question whether the Chrysler

approach relies too much on suppliers and may in the end compromise quality and reliability. Time, as always, will tell.

Ford, by contrast, has chosen to pursue volume and, with it, economies of scale. It is seeking to exploit the aggregate size of the worldwide market. Ford's goal is to consolidate worldwide aggregate volumes with its manufacturing and development resources, and thereby realize vast savings. To this end, Ford is:

- Consolidating worldwide vehicle design into five centers
- Reducing and scaling up assembly operations
- Reducing the number of suppliers, which allows suppliers to gain economies of scale and also benefit Ford[12]

Ford's bet is that the convergence of consumer tastes and environmental regulations, combined with the opening of national boundaries, will make possible the success of "world cars." These cars would be designed at central locations and manufactured at the places that achieve maximum economies of scale while managing to meet requirements for local content and the costs of tariffs and taxes. The danger of this strategy is that the coordination costs of doing a world car will overwhelm its advantages. For its part, Ford believes that advances in information technologies, which reduce coordination costs, have now made such a sophisticated concept feasible. Another risk is that world markets will diverge in tastes and regulation, and that the advantages of world cars will be more than canceled out by products aimed at smaller markets.

Meanwhile, Toyota appears to be seeking new methods in the car business, in some cases roping functionality back in from suppliers. This allows it to graduate more nimbly to advanced process and asset architectures. Interestingly, Toyota continues to eschew high-technology automated manufacturing as an end-all. Rather, it is putting enormous efforts into mechanical engineering, the development of individual and team skills, and the diffusion of knowledge across its supplier base. In some important ways, Toyota is sticking to its roots, focusing closely on how to make cars with ever better coordination and ever deeper human talent and engagement.[13]

The risk to an architect of new methods staying too close to its roots is that doing so may waste time and money trying to improve an ecosystem with diminishing potential for returns on innovation. In some cases, that same effort might be better spent on more radical possibilities. One could argue that Toyota might be wiser to spend the same resources on new transportation systems to replace cars. The other side of this argument is that seeking new methods actually may not be all that expensive. It may be more a matter of mind-set than of resources, something that can come out of normal management expenditures in companies that may also be exploring dramatically different futures.

At the time this book was written, GM was an interesting wild card. In recent years, GM has followed the vertical integration path. During the 1980s, it spent heavily—and perhaps unwisely—on high-information, technology-based reengineering, ultimately acquiring, in part to advance this agenda, Electronic Data Systems and creating the world's largest computer services company. Optimists point out that GM has the scale to match Toyota, and could perhaps play both the Ford and Chrysler approaches by having a portfolio with some world cars for the long run, along with systems-integrated, fast-assembled, low-volume lifestyle offerings. Pessimists, of course, continue to argue that GM's fabled bureaucracy—the legacy of its enormous success in the first automobile age—will continue to hamstring the company.

The auto business shows us that the new, comparatively boundary-free economy creates two great resources in an opportunity environment—a vast community of participants and large aggregate volumes—and that companies can position themselves to exploit these resources. Strategic invention is raised to a higher level, as companies become aware of these resources and position themselves to utilize them. As I emphasize throughout this book, the fundamental lesson of the "death of competition" is that in these sorts of environments, companies need to become able not simply to operate their current business models, but to envision those of the future. Chrysler, Ford, and General Motors are all showing interesting alternative ways to configure their ecosystems, as they move deeply into the new era.

Will "Green" Hypercars Destroy Detroit?

For all of the creativity of the firms in the auto ecosystems, a profound threat looms on the horizon. Almost no one today believes that the automobile is a sustainable technology. Its dependence on oil, among other resources, is probably more than the planet can bear, particularly as more nations become highly developed and demand the best in transportation.

How long the automotive ecosystems last depends in part on how long the overall environment—social, political, economic, and biological—avoids radical transformations. Changes in personal transportation systems are already on the horizon, in part due to environmental pressures. Proven world reserves of conventional crude oil will last only another forty years, according to the best projections. Natural gas reserves are likely to last sixty more years. Unless something happens, the main modes of transportation will have to change over the next few decades.

While the auto business is already experiencing many of the effects of the end of isolation, particularly in how swiftly new paradigms are being adopted and in the coming of electronic technology, on another level its change has just begun. The real end will be when it finds that it must break out of the broadest outlines of its business or be supplanted by other firms, based perhaps in aerospace (new vehicles), or civil engineering (new infrastructure), or computers (new controls), or even residential construction (new towns). This will very likely happen within the managerial careers of many readers of this book.

At least two lines of plausible if radical thinking could undermine the current auto ecosystems—and create new ecosystems better adapted to future opportunity environments. One school of thought goes under the rubric of "intelligent transportation systems" and argues for computer control to coordinate integrated systems of vehicles and highways. The notion is that automated controls will bring about better utilization and loading of both cars and roads, and that this will generate efficiencies that will make the effort worthwhile.

Though experiments have begun around the world, the jury is still out on whether the benefits of this approach will be strong enough to foster new ecosystem development. If we return to the four tests that a potential ecosystem must meet, the approach faces a major hurdle in the value test. It seems likely, then, that intelligent vehicle systems will remain stuck in Stage I until this test is clearly met.

A more radical approach is the "Hypercar." Promoted by the futurist Amory Lovins, among others, the Hypercar combines hybrid gas/electric motors and lightweight carbon-fiber reinforced plastic bodies.[14] Theoretically, the vehicles can drive across the entire United States on a single tank of gas.

Equally fascinating, the carbon-fiber bodies can be made without the capital-intensive dies and stamping presses required for steel-shelled cars. Since this capital intensity is one of the major barriers to entry enjoyed by the current leaders of the auto ecosystems, the erosion of this barrier might permit smaller and radically different companies to assemble cars. For all we know, the car business could become like the personal computer business, with a vast number of small assemblers and direct distributors making Hypercars.

In theory at least, the Hypercar appears to pass the value test. After companies spend a few years producing prototypes, this test may also be passed in practice—at least on a small scale. The more likely challenge for the Hypercar is the Stage II requirement of critical mass. A car business needs a complete network of suppliers for components, even if the body is plastic. More important, customers will want to know that their cars can be serviced wherever they travel. Accordingly, the new ecosystem will have to establish extensive networks of sales and support organizations. The auto companies have these networks, of course, but they may not be motivated to use them to destroy their die-making and steel-stamping advantages. On the other hand, an upstart—that is, an aerospace or computer company—could make Hypercars, but it would find deployment of a region-wide service quite an undertaking.

Stability Is Fleeting

Mastering business evolution means to influence the future. As I emphasize throughout this book, the fundamental lesson of the "death of competition" is that in these sorts of environments, companies need to become able not simply to operate their current business models but to envision those of the future. The way to achieve advances is to marry ideas of what to do to meet customer needs with ideas of how to do it. When a new idea is radically better than what already exists—as the wheel was to the drag sled, or the microprocessor to the mainframe computer—the result may be the creation of a new business ecosystem.

In the broadest sense, business strategy deals with issues of stability and instability in the vast complex system that we know as the world economy. It takes a mixture of factors—technological, capital, managerial, regulatory—to give birth to an ecosystem. The creative leaders seek to harness these opportunities and turn them into successful business initiatives. In so doing, they start to create stability in change: they create a paradigm of integration that is the seed for a business ecosystem. This is the Stage I story. The nascent ecosystem, if successful, becomes hectically alive and sweeps across market territories. In this way, the stability of the integrating paradigm is now applied to a vast number of lives and businesses. This is the phenomenon of Stage II. Table 5.1 depicts this pattern of rolling stability.

STAGE OF THE BUSINESS ECOSYSTEM	I PIONEERING	II EXPANSION	III AUTHORITY	IV RENEWAL
Leading species or companies within the business ecosystem	Emerging	Stable	Increasingly contested	Heavily contested
Business model for the ecosystem	Emerging	Stable	Stable	Becoming unstable
Dominant ecosystem within the boundaries of a given market	Not yet determined	Emerging, contested	Stable	Becoming unstable

Table 5.1

Two items stand out in this chart: first, how small the zone of stability is when viewed across a longer evolutionary perspective; and second, how a company never achieves a state of stability across all four stages. In Stage II, a company's leadership or membership will usually not be directly challenged, but the viability of the ecosystem itself is in doubt, so management is consumed by a dramatic expansion battle. Yet once that battle is won, competition flares riotously among one's partners and allies. In Stage III, so many aspects—the stability of the business model, the conception of value, the architecture of processes and assets—can conspire against those companies that made up the original cabal.

Now turbulence returns to these insiders who founded and drove the ecosystem, and it would not be surprising for them to find themselves pining for the halcyon days of old. These pioneers have much to be proud of. They contributed value by refining a paradigm of integration and stability and by bringing it to a wide array of suppliers and customers, not to mention extending it across a broad set of market territories. But now that the stable pattern is set, it has its own life. The leaders alone no longer speak a new language. Thousands if not millions of participants know the tongue. A community has been established, and it doesn't need its founders. The destinies of the ecosystem and its founders are no longer intertwined. New entrants can readily come into the community. In some cases, they will be cleverer than the founders. Or, in other cases, they will be willing to spend more, or get back less, to play.

Now, if the pioneers are to have enduring value they must buck the populism of the community and lead from principles. To be woven back into the canon, they must force instability in the ecosystem to keep the architecture of the community open to new innovations. They must rally the members to work together to move forward. And they must find means of contributing important advances that are valued by the ultimate customers—indeed, demanded by them. This will encourage others in the community to do what is needed to help bring these advances to market.

Finally, in Stage IV, the paradigm of integration that has served so well runs out of gas. Effective community action no longer is able to deal with contemporary opportunities and problems. Other, better models of integration become more compelling visions and more provocative as the basis for a community. In Stage IV, instability returns to the ecosystem in one of two forms. Either there will be managed instability, which will allow the more or less orderly conversion of assets and processes to a new paradigm of integration, or the community will become rigid in defense of its approach, a calcification that will cause the community to slide quickly and inexorably into decline. The role of a leading company and manager is to provide visions of conversion, to do the hard work of conversion, and, if conversion proves unfeasible, to attempt the arduous task of moving out of one community while doing the spadework needed to form its alternative.

In the following chapters I will more systematically tackle, one by one, the distinct challenges of the four stages. Remember that notably different talents and skills must be summoned in each stage. In fact, astute leading companies are learning how to reenvision their divisions and business units in terms of which stage-related issues they are working on, as well as which markets and products. In so doing, one better tailors management talent, management systems, structure, and culture to those concerns that most gravely burden each stage. Distilled in this way, it is the best means to prosper in the new world.

6

Stage I: The Terrain of Opportunities

For a pioneer, the terrain of opportunities comes in many shapes and sizes, ranging from a solitary microchip to an entire planet. While horse waste may be distinctly unappealing to us, it represents a wonderful opportunity to a fly or fungal spore. The key to successful pioneering is the ability to find new terrain and, once you arrive there, to survive and thrive.

In nature, some plants and animals are considered pioneer species. They specialize in colonizing relatively barren terrain. By and large, they are exceedingly fussy about their choice of location. Many lichens, for instance, colonize only bare lava rock. Some plants restrict themselves to disturbed patches of open soil like landslides and tree-fall gaps. Weedy species of this sort seem always quick to colonize the turned soil in our gardens. To be sure, the process of colonizing a new volcanic island in the Pacific Ocean is much different from colonizing a landslide in the Costa Rican forest, and the characteristics of the successful pioneers are different as well. However, there are also many similarities.

One important trait shared by pioneer species is high vagility—the ability to disperse over long distances and find new places to colonize. Many of these species, however, do not have direct control over their voyages. Some, like dandelion seeds, are subject to the whims of the wind. Others depend on different species for transportation. The seeds of many plants do their traveling nestled inside a bird's gut. Burrs attach to the fur of mammals and hitch rides to new domains. Other colonists, like flying insects, make it to new areas on their own power.

In the biological world, the vast majority of potential colonists are doomed to failure. A mushroom may produce millions of spores, but a minute number find a suitable place to germinate and grow. The reason is that most of these hopeful colonists either arrive in inappropriate territory, where they cannot survive, or arrive too late to compete successfully with those colonists who have already established themselves. Others get to a new land too early, before the essential mutualists they need. For example, a plant may flourish on a new island, but be unable to reproduce because its pollinator is absent.

Some colonizing species bring their essential mutualists with them. A new leaf-cutting ant queen always packs a small piece of fungus from her home garden before leaving her natal nest for a new colony. The queen carries this precious cargo in a special pouch that is the unique product of evolution. When she settles in an appropriate home, she uses her small fungal fragment to start the fungus garden for her new colony. Leaf-cutting ants cannot survive without their mutualist fungus. Indeed, DNA studies show that leaf-cutting ants have been using the same strain of fungus for at least 30 million years.

From Happy Experiments to Directed Learning

Human pioneers who colonize new terrain also bring many of their mutualists with them—the seeds of their cultivated plants, the stocks of their domesticated animals. These pioneers often find that they must change their behavior to adapt to the new land. But human pioneers have another very useful ability: they often can change the terrain itself to fit their needs.

Business pioneers have still more advantages. They can carefully examine new terrain from afar and prearrange local mutualisms before they make their move. Skillful planning can allow business pioneers to anticipate needs and problems that may lie ahead. Nonetheless, a business pioneer must find that new opportunity and capitalize on it. And in a surprising number of cases, chance—including the always unpredictable creativity of individual customers—can play a profound role.

Managers are often amazed at the uses clever consumers find for their products. Radio Shack sells large numbers of marine band radios in western Kansas and eastern Colorado. Why? Because ranchers have discovered that these radios provide an inexpensive and convenient way to talk to one another across the broad expanses of the plains. There is little likelihood of either interfering with a legitimate ship-to-shore signal or of being nabbed and prosecuted by regulators from the federal government. Indeed, one of the most interesting ways to look for new product ideas is to track surprising, and even illegal, uses of technologies.

But erstwhile developers of business ecosystems do not want to depend upon chance alone. They want to give economic experimentation as much help as they can. Indeed, the ultimate aim of business strategists is to manipulate predictably the assembly rules of business ecosystems. The fundamental cycle of entrepreneurship is the conversion of ideas and opportunities into value for customers—and profits for investors. How this value comes about varies with each case. Even with a great deal of study, it is likely that the basic question—"What comes first, with what timing and sequence?"—will remain an essential mystery, played out anew in every case.

But it is impossible to anticipate all that will be involved and transpire in an emerging new business ecosystem. One is moving from the closed, cognitively limited realm of the mind into the infinitely complex, multiply related world of real customers and real business. Probably the best one can do is establish a program of directed learning—that is, strive to reflect deeply upon the experiment as it is being undertaken and become a leader in the race to understand value within the context of the new possibilities.

Figure 6.1. A learning cycle focused on the creation of economic value.

The challenge, then, is to set up a learning cycle, with the subject being the creation of economic value, as illustrated above. The challenge to the creator of a business ecosystem is similar to the biological: there are many ways to realize a mutualistic, self-reinforcing set of relationships—and many ways to fail—and the real assembly rules for business ecosystems are only dimly understood. Out of the available range of environmental conditions and enabling genetic material, the aspiring Stage I visionary must find a set of interdependent relationships through which this fundamental cycle of trapping and converting energy can be established. In business ecosystems, there is a tremendous premium on inspiration and passion to carry the pioneers through inevitable failures, and on imagination and learning to suggest creative solutions and allow improvement based on analysis and experiment.

A Club of Dreamers

Executives often ask me where and how do you start an ecosystem? What is it like at the beginning? I tell them that the Stage I world is alive with the spirit of newness and the brash compulsion to do something different and distinctive. Often its inhabitants are heady with the desire to find the elixir that will change the world. These electrifying dreams may start in the figurative attics or basements of large corporations, or they may bubble forth from small companies or even from the experiments of a handful of ingenious individuals.

It is not uncommon to find hotbeds of Stage I activity on the fringes of the global economy, languid places where little of a commercial nature is percolating. In the desert, it seems, the imagination blooms. In 1975, Bill Gates and Paul Allen, later to be the billionaire leaders of the Microsoft empire, were toiling in Albuquerque, literally in the desert, struggling to get primitive software to run on a cobbled-together computer.[1] The company behind the computer was called MITS, and it was run by a renegade, financially strapped engineer named Ed Roberts. The MITS offices were sandwiched between a Laundromat and a massage parlor in a decidedly downscale mall. The computer was an unreliable $395 hobbyist kit sold by mail order through *Popular Mechanics* magazine. The computer had no storage device and no reliable memory, and it used toggle switches instead of a keyboard. As Bill Gates recounted later, "Every good idea was half-executed at MITS." Such is the stuff of Stage I.

Out in the shimmering heat of that New Mexican desert, MITS built a center of learning and experimentation that would ultimately seduce thousands of co-revolutionaries from across the United States. Tooling around the West in a motor home called the MITSmobile like a computer Ken Kesey, Roberts stoked the fire by helping to establish computer clubs in a number of cities, igniting the ambitions of many youngsters. He articulated a dream quite rhapsodically. Orders poured in for the primitive kit, and for a time MITS prospered.

More important, a learning organization came into being unburdened by tradition, industry, or geography. The possibilities were limitless.

One hastens to add that while all entrepreneurs hope for happy or at least beatific endings, most do not succeed. Part of the essence of radical ventures, transfixing as they may be, is that the bulk of them stall and fail. Even in failure, though, they will often make contributions of great merit, training future leaders who will leave their mark in later incarnations, spawning seminal ideas and providing rallying points for communities of learning that will spray ideas and visions to the wider world.

MITS failed, but it also helped found a nascent ecosystem that succeeded it. Over the next few years, that community worked out the nature of the personal computer. Two of the members of an early computer club, the Homebrew Computer Club in Palo Alto, were Steve Wozniak and Steve Jobs. It was to this club that they took their first Apple. The collective energy of thousands of hobbyists was what stimulated the personal computer revolution and ultimately convinced a reluctant IBM that it had to take part or get left behind.

Stage I is also where pioneers first learn how to galvanize customer support and participation—and create pioneer customers. Because they introduce radical advances into peoples' lives, Stage I efforts always have something of the social movement to them. Sometimes Stage I strategists seize on this as the centerpiece of their strategy-making. General David Sarnoff, the commercializer of radio, deliberately contrived to displace the piano as the focal point of home life. He felt that radio—something that men and boys tinkered with in a garage or basement, hence the term "radio shack"—could become the exhilarating heart of family entertainment. Thus it would also appeal to advertisers. Advertising revenues would fund programming, which—in an endless cycle of improvement—would make the radio even more central to the family.

Ultimately, the radio also further transformed the home by making the parlor the center for news and politics as well. Both world wars were copiously reported by radio directly into the home, and throughout the Second World War politicians like Franklin Delano Roosevelt and Winston Churchill kept people engaged and inspired by touching them through radio.

There is a tremendous value in understanding the Stage I mind-set. The same strain of Stage I thinking that started the revolution in radio or personal computers is being rewarded all around us, every day. Even if we wish, in the end, merely to extend a current ecosystem, we need to know what it will face in the way of Stage I alternatives, and whether in the near or distant future. Put another way, only by taking the Stage I alternatives seriously, and trying to see what wounds they might inflict upon the status quo, do we assure ourselves that we have assiduously examined our own potential vulnerabilities.

Case in Point: Starlight Telecommunications

In the summer of 1994, I was returning to Boston from a business trip to London. On the plane, I struck up a conversation with my seatmate, an adventurous-looking man in khakis, carrying a faded luggage box festooned with travel stickers from every place from Eastern Europe to East Africa. He had much to say that was interesting. He mentioned that he was returning from Somalia to his home in New Hampshire. Somalia? My curiosity piqued, I asked him what he had been doing in one of the scariest places in the world. Of all things, it turned out that he and some Somalian partners owned and operated a private telephone system based in Mogadishu. In fact, their system furnished the only telephone service in the unstable, war-ravaged area. As we talked, it dawned on me that here was a marvelous example of the challenges, the risks, and the inimitable satisfactions of Stage I business development.

Bill O'Brien is president of Starlight Telecommunications, headquartered in a single room rented from the Chamber of Commerce in Salem, New Hampshire. He is a magnetic, courageous man with a bent toward optimism, the sort of person at home with conflict scenarios. His company works with local partners in the back alleys of the world to provide local phone service and a connection to international carriers for long-distance service.

A strong dose of happenstance thrust him into the business. In the early 1990s, he had been contentedly working for GTE as the director of marketing and business development for Eastern Europe, the Middle East, and Africa. As a way to drum up creative strategies, GTE had recently begun a New Ventures group that solicited proposals from employees for new businesses. New Ventures would judge the viability of the proposals and, if they were deemed promising, would fund them.

One day Peter Nielsen, who was in charge of product development for GTE's satellite division, called O'Brien and said he had an idea for a phone business in developing countries and wanted O'Brien to help him work it out. Initially Nielsen had in mind a hardware business that would strictly sell telecommunications gear to these nations. O'Brien convinced him that it would be wiser to be an actual operating company. The pair went bleary-eyed studying the tedious, 600-odd-page manual that New Ventures supplied to guide participants in drafting a business plan. They read the book *Intrapreneurship* by Gifford Pinchot.[2] They looked at the way Cable and Wireless, the British telecommunications giant, went into developing nations and made alliances with local phone companies.

They also studied the rather colorful exploits of Kenny Schaffer, an ex-hippie, rock-star manager, and inventor of the wireless electric guitar. Schaffer had managed to set up a long-distance phone company in the Soviet Union, where phone service was notoriously unreliable. His escapades were among those that thoroughly convinced O'Brien and Nielsen that starting a phone business in another country was not some sort of black art that would require ten years and a hundred million dollars to get the first call made. After all, if a rock-and-roll guy able to speak only a single sentence of Russian ("There are too many big mosquitoes") could do it, how hard could it be. And so the pair put together a plan for a business they called Starlight Communications. Both the men had young children fond of the poem that begins, "Starlight, star bright . . ."—hence the name.

ELEMENTS OF THE STARLIGHT PLAN

The plan spelled out how several important trends could be capitalized on by certain business actions, and how a cycle of reinforcing relationships could establish the basis for a new business ecosystem. The heart of the proposal was the insight that there were many parts of the world—much of Africa, for example—with virtually no linkage to the worldwide telephone network, even though there were customers who could pay to be connected. Moreover, that connection could be relatively easily established by satellite through any number of vendors.

The missing link was local service. Here the pair felt technology offered them a solution. Wireless pay phones, connected by inexpensive radio gear and telephone switches, could be hooked up by satellite to the outside world. If the cost of the gear could be kept cheap enough, it could pay for its capital costs in a few months—and be prudently placed in unstable areas.

Finally, there was their own experience and comfort in the wilder reaches of the planet. O'Brien, in particular, felt that he could effectively create local partnerships in unstable territories and establish Starlight's presence where other, more established firms would fear to tread.

These elements, then, formed the first seeds of the new ecosystem. Their own creative value chaining had led the Starlight adventurers to conceive a particular set of resources and relationships that, if put together, would be far superior to what was currently available in their chosen markets. The potential advantage was strong enough to motivate them to take the next steps and seek support for their plan. It seemed to them that there might be enough theoretical value not only to excite them, but to bring in others—and ultimately to support the creation of a new business ecosystem in Africa.

MOVING INTO ACTION

More than two hundred business plans were submitted to New Ventures; O'Brien and Nielsen were notified that their entry was one of two that was going to be funded. That was the end of the good news from GTE. For a variety of internal reasons, New Ventures reversed itself and decided not to fund the venture. However, it told the two men that they were free to do what they wanted with the business plan. Still infatuated with the idea, O'Brien and Nielsen continued in their jobs at GTE but also began circulating the Starlight plan to outside investors.

Coincidentally, in early 1992, O'Brien got a fortuitous phone call from an acquaintance named Baloo Patel. Patel is a fabulously wealthy businessman based in Kenya, who, among his many ventures, owns the world's largest hot-air balloon fleet, which is used to float tourists on safaris. He had been approached by a group of seven Somalian brothers who operated a business called Qorco Trading. They wanted to start a phone business in Somalia. Patel called O'Brien thinking GTE might be interested. Instead, O'Brien decided to quit GTE in June 1992 and use Somalia as a test of the Starlight concept. If it succeeded, then Nielsen would quit as well and join him. In November 1994, well after the Somalian system had begun returning profits to its investors, Nielsen and another GTE man, Dave Rowe, joined O'Brien to formally incorporate Starlight.

ON THE GROUND IN SOMALIA

When O'Brien made his first trip to Somalia to meet with local powers, he immediately regretted going. He was transported from the airport in a minivan squashed between an assortment of uncharitable-looking men bearing machine guns. Three times he was forced to switch to another vehicle as a precaution against being followed. Fortunately, the brothers that made up Qorco had smoothed the way with the warlords. Still, General Mohamed Farah Aidid, the head of the most visible militia, told O'Brien bluntly that he wasn't sure if he were a war profiteer or a spy. Neither possibility made O'Brien feel particularly secure.

Much of Somalia is a checkerwork junglescape of crumbling houses made of cardboard walls and zinc roofs. The per capita income is about $175 a year (although armed bandits command $50 a day). At this time, Somalia had no recognized government, nor much else in the way of infrastructure, including phone service. It was convulsed by war and mass starvation, and caught in an uneasy leadership standoff between two local leaders that the outside world persisted in referring to as "warlords," though Somalians hailed them as heroes. In a country burdened with overpopulation, disease, crime, and scarcity of resources, most Somalians worried more about where their next meal would come from than to whom their next phone call would go.

CREATIVE PROBLEM SOLVING

Getting the system going in Somalia was a learning experience for all of the Starlight participants. Everything imaginable came up. Consider the following problem: How do you bill for phone calls—even pay phone calls—in a country with no currency (for paying for calls), no reliable mail services (for mailing bills and payments), no banking (for cashing checks), or no legal system (for enforcing collections)? What did Starlight do? It put up pay phones that were operated with slide-in "smart cards." The cards are purchased for whatever hard currency is available—typically U.S. dollars or South African Rands. Often, the money is sent to local Somalians from the overseas compatriots they call.

The cards themselves are marvels of high-technology in a generally low-tech setting. Manufactured in Japan, the smart cards carry embedded microchips. The size of conventional credit cards, they are purchased with a specific face value, the equivalent of about fifteen American dollars, good for a certain number of minutes of overseas calling. The user inserts the card into the phone set and dials his call. While he talks, the phone set debits the face value of the card until the credit is exhausted.

Starlight's local service is furnished through one or another inexpensive wireless radio technology, often some variation of equipment that is used for tasks like dispatching taxis and plumbers in the developed world. Calls are switched by small versions of the digital telephone switches used throughout the world by phone companies and for business PBXs.

International calls are bounced off a satellite from a local ground station operated by Starlight. The signal connects to a large, highly sophisticated teleport run by Norwegian Telecom in Norway. (Whenever I think of this, I always imagine equipment sitting in something that looks like Superman's Fortress of Solitude.) From Norway, calls are routed as normal international long-distance calls and can reach anywhere in the developed world. Incoming calls from other points in the world are dialed through Norway. (At first it was necessary to use the Norwegian country code and numbers provided by Norwegian Telecom, but in February 1995 a Somalian area code of 252 was activated.) These calls are then switched to the satellite circuits and connected to Starlight's bases, and eventually to subscribers.

Starlight and its local partners quickly forged relationships with a variety of local stakeholders, most of whom are also customers. These include leading local companies. In time, a local fruit company, Somalia Fruit, started advertising on the smart cards, paying fifty cents per card to inscribe its logo on them. Others include multinational firms, aid organizations like the Red Cross, hotels and airport concessionaires, and local power brokers. One of the day-to-day concerns was that someone would steal everything. So Starlight had to hire fifty armed guards to patrol its facilities; it didn't hurt in its efforts to gain influence that it picked fifty soldiers from General Aidid's army.

Undeniable risks existed, due to the unstable economy and tenuous political situation. But clearly there appeared to be worthwhile compensations for the risk. The open, chaotic, boundary-free environments of less developed nations are perfect settings for a small group of men to get into the phone business. Also on the positive side, the business services are

sorely needed, modern technology makes the capital investment much less than one might think, and the operating challenges are manageable. The financial returns are extremely
appealing.

GETTING GOING

Starlight began its operation quite modestly, with a wall of a
dozen phones that were installed on the top floor of the Hotel
Olympic in the center of Mogadishu. Outside the hotel
entrance, the company made sure to post a sign warning customers that no guns or grenades were allowed inside. (Patrons
were rather good about checking them with the desk.)
O'Brien started small because he was eager to get something
up and running quickly to get investors their money back,
because it was never far from his mind that at any moment a
stray bomb could wipe out the whole enterprise. On January
27, 1994, Starlight placed its first international call from
Mogadishu, and it was heralded locally as a landmark event. A
Muslim imam blessed the occasion. A bunch of sheep were
sacrificed. And General Aidid himself spoke to a Norwegian
official, though he found he did not have all that much to say.
All the revenues from the first two days of calls were donated
to the local mosque.

Day and night, the phones were available for both outgoing
and incoming calls, and people quickly took to using them.
Families in Somalia frequently would write to friends in other
countries and suggest a convenient time to call. The letters
would then be hand-carried or flown to neighboring countries
blessed with mail service, and then mailed to their ultimate
destination. Somalians are scattered throughout the world,
including the United States and Germany, with quite a heavy
concentration in Canada and the Scandinavian countries. The
recipients of the calls would then show up at Starlight's offices
on the appointed day and begin the inevitable long wait.
Sometimes it could take days for a call to arrive and sometimes
the call never came. Those anticipating a call came by in the
morning and hung around until evening. If the call didn't

arrive, they'd leave and return at first light the following morning. Whenever a call did come, there was invariably unmitigated delight.

PREPARING FOR EXPANSION

From that humble beginning, there has been considerable progress. Starlight today has an expanding network of about a thousand pay phones around Somalia, supplemented by about a hundred and twenty-five private line customers, including the International Red Cross, Reuters, CNN, Medicines sans Frontiers, and various local businessmen. At first local service was free, but now it is billed. Any long-distance call is $2.50. Since there is no mail, bills for private-line customers are delivered in person and they must be paid at once in cash.

In selecting locations, Starlight generally finds the centers of commerce and puts its pay phones there. Acquired knowledge of the local customs has taught it that one of the choicest spots is near a tree that is a traditional center of sheep trading in a rural area. Since the link to Starlight's headquarters is wireless, all the pay phone needs is a minimal power source, either batteries or solar energy.

Granted the business is small, but it is successful from both a financial and a learning point of view. (Also from a military standpoint; there have been no sieges on the Starlight equipment.) Revenues in 1994 surpassed $600,000, and they are much higher now; the gross margins are impressive. Of course, with no insurance, Starlight must remain actively involved on an ongoing basis. But with the service valued highly by its customers, there are great expansion potentials. In fact, Starlight has legitimate hope for creating the basis of a worldwide service business.

The conditions Starlight seeks exist in more places than even O'Brien imagined when he first dreamed up his system. Somalia is merely the beginning. Starlight also has an operation in Uganda, initial licenses in Swaziland, and is working on a program for the homelands of South Africa. In addition to other opportunities in Africa, O'Brien imagines moving into Eastern

Europe, Russia, and the Commonwealth of Independent States. As O'Brien told me one day, "Before long, we'll have this portfolio of small phone businesses. Which is the way communications evolves. If you look at the history of the phone business in New York, there were like two thousand phone companies at the turn of the century. We've all seen the episode on *Little House on the Prairie* where the general store gets the first phone. That's sort of what we're doing."

SEEING OPPORTUNITY WHERE OTHERS SEE RISK

What makes this such a compelling story is that most people looking through this same prism would not see the opportunities that O'Brien and his partners did. The last place they would consider starting a business would be the African nation of Somalia in 1994. A businessman would be thinking more about how to avoid getting shot than how to make profits.

But not Bill O'Brien and his business partners. They envisaged a beckoning opportunity environment, around which they felt they could assemble a sound business. It is well worth reviewing each of the opportunities as they saw them in order not only to understand Starlight but to grasp the method required to mine Stage I opportunity environments for clues to successful Stage I business models.[3]

Choose Customers and Customer Segments That Support Learning

The thick literature of new offerings often mentions "early adopter" customers without defining the concept particularly well. In my view, certain Stage I customers are better than others. The goals of Stage I primarily have to do with learning— learning what value proposition works and learning how to provide it. Consequently the ideal customers are those who will tolerate a primitive version of the final offer, knowing that even in the rudimentary form the value is sufficient to improve their lives or businesses.

Somalians nicely fit the bill. They will patiently wait days to get a phone call because the alternative is not talking to certain people at all. Moreover, they will provide useful feedback about the service and how to improve it, and they will often contribute to its improvement by creating support systems of their own. Finally, even though they are early adopter customers, they are representative enough of other sorts of customers that any information gleaned from them can be applied more broadly when the ecosystem expands in Stage II.

To be able to effectively pick the brains of customers, you really need a situation that is conducive to learning. Two factors are important. First, intense customer interaction to find out how customers think and to get clues to how they want to use your product. Second, customers who are challenged to provide that value. Stage I situations commonly boast what can be called sponsor/patron customers. These are people who are committed to helping the core offer evolve fruitfully. Though not necessarily loyal to any given product or service, they are faithful to the process that produces it. If they are not disappointed, they will become quite firmly tethered for a long time.

A buzz of early customer interest can be an important catalyst for an ecosystem. What generates this enthusiasm is the ability of early adopter customers to perceive the dramatic potential of the innovation even during this embryonic period when it is only partially formed. The fervor for MITS began with a fortuitous cover story in *Popular Electronics*. The article stimulated thousands of orders and kicked up a lot of excitement. With such a heady brew of enthusiasm an extensive learning community can sometimes be established.

By no means are the people living and working in Somalia typical of early adopter customers in the developed world. But they are people who saw the appeal of the value proposition of even a crude service. In that respect, they met the criteria of a good Stage I customer.

In fact, several types of customers in Somalia had a strong need for telephone service to other nations. The international aid organizations—the Red Cross, Medicines sans Frontiers,

UNISOM (the UN mission)—had to communicate both with one another and with the outside world. Second, many Somalians have friends and relatives as well as business interests sprinkled throughout the world. They are concerned about each other and like to stay in touch. Third, a certain amount of international business is carried on by firms within Somalia, and, as the country rebuilds, this will obviously increase. A country on the mend invariably attracts oil and gas companies, construction companies to build roads and power systems, and consumer goods distributors. Fourth, a recognized government will eventually come to Somalia that will need to talk to the world. In 1995, there were two competing quasi-governments with not much interest in getting on the phone to other countries, but this condition is bound to change.

To be sure, all of these promising segments also pose difficulties. The aid organizations are in Somalia temporarily, and while valuable during the first flush of phone service, they will not last as customers. The citizens are hard-pinched and make do with meager incomes, though they do get supplementary money from outside the country that can be used for calls. More troublesome, there is no reliable postal service and banking in the country. Billing practices standard in the developed world become farcical in today's Somalia. Finally, there is no meaningful local currency.

Business and government sectors are just emerging. On the other hand, some powerful players in this arena are already circulating in Somalia trying to get the lay of the land. They can be courted for future relationships.

The resourcefulness of Starlight shines through in how it has nimbly transformed these initial customers into important allies and sources of learning, and in how it has found ways to both serve them well and make a decent profit.

Start in Naturally Bounded Markets

Here the question to address is, "What are the naturally occurring markets and market boundaries within which we might operate?" In Stage I, it helps if markets are relatively free of competition, as well as isolated from the prying eyes of potential competitors. This allows learning to go on without being appropriated by others. For maximum learning, nothing beats a one-way view into the work and learning of other competing firms and competing ecosystems. Starlight's pioneers can easily study the organization and technologies of communications services in the United States and Europe, applying what they learn to Africa. However, it would be unlikely for competitors to go to Somalia to inspect what Starlight is doing. Similarly, Wal-Mart's Sam Walton spent a good deal of time visiting other retailers, analyzing their methods. In the early years few reversed the process and went to rural Arkansas to study him. By operating in this manner, the hidden company not only has its own integration laboratory, but a rich source of ideas from other labs that it can borrow from without having to fund or manage those labs. Certainly Somalia fits the bill. There are no other phone services and no interest from rival carriers for getting into the market. Somalia is well off the beaten path, even within Africa.

But markets also need to be fundamentally stable—at least later if not sooner. Starlight is betting that Somalia will not always be a political and economic mess. As it replenishes itself, telephone service should play a central role in its reconstruction, and that will benefit Starlight mightily.

Until that happens, Starlight assumes significant risks. International trade insurance is unavailable except at great expense, so if equipment is destroyed or stolen, Starlight must eat the cost. It would not be unknown for some telephone equipment to be blown up by bombs. Furthermore, purchases have to be made through the United States, rather than directly by the Somalian partners. And since no effective local government exists, another rival could enter the market simply by choosing to do so.

Finally, there are no guarantees that Starlight will be the telephone system of choice once the nation stabilizes. If the government leaves the market unregulated, another rival could overtake it. Or the government could decide that it wants to control the telecommunications franchise itself. The government could then strike a deal with another carrier, or even set up its own system by hiring engineers from the ranks of foreign-trained Somalians wishing to return to secure jobs at home.

It is pretty clear that Starlight is competing in the ultimate unstructured market, unstructured even to the extent that the future of regulation cannot be predicted reliably. Starlight's answer to this problem, as we shall see, is to ally itself with the likely power elites so that it will be tucked securely inside the social establishment as it forms.

Offer Precursor Products That Can Expand and Evolve

Stage I offers, as pointed out, need not be comprehensive. But they must work. In general, "working" means that they accomplish the following:

- At the core of the offer there must be a product or service so valuable to certain customers that they will purchase it even though it is incomplete.
- Offers must be able to be integrated into the culture and lives and businesses of the customers. The provider needs to do its part by making available a Stage I offer in a manner that encourages customers to solve problems by incorporating it into their worlds.
- There needs to be a clear plan for product and service improvement that the customer can believe in, so that the customer helps to improve the offer and tolerates its limitations just to maintain a relationship with the provider.

Starlight felt it could begin with no more than wireless access to the international long-distance system on a dial-out basis. It provided this through pay phones activated by debit cards. For organizations, dial-in service could also be added, allowing others around the world to initiate calls. Local service between subscribers would also be possible but would be of much less value to customers, since they could already reach one another through various forms of radio communications gear. But from this beginning, Starlight and their initial customers both had the hope of more and better service as time went by.

Product and service improvements are where a Stage I effort must excel. The supple way in which assets and activities are deployed must add up to significant benefits for both customer and producer. Customers betrayed by a marginally beneficial service will be quick to blame the provider.

Here is where Starlight displayed its great talent. It showed how technology could be integrated to create a low-cost infrastructure for offering phone service. At least in principle, wireless local service was becoming easier to provide. "Mobile trunked radio," the same basic equipment that is used to dispatch taxis in the developed world, could serve as inexpensive wireless connections for a small number of customers. The technology is ideal, being well understood, easy to maintain, rugged, and cheap.

It is relatively straightforward to link a network of customers through a ground station to a satellite, and from there back down to a point in a developed nation, and finally, out to virtually anywhere in the world through the wonders of conventional international long-distance circuits. Therefore connecting Mogadishu to the rest of the world was achievable without much difficulty. Starlight was able to establish a strategic relationship with Norwegian Telecom, which provided satellite-based connection to the worldwide telecommunications grid. Calls made to Starlight in Somalia would initially be made by dialing the Norwegian country code and numbers supplied by Norwegian Telecom, which would then be routed to the Somalian service.

The most complex and potentially expensive piece of equipment needed was the telephone switch, the device that would connect the various radio circuits together and permit dialing over the satellite uplink to the rest of the world. Here again, technology and economics militated in Starlight's favor. Small digital telephone switches—miniature variations of the PBXs used for larger companies in the developed world—were readily available from a variety of suppliers and at shrinking prices.

Invest in Business Processes That Can Eventually Be Scaled Up

In Stage I, the business processes tend to be about experimental learning. At this juncture, the processes are primordial and do not exist in any distinct way. Everything is up in the air and fluid. The overarching business processes are design, experimentation, and reflection. Eventually, the seeds that get planted from these actions will grow into the traditional processes like product development, marketing and sales, and customer service.

The largest potential operating cost and start-up issue for Starlight had to do with how to get trained, expert people working in the local areas. Starlight concluded that it might be able to begin business with pay phone services, located in public areas like airports and hotels, that would be linked with its central office wirelessly, by radio. This service offering would have the advantage of not requiring extensive billing capabilities, because services would be paid for as used. Moreover, the wireless network would require little in terms of a field service force. What ongoing technical talent was required could be hired or borrowed from the local PTTs, with training and support from Starlight expatriates. The major need for expert personnel would be at the initial installation or expansion of a system—and not for ongoing support.

A strength—and a weakness—of Stage I situations is the amount of business process knowledge that is carried around in the heads of a few people. In Starlight's case, crucial business processes started with the perspective and knowledge that O'Brien brought to a fast-moving situation. As a company goes forward, it must find ways to create the organizational differentiation and sophistication necessary to grow.

Establish an Organizational Architecture That Creates Allies

In reality, few business strategists work their Stage I businesses in isolation. They operate in a world of other ecosystems— some established, others emerging. In most cases, a new ecosystem emerges on the edge of a more established one, or is grafted on to it, or else it comes about through the transformation of some aspect of an existing business. Cable television grew up to extend broadcast television to rural areas and now rivals broadcast itself. The home video ecosystem arose on the edge of the television and movie ecosystems. At the same time, Stage I ecosystems depend upon the generation and coevolution of multiple new organizations. Thus part of the challenge is coming up with an initial organizational architecture that gains the Stage I ecosystem the support that it needs, without swamping it or unduly distorting its operations.

A Stage I system must find members to supply the necessary assets and processes. In some arenas, this means more partners; in other arenas, it means more vertical integration. But in all cases, the community of customers and suppliers must work harmoniously because they are creating something new. The ability of the network to learn together is crucial. The members must regard the system of governance to be fair and powerful so that it can be effective in arbitrating disputes.

To cling to its role over time, the lead company must do more than merely suggest that the community come together. It must provide three sorts of value: It must provide the structure for the alliance; it must provide end-to-end performance oversight; and it must make sure that a key portion of the value cannot be replicated by others and is not a likely future target of competitors.

Starlight is the catalyst of its ecosystem, bringing oversight, knowledge of how to design and operate the end-to-end whole, and the ability to work across several cultures: establishing services in Africa; buying equipment in the United States, Germany, France, Japan, Taiwan, and Singapore; making partners with Norwegian Telecom and drawing in U.S. investors. Under its arrangement with its Somalian partner, Starlight gave the local Somalian partner 40 percent of the local company set up to manage its system.

Starlight has several symbiotic relationships. First and foremost, it is tied to Norwegian Telecom's satellite services ecosystem, which in turn is connected to the global network of long-distance lines. For equipment, it depends on other business ecosystems, principally companies in Japan and the United States that peddle telecommunications gear. Part of the beauty of Starlight's plan is that it is feeding off these other ecosystems, benefiting from their economies of scale and scope and cumulative learning.

But intentions do change. Players decide they want a larger chunk of the profits. Relationships sour. One of the major issues facing Starlight will be how to keep Norwegian Telecom from snatching its role, should it eventually acquire a large number of end-point relationships. On the other hand, Starlight could at some point vertically integrate itself into the services that Norwegian Telecom provides, perhaps in a venture with another worldwide carrier.

Another concern is rivalry between the new and the old. In Somalia, Starlight faces no competition from an existing local phone company because there is none. In other parts of Africa, however, Starlight has had to make alliances with existing ecosystems to avoid a nasty and probably destructive fight.

A final worry is direct competition to create a new and similar ecosystem. But Starlight has been wise to pursue areas deemed too risky and complex, as well as too small, for more established competitors. This buys it valuable time to learn and establish itself.

Use Ownership and Other Forms of Stakeholding to Cement Relationships with Key Supporters

Stakeholders have their own view of their destiny and what they must do to secure control over that destiny. Five conditions define the ideal stakeholders. First, they need to be real movers and shakers in the broader environment and marketplace, though not necessarily in the traditional industry, since that is where the collaboration will happen. Second, their support, if possible, must preclude involvement in competing ecosystems. Third, in their minds, the collaboration should seem central to their overall interests. Fourth, among themselves, they need to have reasonably complementary rather than competing interests. Finally, they need to have a shared ethic—or ethos—that allows them to work together without cheating each other.

Granted that for a European or an American, operating Starlight's Somalian branch would be risky indeed. But for O'Brien's Somalian partner it was sheer opportunity. As he pointed out, "I live here in Mogadishu. I'm not increasing my risk by working with you." So O'Brien chose a local figure savvy about how to handle himself in the operating environment.

Besides supplying satellite downlink services, Norwegian Telecom promised to be an important strategic ally. In recent years, Norwegian Telecom has itself made an interesting strategic decision in business ecosystem terms. In a boundary-free, deregulated telecommunications world, much of the international traffic in the developed world is expected to flow through regional hubs such as New York, London, Berlin, Hong Kong, Singapore, and Tokyo. This concentration is accentuated by the global banking and financial service centers and headquarters of major multinational corporations that are based in these cities.

Recognizing that it doesn't have the wherewithal to compete in this high-level game, Norwegian Telecom has chosen to specialize instead as the satellite-based hub for connections between the developed and less developed corners of the world. Norwegian Telecom, working with entrepreneurs like O'Brien, has learned how to handle difficulties like billing and numbering, as well as how to deal with a diversity of end-station capabilities in the nations that it serves. To solidify the relationship between Norwegian Telecom and

Starlight, Norwegian Telecom is also a minor financier of O'Brien's operation.

Not every mainstream company has been as willing to be involved as Norwegian Telecom. For example, when O'Brien approached AT&T about seed money for his project, the AT&T representative said that he could not invest money in any country that did not have an official privatization program. O'Brien looked at him askance. He explained that Somalia didn't have an official anything.

Do All You Can to Create Symbiosis Between Yourself and Those Who Shape Societal Values and Government Policy

Most strategists give scant thought to their relationship to government, or to the overall society represented by government. This oversight is a mistake. The early leaders of small entrepreneurial ventures are sometimes so emphatically anti-government that they devote virtually no management attention to the relationship. On the other hand, government relations in very large firms are often the province of a specialized department or are part of the workload of the corporate counsel and are rarely blended into the strategies of specific units. I can't stress enough that leaders ignore this dimension at their peril. Ecosystems trigger social change. Social change always stirs up reaction from society, and almost always from government. It is crucial for the strategist to try to anticipate and manage these reverberations so that they are as supportive as possible of the ecosystem's success, and also to prevent them from being a reason to confiscate the gains if the ecosystem flourishes.

Of course there is virtually no formal policy—or government—in Somalia at this time. However, there are power elites who represent a fledgling establishment, and Starlight works diligently to support those in this group who appear both strong and fair. It keeps in close touch with local leaders, as well as UNISOM and the major foreign consulates (and, as I pointed out, it hired members of one of the lead armies to work as its security guards).

Longer term, Starlight worked through Norwegian Telecom to have the International Telecommunications Union restore the Somali country code to active status so that Starlight's system can be dialed direct. This has been one of many efforts to involve Starlight as a constructive and central member of the emerging society as well as the government.

The dimensions of business issues and of the developing business ecosystem that you need to consider are summarized in the chart below, along with the ideal conditions that you want to test for and aim for.

DIMENSIONS OF THE BUSINESS ECOSYSTEM	GENERAL QUESTIONS	IDEAL CONDITIONS	STARLIGHT EXAMPLE
Customers: Customer interest and participation	What groups of customers can we serve in distinct ways?	Customers who are willing to contribute to learning, and for whom even a primitive version of what is possible is still attractive	Multinational organizations; the public; local quasi-governmental organizations
Markets: Market boundaries and agencies	What are the naturally occurring boundaries within which we might operate?	Find some bounded markets or relatively hidden markets, but not so idiosyncratic as not to provide for standardized learning, and enter, learn, and eventually dominate	Eastern Somalia
Offers: Product and service architecture	What are the total offers that we can make?	Partial, but with the core value delivered	Local service and access to international service
Processes: Business process architecture	What sort of business process architecture can we build to provide this offer with radically better price/ performance than what already exists?	The business process architecture must have truly revolutionary potential—and show enough of this potential to excite early customers and fund further work	Local wireless network, smart-card pay phones, and satellite link to Norway and the world
Organizations: Organizational architecture	What roles will stakeholders play in putting forward major contributing businesses, and how will the relationships be structured and orchestrated? How are conflicts resolved?	An ability to put together the value proposition and business process architecture and to work together to learn to evolve it	Shared ownership, under the direction of Starlight officers
Stakeholders: Owners and other stakeholders	Who are the stakeholders, what are their wider interests, and how does this ecosystem fit into their plans? Where are the stakeholders aligned and not aligned?	Need strong supporters aligned with and in favor of the venture, who are not in conflict over the aims of the venture	Somali nationals, Starlight, Norwegian Telecom
Societal values and government policy	How can a relationship to the public and to the government be established so that innovation will be valued and a strong return on innovation supported?	Establish a social contract whereby you can gain a return on your innovation contributions	Working to be a valued contributor and respected player in the local informal power structure, hoping to become a recognized part of any emerging formal structure

Table 6.1

In a very real sense, Stage I adventurers are surfing on waves set in motion by the convergence of multiple trends. Timing is critical. If the wave arrives too early, or too late, the Stage I effort may either fizzle for lack of support or be knocked down by unexpected force and turbulence.

In Starlight, these Stage I challenges stand out in sharp relief. Starlight understood the theoretical potential of the telecommunications technologies they were betting on. Starlight was convinced that these trends made phone service in remote regions feasible. Moreover, Starlight felt that the timing was right to move.

The theoretical potential of trends is obviously necessary but not sufficient for Stage I success. Implementation—the equivalent of the working out of assembly rules in biological ecosystems—is everything. Even in the best of circumstances, theoretical advantages cannot always be realized. Certain technological architectures that appear straightforward enough to implement prove to be exceedingly difficult. Some operational and market development problems turn out to be nearly intractable.

Stage I ventures always bear a profound implementation risk. The task of the Stage I adventurer is to gauge the theoretical potential and work to mitigate the implementation risk as quickly as possible. The individual and organizational learning that results from these efforts is the major competitive advantage to be gained in Stage I. Later entrants have the "second mover advantage" of being able to draw on the spadework of early Stage I ventures in proving a concept and testing options. On the other hand, whatever implementation knowledge that can be kept secret or hard to duplicate affords a genuine edge to the Stage I pioneer. For Starlight, the technological issues are comparatively straightforward and may not provide much advantage. However, there is a good deal of knowledge in the business relationship and operational sides of the project that work in its favor.

Look into the Future, and Anticipate Its Requirements

It is critical to remember that:

- The world is not going to stand still for Bill O'Brien. His stakeholders, his customers, and their society will change.
- The goal of Stage I is in large measure preparation for Stage II. As O'Brien moves forward, he will confront Stage II.

Table 6.2 illustrates some of the issues that we can anticipate hitting O'Brien and his friends. More to the point, it is important that they strive to make and continually update such a chart for themselves.

All of us, in working within business ecosystems, need to periodically take stock of what is coming. It is worth considering some of the highlights of the Starlight chart, because they may suggest issues of importance to managers in other situations. You need to anticipate what is going to hit you and then start investing in the competencies needed to respond.

O'Brien's customers are going to mature—in their lives and in their needs for services. Over time, local service and outgoing international calls—now a small part of the business—will grow in importance. The quality of calls may become an issue. It is critical for O'Brien to stay close to his customers and begin to put in place road maps for the evolution of his services, matched to the development of the society. He needs to continue to understand his customers and work with them to transform life in Somalia.

The markets in which Starlight is offering services are now virtually free of other entrants, but this may not last forever. Starlight will need to extend its relationship with the local government as it becomes established and defend its franchise, if possible. Moreover, it will need to meet as much customer demand as possible to preclude other entrants. There will be increasing social and political stability, and eventually eco-

DIMENSIONS OF THE BUSINESS ECOSYSTEM	KEY QUESTIONS	ANTICIPATED CHANGES OVER TIME	REQUIRED STARLIGHT RESPONSE to deal with exogenous challenges and to deal with growth and succession.
Customers: Customer interest and participation	How will customers and customer segments change over time?	Customers will be less tolerant of a primitive system.	Starlight will need to develop better segmentation and more complex plans for responding to advancing customer needs and interests.
Markets: Market boundaries and agencies	How will markets and market boundaries change over time?	As the current deterrents to business decline, other entrants may want to come in. Government will become stronger, its policy will become more enforceable and more salient because of the natural decline in impediments.	Starlight will need to extend its relationship with any emerging government and defend its franchise if possible. Moreover, it will need to meet as much customer demand as possible to preclude other entrants.
Offers: Product and service architecture	How will the offer change? What product and service architecture changes will be required?	Greater full offer will be expected—such as directory, customer support.	Starlight will need to make significant investments in its service platform and human resources.
Processes: Business process architecture	How will the organization and its skills need to change? What will be required to handle the demands of a growing, evolving, maturing business?	Customers will come to expect consistent marketing and sales, customer support, and the regular introduction of new and enhanced services.	Processes such as customer service, operations management, service development, and marketing and sales will need to become more systematic and professionalized.
Organizations: Organizational architecture	How will roles and governance change across the supply chain?	The continuing evolution of technology and businesses will likely cause struggles over the value across the end-to-end system.	Starlight will need to ensure that it keeps important parts of the supply chain in portions owned or closely controlled by it and its owners.
Stakeholders: Owners and other stakeholders	How will stakeholders and their agendas change over time—for example, become more or less aligned?	Norwegian Telecom may want more participation. The Somalia-based portion of the system may eventually be sold to acquirers. More sophisticated equipment will require more capital and closer relationships to equipment companies.	Starlight will need to continue to lead the community. Moreover, it will likely want to standardize its supplier relationships across its several markets, gaining integrated buying and bargaining power.
Societal values and government policy	How will societal values and government policy change over time?	At this point the society and its government, to the extent there is any organized government, are content to leave Starlight alone. Over time, the society and/or government may want more of the golden eggs.	Starlight will need to promote itself as a leader of the development of Somalia and a trusted contributor in the improvement of the daily life of the people—in order for its contributions to continue to be respected and supported.

Table 6.2

nomic development, in Somalia and other nations like it in sub-Saharan Africa. With luck, Starlight will grow up with these national ecosystems as one of the established players.

Starlight will need to make significant investments in its service platform and human resources. Processes such as customer service, operations management, service development, and marketing and sales will need to become more systematic and professional. If O'Brien truly wants to become the Wal-Mart of telecom across Africa, he will have to standardize his approaches. As we will see in the next chapter, scale, volume, and replicability must be his watchwords, if he is to move to Stage II market coverage.

Advances in technology will lower the costs of providing local and global service. These include cheaper switches, remote switching capability out of Norway (so-called Direct Access Mesh Architecture), and better and cheaper wireless systems, taking advantage of the high volumes of wireless equipment and semiconductors being manufactured for the wireless revolution in the developed world. O'Brien needs to be on top of these trends and make sure they are incorporated into his ecosystem, rather than becoming the basis for others.

New competition will inevitably develop. Direct satellite communications are being developed for global use. The iridium service, from a consortium led by Motorola, is one. These will create some services that could substitute for Starlight's offers, albeit probably at higher prices and lower quality. There may be other wireless local carriers who are willing, in later, more politically stable times, to put in more capital for more integrated, sophisticated systems.

There will be a need for change in the business model as the ecosystem matures, since initially it is tuned for Stage I. What will it need to do to deal with expansion? Where should directories reside? What about a numbering plan? How about evolution of the system? Broadband? Mobile satellite? A lot of decisions must be made.

All in all, a kind of all-purpose glee greets the conclusion of Stage I. But there is also a sensation of inscrutable equipoise.

One becomes torn between reveling in the moment and an equally powerful desire to get other activities going. For the future, implementation means that one needs to make and manage the relationships to other ecosystems. One must establish the roles and get people to perform. And finally, one must address other relationships with stakeholders and the society and government.

The more general issue is to decide how to lead the revolution. In other words, a strategy and tactics must be mapped out to recruit others to help create a full, rich ecosystem. Precisely how others are enlisted has important implications for the emerging architectural structure of the ecosystem. These initial conditions can have a profound effect on how the subsequent stages play out, and on what specific challenges face particular players in the future. For Starlight, it is found in its relationships to power centers—local business people, local customers, the emerging government, and to Norwegian Telecom and other suppliers of equipment.

In every respect, Bill O'Brien and Starlight represent the quintessential Stage I situation. They bring together good ideas, with the potential for radical price and performance gains and radically new benefits. More than anything else, Stage I is about defining opportunity. In this partition-bare world of many resources, Stage I is about taking the time and care to examine more closely than others what can be brought together into an ecosystem that will create new value. It is when bare land gives way to glorious life.

7

Stage II: The Revolution Spreads

A new ecosystem has been colonized. Pioneer microorganisms and fungi have established themselves. The territory has become flecked with mats of vegetation and clumps of small bushes. If nothing more were to happen, few would take note of the life so far. The habitat would be simply an ecological blip. For an ecosystem to gain distinction, its population and species must expand to the extent that the ecosystem literally teems with life—a perfect description for what happens during what I call Stage II of the evolution of an ecosystem.

There is a fascinating subfield of biology known as biogeography, the study of which sheds some light on the circumstances that allow an ecosystem to really take off. In large part, this subfield dwells on the processes of colonization, the means by which an initial community of pioneer species transforms itself into a robust, dynamic ecosystem at climax. Some of the essential principals of biogeography have special relevance for managing the expansion of business ecosystems.

One of the central observations of biogeography is that ecological communities mature in at least two ways. First, they expand in biomass. Grasslands get denser. Trees grow taller. Populations of animals multiply. As organisms die and decay, the organic matter in the earth increases and soils are enriched. Overall, energy from the sun is converted by photosynthesis into biological structure. As this energy continues to pour in from outer space and illuminate a particular patch of earth, the local biomass keeps expanding.

The second way ecosystems mature is through increased genetic diversity: they add species, elaborating synergistic relationships and becoming ever more artful and lively in turning resources into community life. Genetic diversity is generally a very good quality of an ecosystem. If the ecosystem is faced with a challenge—a shift in climate, or the introduction of an aggressive disease—keystone species and important symbiotic relationships may be threatened. In such times, it helps to have other species to turn to.

There is an interesting hypothesis about how genetic diversity relates to the size and range of the ecosystem. This hypothesis, originally developed by Edward Wilson and Robert MacArthur while observing islands in the Caribbean Sea, says that the bigger the island, the more the species. This phenomenon is known as the "area effect," and it has now been observed in many other ecological situations. For example, it is currently cited as a rationale to keep natural preserves from being carved into pieces too small to support essential species.[1]

The area effect partly derives from the fact that many species—particularly predators at the top of the food chain—require food contributions from a very wide contributing territory. A single jaguar, a top carnivore of Costa Rica, has a home range of about twenty square miles. A sustainable population of jaguars may require at least 700 square miles of forest. The larger the contiguous area that an ecosystem colonizes, the more species will find what they need. These species, in turn, may provide shelter or food for still others.

Promote Diversity in Business Ecosystems

In business ecosystems, there is also an advantage to diversity of people, organizations, and ideas. In general, the diversity of members in a business ecosystem makes it more robust and resilient, providing variety to its offerings, alternative sources of supply when bottlenecks arise, and a host of creative ideas to help spawn further evolution.

In business ecosystems, there also seems to be an area effect. There are threshold levels of critical range or volume of trade beyond which a given economic community can support additional types of members, who will then draw in new customers. One certainly sees this in the difference between small town and large city economies. While small towns often husband important values and unique cultural resources, in terms of diversity they provide no match for the sheer chaotic range of an urban center. We also notice this in the competition among consumer electronics formats, where a vast range of prerecorded programming is available on VHS tapes, audio cassettes, and compact discs, and much less on 8mm video and MIDI disks.

Business diversity, of course, is not limited only by the volume of trade in an ecosystem, but also by how open or closed the business community is to new ideas, people, organizations, and processes. The same is true in biology. Some biological ecosystems are much more isolated than others from invasions of new biological material. Biologists note that the farther an island is from continents and other landmasses, the fewer the species that live on it. This is because the more remote islands fill up more slowly, since species have to travel greater distances to settle there. Biologists call this phenomena the "distance effect." While this concept may seem obvious, it has an important parallel in business, for it demonstrates the costs of isolation during expansion. All too often the limits to growth of a business ecosystem have a lot to do with the unwillingness of those in charge to accommodate others who wish to participate.

In business ecosystems, as in biology, the expansion stage is one of both increasing volume and scale, as well as the diversity of species of organizations and individuals that come together to make it happen. It is also a period of defensive action, because the expanding ecosystem will almost always face competition from either entrenched incumbents or from newly formed alternative ecosystems. From a management standpoint, three big questions are central to Stage II: Is our idea ready for prime time? What sequence of initiatives will be required? At what rate should we try to make this ecosystem grow—that is, how much business do we want in a given time frame, and how many different participants can we handle?

Design a Compelling, Scalable Vision of New Value

Readiness is the first issue. Generally speaking, Stage II expansion requires a compelling vision of value and the ability to scale up the ecosystem to provide that value to a broad base of customers. As discussed in previous chapters, sometimes a concept does not promise enough economic value to allow expansion, at least not at the costs currently envisioned. In such cases, the concept should return to Stage I until its value proposition makes more sense. Unfortunately, enthusiasm can cause blindness. The new product landscape is littered with offers of limited value that were forced into senseless expansion.

Sometimes more than enough potential value is found in the core concept, but achieving this value and delivering it to customers depends upon the ecosystem reaching a particular size or richness. In these cases, it may be necessary to provide a special price or other incentives for the first participants to enter the ecosystem, and they then provide an attraction for those who come later. One sees this phenomena often in clubs—health and social clubs—where the first batch of members must be lured by substantial incentives.

A related problem is when the customer or supplier experiences prohibitive start-up costs, even though participation in the ecosystem will be of great value to them over the long run. Sometimes it makes sense for one of the larger members to subsidize the entry of these players with some sort of long-term loan. Look at the availability of "free" cellular phone sets. They help customers over the hurdle of the high initial costs, but they eventually are paid for by way of revenues from the customer's subscription to the cellular service.

Replicating and scaling up the value proposition is a second challenge. Ford's cars, McDonald's burgers, AT&T's telephone service, Intel's microchips, and Fidelity Investment's customer service are all distinguished by the fact that their value can be consistently delivered at vast volume. This volume enables these companies to anchor huge ecosystems. Smaller ecosystems can be anchored by less mighty firms. But even the neighborhood restaurant that aspires to create a local business ecosystem must deliver its meals with consistency. Moreover, it must be able to realize economies of scale, which will provide profits as a result of expansion—which in turn can be reinvested in growth and in maintenance of the community.

If you want to test the readiness of a business idea of your own, ask yourself this: Given my own aspirations for creating economic ecosystems based on the virtues of my company, have I and my associates learned how to consistently and reliably deliver our value on the scale required? What would it take to do so? The answer to these simple questions can go a long way in helping you prepare for your own Stage II expansion campaign.

Create a Sequence of Initiatives to Expand the Ecosystem

Assuming value and scalability, one confronts an array of Stage II implementation challenges. The main ones have to do with sequence: what needs to be done now and what can be done later? A strategy for expansion must consider initiatives that touch all seven levels of the business ecosystem. Some of the challenges are external: How do we differentiate our ecosystem from the alternatives? Often the answer to this question is found in paying careful attention to the sequence of customers, markets, and products pursued. With what customers and markets will you begin—and where and to whom will you move next? You need to consider the nature of your initial customer sets and markets—and the differences in buying patterns, needs, and attitudes of your subsequent customers and markets. Your ecosystem must adapt to serve successive groups. Your initial product and service offers will become precursors of later offerings, and perhaps should be consciously designed that way to hook customers into your ecosystem and subsequently deepen their participation.

Many of the challenges are internal: How do we keep from imploding under the weight of new growth? During Stage II, many of the biggest internal challenges are at the process, organizational, and stakeholder level. Scaling and replication require well-designed, standard processes. These in turn depend upon well-managed organizations. Taking an organization through aggressive growth requires risk capital, which must be provided by stakeholders with deep pockets.

The priorities of major investors of capital are in turn deeply shaped by government policy—everything from direct interventions into pricing and business ownership to tax preferences, banking and securities regulation, interest rate policies, and support for the local currency. In 1993 we saw the collapse of billion-dollar mergers of cable television and regional telephone companies, aimed at creating information superhighways, in part because the government capped cable television prices.

Stage II expansion is a very serious game. It requires substantial financial resources, a key difference from the pioneering stage. Managers and organizations need to anticipate and take action to prepare for the effects of making such a dramatic transition.

Manage the Rate of Ecosystem Expansion

Rate of expansion is a key dimension of choice in the development of business ecosystems, just as it is in the growth of companies. You can try to expand rapidly, or you can try to cool down and make growth more measured. Obviously there is no formula for determining how fast to grow a business ecosystem, but a few factors are important to consider—again separable into external and internal.

Externally, if your business ecosystem is sheltered from direct rivals, you can take more time to expand. In the expansion stage slow growth can yield real benefits, as it allows you to take some care in turning the theoretical advantages of your business model into realities. As we will see later, Wal-Mart spent many years building a solid foundation for its ecosystem, partly because it avoided the direct competition that nettled its big city brethren. This enabled it to create a depth of customer allegiance, individual and organizational skills, and of systems and procedures before facing aggressive, head-to-head combat. Similarly, the Japanese auto-making ecosystems have created their core capabilities behind high walls of economic protection—waiting until they had honed their skills and established economies of scale and scope to make them competitive in the world market before they exported their species and ecological model to the United States.

Protection, of course, cuts both ways. It can be essential in Stages I and II as new ideas are nurtured and brought into reality. On the other hand, too much protection can result in what we are calling Hawaiian ecosystems—vulnerable, inwardly focused, and uncompetitive. The right answer to how much protection is optimal is that managers who lead in the development of business ecosystems need to pay attention to two imperatives. First, they need to make sure that their nascent ecosystem has access to all of the best business species the world has to offer and can synergistically coexist in the expanding ecosystem. The idea is not to create an isolated island—but rather one where introductions of new ideas can be to some extent controlled by the equivalent of a wildlife manager. The leader is shaping the ecosystem. Second, the leader must make sure that the benefits of early protection are reinvested in world-class competitiveness. The Toyota auto ecosystem, described earlier, did a good job after World War II of appropriating know-how from ecosystems outside Japan. It used protections to build capabilities that ultimately allowed it to thrive beyond its original island home. The leader's intent must be clear. The temporary greenhousing of the ecosystem must support the ecosystem's preparation for breaking out into the wider opportunity environment.

In some markets, and at some times, the protection issue is nearly moot. This is often the case in high technology. When companies quickly come together to lock in particular standards, lightning speed in entering and dominating the wider opportunity environment can be critical. Starting in a protected micro-environment may be of limited use. In the Internet world, for example, Netscape Communications moved in the early months of 1995 to position itself as the standard for server and "browser" desktop software for companies and individuals engaged in electronic commerce. In order to establish itself as the de facto standard software supplier, it gave away thousands of copies of its introductory desktop browser. At the same time, it made server sales to a multitude of major companies looking to put content on the Internet, rounded up substantial investment capital, and managed to incorporate into its software base every significant new innovation that hit the market. Inside of a year, the Netscape software-centered ecosystem became dominant, and Netscape executives established a basis for community leadership. The question that now confronts them is: Can Netscape turn this leadership into a real business model, with revenues, scale, and profits—just to make it sustainable? Can they establish a viable business in the face of sustained opposition from Microsoft and others with already established core businesses—and massive abilities to invest?

Even if the external environment dictates rapid expansion, you must balance your desire for speed with an appreciation of the risk of internal collapse. One of the best ways to manage internal risks is periodically to use the seven dimensions of the business ecosystem to assess one's rate of ecosystem growth. For example, in the customer dimension, you want to stimulate demand in the end-user customer base, to stay ahead of rival ecosystems. On the other hand, you do not want to have demand far exceed the capacity to supply it. Otherwise, paradoxically, that demand may seek out your rival as a second choice, and your investment in demand stimulation will help your opponent. Apple Computer, in 1995, dropped prices and stimulated demand for its Macintosh offering. Unfortunately, chip supply problems prevented Apple from meeting this demand—and analysts now believe many of those customers ended up purchasing new machines from the opposing Microsoft/Intel ecosystem. In the market dimension, you want to sign up many channels and agents. But you do not want to move so quickly that you lose control over what they actually deliver to customers—or worse, lose control of the customers themselves, allowing the intermediaries to start new ecosystems.

Processes must be scaled up to meet demand and to create the economies that your business model promises. On the other hand, if you stretch too fast and far, quality and reliability will collapse. Suppliers and stakeholders are critical, but not if their price exceeds their added value—or if the overall network of suppliers cannot create a high-quality offer. In 1993 Chrysler Corporation introduced its LH-series cars, which were beautifully designed and became very popular. They were created by an extended community of suppliers—an ecosystem—that took responsibility for an unprecedented range of functions, including not only manufacturing of critical components and subassemblies but design. Chrysler, coping with its small scale relative to other world automakers, sought to strengthen its ecosystem and lower costs by relying on these outsiders.

Unfortunately for Chrysler, getting a quality product out of such a distributed supply chain turned out to be more challenging than its executives had anticipated. By 1995 *Consumer Reports* had taken the LH models off of its recommended list due to reliability problems that Chrysler acknowledges resulted from its limitations in managing the network. Warranty costs had almost doubled. Chrysler executives remained committed to their ecosystem design, but sobered about what it took to manage the creation of a culture of quality across an array of linked, but independent, organizations.

Sometimes funding for fast growth comes at a high cost in terms of interest rates or managerial control. In some instances, the government mandates that an ecosystem grow quickly, particularly when—as in the personal communications services

(PCS) licenses that were sold in 1995—it is offering statutory monopolies or oligopolies. In the case of PCS, government took a novel role not only in the stimulation of business ecosystems in a new opportunity environment, but by making billions of dollars for the public by selling the rights to the radio spectrum required to enter the environment.

All in all, as an executive you need to pay attention to two objectives: mastering the internal challenges of direct expansion and growing fast enough to colonize the available range before other ecosystems do. As we shall see in chapter 8, there are ways that you can accentuate market boundaries to enhance your ability to defend against rival ecosystems. However, in ecosystem-to-ecosystem competition, as in many other games, a good offense is—if not the best defense—a very important element.

Stage II, then, is about the race to move from a set of core synergistic relationships to a rich, robust ecosystem. It is about combining a wide range of value elements, and even aspects of competing ecosystems, into an economic system that can capture market territory and defend it against rival business ecosystems.

A story from the early days of the personal computer business—the race between Apple and Tandy—adds two values to this discussion. First, it illuminates in a nice compare-and-contrast example how traditional thinking, as illustrated by Tandy, does not work in a world of business ecosystems. Second, and more important, it was the experience of this battle that taught many of the pioneers of personal computing these lessons—and in fact set the stage for subsequent rounds of ecosystem-to-ecosystem-based competition in the computer business and in other businesses that have been touched by it. The battle itself, and the appreciation of the battle, both have had widespread subsequent impact on the world of business.

To Create a New Ecosystem, Change Lives

I have fond memories of my first personal computer. It was a Tandy TRS–80 Model I (a "trash 80" to its detractors) that I acquired in 1982. I was its third owner. It had helped auto-mate a trucking company, computed the heating and cooling calculations for a consulting engineering company, and now it was going to help me get a graduate degree from Harvard. In today's terms it was a puny machine—with only a small amount of memory, a slow microprocessor, and a few pieces of software.

Despite its limitations, my TRS–80 was a revelation. As a student on a shoestring budget, I did research and writing for faculty members to support myself. With my trusty personal computer, I became six times more effective than without it. Since most of my fellow students did not yet use personal computers, I seemed like Superman to my customers. My income began to rise.

Personal computers were more than handy devices for poor grad students. They represented the liberation of electronic computation. I had previously journeyed to the university computer center to use terminals attached to a mainframe that was controlled by the intimidating staff of the "Office of Information Technology." With the TRS–80, I could work com-fortably in my own apartment, without interruptions or any time-sharing expenses. The TRS–80 was mine, and it became what Steve Jobs astutely called "a bicycle for the mind"—ubiq-uitous, omnipresent, an extension of my mental capacities. The TRS–80 sparked a personal revolution in my life—and in the lives of millions of others like me.

As I emphasized in the previous chapter, innovations that have the potential to create major business ecosystems stir these sorts of revolutions in people's lives. Automobiles, telecommunications, television, pharmaceuticals, and air travel all had these effects. Currently the Internet repre-sents the liberation of global telecommunications in the same way that personal computers liberated electronic com-putation—and promises to set off a similarly vast economic revolution. In 1982, as I delighted in my TRS–80, I was par-ticipating in a broader revolution—a business revolution—that in hindsight can be better understood than it was at the time.

Complete the Total Product, Process, and Organizational Architecture

As is so often the case, the revolution began in fits and starts. In the early 1970s, a new technology—the microprocessor— emerged with the potential to spawn vast new applications and dramatically reduce the cost of computing. Yet this innovation sat dormant for several years. By 1975, hobbyist machines like the Altair and IMSAI had penetrated a narrow market. But these computers were not products suitable for the average person.

Starting in the late 1970s, Tandy Corporation, Apple, and others introduced early versions of what would eventually become the personal computer. The seed innovation they chose was the microprocessor, but these first designers also recognized that other products and services had to be created to tie the whole package together. These ranged from hardware components to software to services like distribution and customer support. My TRS–80 Model I was a product of these efforts.

Apple and Tandy each had a different strategy for creating a full, rich ecosystem. Apple worked with business partners and talked about "evangelizing" to encourage coevolution: identifying partners, exciting them with its vision for the whole world of personal computing, and providing moral and other kinds of assistance to get the partners going. While the company tightly controlled its basic computer design and operating system software, it encouraged independent software developers to write programs for its machine. It also cooperated with independent magazines, computer stores, and training institutions—and even "seeded" a number of school districts with Apple IIs.

Tandy, on the other hand, took a more vertically integrated approach. It attempted to buy and then own its software, ranging from the operating system to programming languages and applications like word processors. The company controlled sales, service, support and training, and market development by selling exclusively through its Radio Shack stores. At the same time, it discouraged independent magazines devoted to the TRS–80 machines. Therefore, Tandy's simpler and more tightly controlled ecosystem did not foster the excitement, opportunities, and inner rivalries of Apple's, nor did it harness as much capital and talent through the participation of other companies.

Table 7.1 compares the Apple and Tandy approaches to external and internal control of major value elements.

Tandy's approach got the company out front fast; in 1979, it reported sales of $95 million compared with Apple's $47.9 million. However, Tandy's tight control ultimately led to slower growth at a time when establishing market share and a large user base was essential to success. By 1982, Apple's $583.1 million in sales had decisively passed Tandy's $466.4 million. Within another two years, the Tandy-centered ecosystem had collapsed in the face of the IBM personal computer initiative—and Tandy had become just another clone player. Apple, because of its wide base of entrenched support, was able to hold on to substantial market territory into the mid-1990s—more than a decade after IBM's entry.

Within the computer industry, this comparison was keenly appreciated by leading executives. Several lessons became clear: Innovation touches off races between alternative implementations. A vital aspect of the race is filling out the total value package. Species diversity attracts customers—customers like a wide range of third-party software, hardware, and services. Early customers support the addition of more diverse elements and offerings. A virtuous cycle of expansion is established.

Perhaps most important, much of the new value that is created cannot be anticipated by the originators and orchestrators of the ecosystem. Instead, new value is often identified and pursued by outsiders who come to the ecosystem seeking help for their own purposes and manage to adapt the offerings to meet their needs. In this way these outsiders become insiders, and the ecosystem and its species multiply. For example, Apple did not so much seek out the educational market, for example, as allow itself to become the darling of educators and students.

Which organizations were responsible for key elements of the product architecture?

PRODUCT ELEMENT	APPLE	TANDY
Application software	Zealous community of independent developers	Smaller community of independent developers, under license to Tandy
Programming languages	Both self-developed and independently developed	Purchased languages from outside developers, made available only through Radio Shack stores
Operating system software	Self-developed	Self-developed
Displays	Sourced from third parties, and relabeled	Self-manufactured
Storage devices	Sourced from third parties, and relabeled	Sourced from third parties, and relabeled
Input devices (e.g., keyboards, etc.)	Sourced from third parties, and relabeled	Sourced from third parties, and relabeled
Basic computer hardware platform	Own manufacturing	Own manufacturing
Microprocessor	Motorola	Zilog

Which organizations handled major business processes?

BUSINESS PROCESS	APPLE	TANDY
Customer support and service	Network of independent dealers	Company-owned Radio Shack stores
Sales	Network of independent dealers	Company-owned Radio Shack stores
Marketing	High-profile national advertising, using outside ad agencies	Low-profile advertising supporting Radio Shack stores, using internally developed ads
Magazines, training products and services, consumer education and information	Encouraged independent magazines, pundits, support organizations	Self-published materials. Discouraged independent magazines, pundits, support organizations

Table 7.1. Comparison of Apple and Tandy approaches and external and internal control of major value elements. Internal controls are underscored.

Similarly, the desktop publishing business essentially found the Apple Macintosh—with its superior graphical interface, its early laser printers, and software developed by independents like Adobe and others.

Ecosystem Leadership Means Creating a Framework for Participation

A second lesson became evident to savvy observers of Tandy and Apple: Expansion is fundamentally about getting new partners to join in the economic community. Expansion of an ecosystem is only secondarily about growing one's firm. Working with partners provides the wherewithal to grow one's company. Partners help to rapidly fill out and enrich the ecosystem's total package of value, and they can do so in creative, unpredictable ways. In addition, having key partners in one's camp may preclude them from assisting the other expanding ecosystems—a crucial aspect of defending oneself. How fast an ecosystem incorporates new contributions is a function of the openness of the framework for contribution—and of how many new contributors have the motivation and ability to join up.

Apple's real contribution was in showing that leadership of business ecosystems is mainly about establishing a framework for participation that brings in others and organizes their activities in synergistic ways. Apple is often given credit for inventing the personal computer—a spurious claim, given all its predecessors and contemporaries. On the other hand, Steve Jobs, as founder and key shaper of the Apple organizational vision, did much to invent evangelizing as a way of doing business—that is, deciding who else needs to be involved, finding ways to recruit them, and maintaining structure, incentives, and fair play in the community. As one insider has commented, "Steve Jobs wanted to be a rock star, and carried those aspirations and methods into the business." By creating groupies and fans, by working with promoters and the media, by seeking to create fame and celebrity and the allegiance—even the defiance—that characterized rock and roll communities of the time, Jobs and his friends at Apple established a new way of doing business—beautifully matched to the new world of boundary-free, modular, value-chain-creating business ecosystems.

Ironically, it was the failure of Apple to keep pace with the framework race that ultimately caused its decline. By the late 1980s the ecosystem that was spawned by IBM was being led by Microsoft and Intel—and had developed an extremely open, very effective de facto framework for participation. Thousands of suppliers and millions of customers streamed in to join it. Apple, now no longer led by Jobs and his original band of rock and rollers, became the relatively more closed and difficult ecosystem to join. Application software companies found it hard to compete with Apple word processors and drawing programs that came bundled with its machines. Hardware companies were blocked by Apple's insistence on being the only one in the ecosystem—and by Apple's unwillingness to license its software operating system to run on other machines. Meanwhile Microsoft software, Intel chips, and other associated components were available to anyone who wanted to join their ecosystem. Innovation rates slowed in the Apple ecosystem, prices stayed up, and value leadership moved to its rival system.

The most effective leaders of expanding business ecosystems put their efforts into creating frameworks for participation that draw in and coordinate the efforts of disparate actors. In the best cases, the ecosystem becomes so attractive that resources self-identify and seek out the leaders, asking to join up. Moreover, the effort is most effective when the leader is open to being surprised by some of the resources that appear—and allows serendipity and the creativity of the resources themselves to play a major role in suggesting and developing new avenues of growth.

The biological parallel here is rather striking. As we noted, islands lying far from other land develop slowly. In business, you can essentially move your island farther or closer to sources of new contributions—and thus manage the introduction of novelty.

For a time, Apple created an ecosystem that was open to new species, and indeed saw its reason for being as inviting and orchestrating such contributions. This yielded a great diversity of business species and helped Apple's ecosystem to grow in richness—ultimately to defeat Tandy in size as well.

Tandy in effect became isolated by pushing itself farther from the coast, becoming a victim of the distance effect. Its ecosystem permitted fewer species to enter it and therefore it was not as vibrant and as strong. In business as in biology, the ecosystem with more diversity is almost always going to be the preferred ecosystem.

To be sure, there are risks in taking partners. Partners in ecosystems, like partners in anything else, may grow powerful enough that they will seize the leadership of the collective enterprise. One must not only take partners, but one must also establish a strategy for long-term leadership and control of the partners. This lesson, however, was not cemented firmly in the consciousness of the early leaders of the personal computer revolution. As we shall see, it took the later experience of IBM, which found itself economically gutted by its erstwhile partners Microsoft and Intel, to drive this point home. Later, we will consider in detail the important matter of the risks of partnering. Suffice it to say that after what I call the death of competition partnering can hardly be avoided, and so its challenges must be mastered rather than denied.

Capitalize on Precursor Ecosystems if Appropriate

In a certain sense it matters not whether an ecosystem is built from scratch from the ground up, or from pieces adapted or borrowed from others. What is important is that a new framework for cooperation and coevolution—a new set of synergistic relationships—is formed and maintained and provides competitive advantages over alternative arrangements. One of my favorite biological examples is the microecosystem established by peregrine falcons in New York City. It happens that peregrine falcons are extremely sensitive to the pesticide DDT and similar chemicals. These chemicals, most of which have been banned in the United States, cause falcon eggs to develop with very thin shells—such that most of the eggs crack before new chicks can hatch. The falcons themselves don't usually directly ingest DDT, but they sometimes eat birds that have eaten insects that have become contaminated with DDT. At each level in the food chain DDT is concentrated, to disastrous effect on the falcons.

It turns out that the pigeons in New York City are surprisingly free of DDT, even though they feed on the detritus of the city. Several years ago a few peregrine falcons became established in New York, nesting in the skyscrapers and swooping down to take pigeons when hungry. They now are thriving in this microecosystem that borrows from old and new, and has now expanded throughout the towers of the city. What matters is not the source of the elements or their previous relationships, but the new framework for cooperation that links falcon, pigeon, and garbage into a synergistic, self-maintaining system.

Adroit utilization of existing ecosystems and ecosystem elements can provide powerful advantages to a new ecosystem. In the previous chapter, Starlight Telecommunications was starting up telephone service in Somalia. It cleverly made use of resources from established systems—ranging from the inexpensive taxi radios for its local wireless connections to its hookup into the worldwide network of long-distance services by way of a satellite link to Norwegian Telecom. The key to success is to take advantage of the scale and other established capabilities of the existing ecosystems—without getting caught up in their old-line ways of thinking and operating. The art is in using the resources, while staying true to one's own vision and values—and embodying these values in a new and appropriate framework for cooperation that can drive the establishment of creative new relationships in a new and distinctive ecosystem.

A little-remembered fact is that the IBM personal computer ecosystem was itself founded upon the piece parts of a previous personal computer ecosystem—the so-called CP/M world. In the early days of personal computing, a third ecosystem almost took off, but then collapsed. This third ecosystem centered around two software companies: Digital Research and Micropro. In 1977, Digital Research made its software operating system CP/M available independent of hardware. That separation allowed almost any small manufacturer to assemble components and put out a usable personal computer. Overnight, a variety of small companies entered the business, building on the same Zilog microprocessor used in the early Tandy machines.

In 1979, Micropro brought out a word processor that ran on CP/M-based machines. Wordstar was the first truly powerful word processor, and it took an important group of potential PC customers, writers and editors, by storm. Demand soared for Wordstar, CP/M, and the hardware of small companies like Morrow and Kaypro.

Unfortunately, there was such intense rivalry among the hardware companies that none could really make enough money to reinvest in community leadership. Neither of the two software companies learned how to play a community leadership role. There was no one to study the market, define new generations of functionality, and orchestrate suppliers and partners to bring improvements to market. The CP/M ecosystem floundered as it struggled to move beyond its early incarnation.

When IBM entered the personal computer business in 1981, it picked up the pieces of this ecosystem. In contrast to its own history and culture of vertical integration, IBM followed and extended the Apple model of building a community of supporters. IBM took on partners and opened its computer architecture to outside suppliers. Moreover, it adopted a microprocessor from Intel that incorporated all of the instructions available in the Zilog microprocessor in Tandy and CP/M machines. IBM licensed MS-DOS, a software operating system, from the then tiny Microsoft. Microsoft, in turn, had purchased MS-DOS from a smaller firm, Seattle Computing, which had created the operating system as a near clone of CP/M. As a result, Wordstar and other popular application programs could easily be ported over to the IBM PC.

What essentially happened was that IBM grafted major elements of the CP/M ecosystem to its own efforts. At the same time, IBM "lent" some of the competitive advantages of its own traditional mainframe-centered ecosystem to the new effort. IBM used its deep pockets and scale to establish a successful personal computer–centered ecosystem. The resulting ecosystem had tremendous relative competitive advantages, in terms of expansion, in comparison to the efforts led by Apple and Tandy. IBM stimulated demand for its new machine through a combination of heavy brand advertising, distribution through Sears and other channels, and building its own network of specialty stores. It helped Microsoft with management advice and systems, as well as with money. It provided Intel with a high-volume microprocessor business, and even went so far as to provide Intel with $250 million in 1983, so that Intel could build chip fabrication capacity. By any measure, IBM's approach to expanding its PC ecosystem was a major success. Its personal computing business grew from $500 million in 1982 to $5.65 billion by 1986, and the company and its ecosystem rapidly dominated the market.

Conventional wisdom tends to see the relationship of old and new ecosystems in terms of the old swallowing up the new. Large companies, often rightly thought to be poor at innovation, wait until an idea is proven, and then take it over and make it a success. Indeed, that is how the IBM personal computer story is often told. I would suggest that a more creative point of view is that new ecosystems can gain a great deal by working with the old—and that often it is the denizens of the new who end up on top. In the IBM case, Microsoft and Intel became the winners, and one reading of history is that they grafted IBM's resources on to what was always in reality more their effort, leadership, and vision than IBM's.

Similarly, Federal Express could not exist without the telephone and air transportation infrastructures that it has organized to its purposes. Retailers focused on dominating narrow categories of goods succeed in part because the customer can supplement their offerings with those of other general-purpose stores. The Home Depot offering is supplemented by local hardware stores and lumberyards. Grocers offering organically grown foods play into an overall market that also includes traditional supermarkets. The customer often shops at both. In the new world of business ecosystems, a key element of strategy is which pieces of the old world do I want to incorporate—and how?

Consider Your Own Situation Within Expanding Ecosystems

Now that you have explored some of the challenges of expansion, it is worth pausing to consider the wider world around your own business and your opportunities for stimulating ecosystem expansion, as well as the expansion of your company. The familiar seven-level chart on page 158 summarizes some of the points worth considering during expansion. You may want to ask your management team to consider the following questions as well. In fact, true to the spirit of creating an expanding community, you may want to define "team" more broadly and include other key leaders from across the ecosystems that you participate in.

To deal with these questions, you have to consider broad issues: To what extent is my business a part of a larger business concept—of offers, processes, and organizations—that bears expanding in a conscious way? To what extent is my business a part of a new, coevolving idea of linked products or services—new functions and solutions—that customers can join to create and develop? The answers may suggest other players to partner with—or standards and complementary products or services that could be more closely integrated with your offerings. The answers might also suggest promising lines of research and development aimed at strengthening the synergies and operational connections among these elements. The overall challenge is to create a framework for cooperation and coevulotion in all seven dimensions of the business ecosystem—and that helps toward the achievement of competitive advantages for the ecosystem.

If you do share these questions with your associates, the points of disagreement among members of your team will be very interesting, as well as the areas where you agree. Discord about expansion strategy at the ecosystem level can be invisibly crippling because it causes people to work at cross purposes, and to do so in a dimension of leadership that may fall out of the range of the normal management systems and tar-

DIMENSIONS OF THE BUSINESS ECOSYSTEM	QUESTIONS A FRAMEWORK FOR COOPERATION AND COEVALUATION MUST ADDRESS	COMPETITIVE ADVANTAGES TO BE ACHIEVED
Customers	What changes in aspirations, in self-image, and in buying habits and vendor loyalties will my ecosystem need to capitalize on, and perhaps help galvanize, in order to expand?	Deep identification of customers with their membership in the ecosystem; many active connections to other members
Markets	What sequence of markets do I want my ecosystem to expand to fill? How will my expanding my ecosystem help it contribute to the aspirations of the people and organizations within these markets? What local species of offers, activities, and organizations may need to be involved in my network of synergistic relationships—or be supplanted by my expanding contributions?	Dominance of marketing channels and the bounded markets they serve
Offers	What complementary products and services will help the ecosystem expand? How can I help promote the linkage of my offers with these associated contributions—and assure their availability and continuous improvement?	Offers that provide a rich, full package of value, such that the customer is not tempted to go beyond the ecosystem for related products and services
Processes	What is the total ecosystem of processes, managed by others as well as myself, upon which my business must depend for expansion? How might the expansion of this architecture of business processes be improved by conscious cooperation among the parties?	Processes that have been well implemented, that have achieved economies of cumulative learning over those in alternative ecosystems, and/or processes that reflect more efficient or more effective underlying technologies and design
Organizations	What set of organizations and inter-organizational relationships will be necessary for the expansion of my business and the ecosystem within which it lives? How might the architecture of cooperation among such organizations be improved in order to support expansion?	Organizational arrangements that bring to this ecosystem maximum economies in terms of scale, scope, and innovation
Stakeholders	What stakeholder support, including financial contributions, will be necessary for expansion? How can this support be assured?	Maximum resources as needed, at minumum cost; in particular, financing that is not onerous in terms of cost or control
Values and policy	How is the expansion of my ecosystem and business consistent with public values and government policy? How can I strengthen these ties, as well as better explain to the public and to important government leaders the virtues of expanding my ecosystem?	Maximum alignment between the aims and values of the ecosystem and those of the surrounding society, and with those of the power elites within the society, including government officials and agencies

Table 7.2

gets of the firm. On the other hand, alignment that explicitly involves the framework for cooperation and coevolution that you are creating and managing can do wonders for the effectiveness of a management team. It can suggest new resources, new ways of harnessing the resources to the cause, and potential areas for breakthrough success.

To a large extent, succeeding at leading the growth of a business ecosystem is a matter of shifting your leadership mind-set—and that of your team. At its most fundamental, the shift is from entities to frameworks. That is, from thinking primarily in terms of business entities—companies, people, skills, and assets—to seeing business in terms of the frameworks of cooperation and coevolution within which these entities work together and coevolve into the future together.

There are several related cognitive shifts that are required in moving from an entity point of view to one that makes frameworks of cooperation and coevolution central. These shifts are summarized in the following chart:

Cognitive Shifts Required to Lead Expanding Business Ecosystems

FROM	TO
Establish individual companies, and help them grow.	Establish frameworks of coevolution that bring together the competencies of many firms—and help these communities to grow.
Seek to do a better job of meeting needs that are already being addressed, with resources that are already harnessed.	Identify powerful unmet needs and fragmented, underutilized resources—and invent new value chains that bring resources and needs together in creative ways.
Identify resources primarily within your own company and industry community.	Look for creative ways to incorporate resources that are resident in companies and industries other than your own.
Exercise management and leadership principally through the control of inanimate assets, and through coercing people and organizations into going along with your plans.	Inspire talented people, organizations, and companies to join you in realizing a common set of goals.

Table 7.3

We need to go further than our current emphasis on organizational networks, standards, and architectures—although these describe important aspects of what must be done. The job of the leader must be recast. That challenge is to design and promote frameworks for cooperation and coevolution that bring innovative value to customers, and within which the leader can find an enduring role and contribution. We need to make a fundamental change in management thinking so that our business strategy starts from this point of view, rather than edging toward it when our entity perspective fails us.

8

Stage II Continued: Defending the Revolution

Looking at satellite photographs of the earth, you see broad swatches of color and pattern, marking vast ranges of similar communities of plant and animal life. A hardwood forest-based ecological order still occupies much of the eastern and midwestern United States.

But if you look more closely, you behold a different picture. Within those broad regions, there is remarkable variation. Sand dunes hug the shores of Lake Michigan. Marshes abut meadows. Plots of suburban bluegrass slice up forests.

This closer look brings you eye to eye with the intricate mysteries of what biologists call a microclimate, the local conditions of a little habitat. On the same day—indeed at the same moment—the temperature can fluctuate many degrees from the south to the north side of a small hill. Soil conditions can vary dramatically within just a few square meters. Rivers course through the landscape, creating rich conditions for aquatic ecosystems and wetlands, adjacent to bone-dry rock formations.

In a world of fast-expanding business ecosystems, converging industries, and exotic, industry-breaching technologies, we sometimes fail to appreciate—or take advantage of—business microclimates. Yet microclimates can provide critical protection for fragile business ecosystems. We may celebrate the richness and vibrancy of the business ecosystems we have dubbed Costa Rica style. However, if you intend to establish a new order, Costa Rica would hardly be the place to start. Rather, you would probably want to find more sheltered territory, introduce the key species, and let the processes of succession create a rich, highly synergistic community.

Thus with the mega-boundaries of nation and industry falling, sometimes the wisest strategy is to start small and build an ecosystem exquisitely tailored to specific micro-conditions. Some of the most powerful companies in the post-industrial world—including, as we shall see, Wal-Mart—created their empires by beginning with micro-opportunities. Once they established themselves in several of these opportunities, they were able to string their creations together like beads into elaborate networks with vast economies of scale and scope. This strategy is highly important in the new world, and warrants elaboration. But first let us revisit the conditions of ecosystem-to-ecosystem competition that in many cases demand such an approach.

The Perils of Ecosystem-to-Ecosystem Competition

With traditional boundaries either collapsing or becoming increasingly permeable, most firms find themselves adrift in broad opportunity environments, facing competitors traditional and new. The most creative firms put together business ecosystems to offer the support and multiple capabilities required to satisfy customers and harness new innovative ideas. But the act of creating a business ecosystem does not by itself stave off competition. Indeed, in the new world of business, there is considerable ecosystem-to-ecosystem competition.

Ecosystem-to-ecosystem competition is more or less unique

to business—and has no direct parallel in biology. The closest analogue would be a gardener's battles with weeds and wilds. In business, however, leaders pose alternative conceptions of the future and relationships among members—and customers, suppliers, and others are asked to choose sides. Ecosystem-to-ecosystem battles are central to most Stage II growth in business. Given that ideas travel fast and traditional barriers to entrepreneurship have toppled worldwide, any idea progressing from experimentation to expansion will stimulate counter-communities. The very existence of an expanding community of alliances signals to other, perhaps less prescient strategists, that action is afoot, and that maybe they should start similar ecosystems.

Given this reality, we cannot make meaningful strategy for Stage II expansion without addressing how to promote the widening and deepening of our own network of synergistic relationships, while also defending against infringements of others. Some of the most interesting competitive situations involve these collisions of expanding universes. I find myself fascinated watching the last gasping days of the Wal-Mart/Kmart conflict. As Wal-Mart steams along, Kmart struggles to avoid total collapse of the now fragile synergies it depends on.

Any competitor to your expansion is not trying simply to beat you at your game. The competitor seeks to usurp enough of the available territory—absorb enough of the ecological carrying capacity of the range—so that the business model of your ecosystem fails. The competing expansionist wants to keep you from growing to where your ecosystem benefits from wide membership, scale, and continuous innovation. This new competitor wants to stunt your ecosystem's growth, ultimately causing its system of advantages to falter and break down.

The point of ecosystem-level matches is to secure key customers, critical mass and market momentum, and relationships with important suppliers and other potential allies. Make no mistake, these are dogged zero-sum games. My sign-up is your loss. Not only am I trying to involve important contributors, but I am trying to deny them to you and other ecosystems.

Thus you must reach two goals to succeed today. First, you must make your ecosystem higher performing, more diverse, and more robust than competing ecosystems. To accomplish this, you must master the distance effect, metaphorically nudging your ecosystem closer to other potential participants and encouraging them to contribute. You must take advantage of the area effect, injecting diversity and richness as you grow in size. And you must seek links to other ecosystems, subordinating them into your network and accelerating the growth of a world of mutually beneficial relationships. These were the topics of the previous chapter.

Second, you cannot depend upon whatever boundaries already exist to shield your ecosystems from the thrusts of others. Instead, you must create and defend ecosystem boundaries, building them where none exist, and shoring up those that do. This concern is the focus of this chapter.

There are three major ways of establishing defensible boundaries. First, find ways of deeply involving customers in your ecosystem. Encourage psychological identification and membership, day-to-day dependence, and recurring, regular engagement. Second, dominate the market and the marketing channels. Absorb all the demand within a market, and price to keep others out. Third, create offers that provide total solutions, which meet all of a customer's needs in a particular category. Don't make the customer look to someone else for products and services that complement those of your ecosystem, because the customer may stumble into the snare of an alternative ecosystem.

Boundary-making can be extremely difficult if you seek to achieve a dominant position in a wide swatch of the total opportunity environment. On the other hand, boundary-making can often be accomplished more rapidly and surely by narrowing your initial ambitions and focusing on what amount to economic microclimates that one can dominate. Successful ecosystem expansion often starts with identifying submarkets within which the ecosystem can establish defensible dominance over a subset of the total territory. In the best of cases, such partitioning of the market allows many defensible positions to be established that can ultimately be linked together to enable successful colonization and defense of much of the total territory.

Let's consider a case of Stage II expansion that seemed wildly successful at the time, but was undone by lack of attention to building defensible market boundaries.

Remember the Cautionary Tales

When the heady days of Stage II expansion arrive, it is easy to be swept up in blind enthusiasm. Evangelism and tent meetings, T-shirts, mugs, baseball caps, and rapture are the order of the day. During these times, it is wise to meditate on some cautionary tales. One of my favorites is that of People Express, a famous story worth examining from the ecological perspective. The darling of business school faculty, the hope-filled dream of its employees, the savior of thousands of backpack-carting passengers, the airline found its feet knocked out from under it just when it was most vulnerable.

People Express was founded to take advantage of the 1978 statutory deregulation of the airline industry in the United States. By 1982, deregulation had stripped the industry of many of its traditional protections and supports, and had opened the boundaries of the world's biggest airline services market. From 1982 on, many rivals flocked to the business. Most failed almost immediately. Not People Express. In many ways, People Express founder Donald Burr did everything right: he focused on price-sensitive customers, dominated underserved niche markets between secondary cities, developed innovative ways to run the airline with a dramatically low cost structure, got employees to accept stock instead of direct compensation, and built a reasonably happy customer base in several important markets along the eastern seaboard of the United States. Between its first service date in 1981 and 1985, People Express grew to revenues of almost a billion dollars a year.

In 1985, however, People Express moved beyond the secondary markets and began flying between large cities, competing head-to-head with the major carriers. This required larger planes and a heavier debt load. In October 1985, Burr bought Frontier Airlines to replicate his success in the western part of the country.

At the peak of People's expansion-related vulnerability—with challenges ranging from integrating Frontier and transforming its corporate culture to paying for the debt taken on to do the deal—American Airlines attacked. Using information from its computer-based reservation system, American loosed a concerted set of pricing actions designed to drastically reduce People's cash flow. This impaired People's ability to continue its expansion, causing a crisis of confidence to ripple across the People Express ecosystem and ultimately precipitating its collapse.

What could People Express have done? It might have stuck with the East Coast markets where its position was strong and focused more tightly on bonding with its discount customers for whom American and other major carriers were unlikely to provide attractive long-term alternatives. Or People Express might have hoarded more cash to withstand temporary discounting by the major carriers. Instead, it took on debt and expanded beyond its defended niches. Had People Express protected its stronghold, attacks like American's would have been very expensive to mount, and might not have been tried at all.

Just this sort of focus powered the rise of many discount carriers, like Southwest Express in the 1990s. These carriers identified small niches that could be saturated—such as the route between Dallas and Fort Worth—and compete as much with bus and auto travel as with the major airlines. While the opportunity environment within which they play is open to many competitors, these carriers have carefully identified territories, saturated demand, kept prices low, and stockpiled enough funds to withstand temporary price wars. That has allowed them to build reasonably defensible niches from which to pursue further expansion. Their ultimate success probably depends upon whether, once they achieve a limited level of success, they can figure out how to unite these positions into a system with economies of scale, while still staying defended against the big carriers. In this regard, they could do worse than try to learn from Wal-Mart.

An Expansion Success Story

Perhaps the ultimate story of boundary-making as a basis for sustainable expansion in a hotly contested opportunity environment is that of Wal-Mart, the fabled discount retailer headquartered in Bentonville, Arkansas. There is a great deal of popular interest in the Wal-Mart story, because of the wealth created since its founding in 1962 and because of the well-promoted Horatio Alger–like story of Sam Walton.[1] Until his death, he was the richest man in America, and the collective wealth of his family still far exceeds that of Bill Gates.

There are two versions of the Wal-Mart story. The first is a simpleminded account of customer focus, centering around the use of "greeters" who bring warmth to the buying process. The alternative is a tale of a corporate behemoth trampling on the gentle ecologies of picturesque small towns. To me, both accounts miss the most important point: Wal-Mart is neither saintly nor rapacious. It is very effectively managed at the ecosystem level. It reaps the benefits today of the boundary defending that it implemented years ago.

Wal-Mart has come far from its "Boots for good ol' boys" roots. While most people recognize that Wal-Mart is nearly ubiquitous in the United States, few truly appreciate the exact dimensions of the total enterprise. Wal-Mart is the largest discount retailer in the United States. In 1995, it boasted of 2,874 stores with revenues approaching $100 billion. With all these stores linked to one of the most sophisticated marketing information networks in the world, Wal-Mart is likely the largest private purchaser of massively parallel computers in the United States. Only the government buys more. Wal-Mart uses these computers for high-speed data mining—that is, for trolling for patterns in the buying habits of millions of Wal-Mart customers and responding to shifting customer desires immediately through pricing and promotion actions. Thousands of point-of-sale terminals feast daily on sales data and then serve it each night to Wal-Mart headquarters in Bentonville.

On the supply side, Wal-Mart has an integrated logistics system second to none. Wal-Mart's cost of distribution, for example, is under 3 percent of sales, compared to the 4.5 to 5.0 percent of its discount competitors.[2] Handling approximately 15 percent of the total North American sales for several major consumer goods companies, it is one of the world's most powerful bulk buyers. It has wired 1,800 suppliers into an integrated system for matching demand in the stores with inventory—both merchandise in warehouses and in transit across the network—and for stimulating supplier production. With this system, Wal-Mart wields unprecedented control over the manufacturing, movement, and pinpoint deployment of products to customer outlets.

But to appreciate Wal-Mart fully, you need to visit an actual store. I have been both a student of Wal-Mart's business model and an admirer of its contributions to small-town America. After all, I grew up in the small- and medium-sized towns of the central Midwest where Wal-Mart planted its first stronghold.

On a recent Fourth of July weekend, I drove down from Chicago to visit my grandparents in the small central Illinois town of Mattoon. My grandparents, 98 and 99 years old, were still living in their own home, albeit with difficulty. I arrived in Mattoon on a swelteringly hot day. The temperature hovered around 100 degrees, and the humidity approached 100 percent. Around Mattoon, the custom is to remark on how fabulous the weather is for the corn. Corn is almost all that you see from horizon to horizon. On the outskirts of town, as I left the Interstate and turned onto a smaller state highway, I noticed a giant Wal-Mart squatting in the middle of a parking lot and covering several acres—quite a sight in Mattoon, population 12,000 and shrinking.

The next day, my grandparents and I were sitting around

wondering what to do. There are not a lot of choices in Mattoon, especially for people pushing 100. Someone suggested that we go to Wal-Mart. The Mattoon Wal-Mart, like many others, is open 24 hours a day, 365 days a year. This time of year, it is deliciously air-conditioned.

Much to my surprise, the Mattoon Wal-Mart proved a revelation. It was then the largest Wal-Mart in North America. At 225,000 square feet, it seemed like a covered football field. But its size was not as impressive as its upscale appearance, when considered from the perspective of what is normally available in a small midwestern farm town. I remembered my childhood of white bread and last year's fashions, sold by Main Street merchants who held virtual monopolies with indifference toward customers. In contrast, this Wal-Mart sold live lobsters and several types of gourmet cheese. It offered well-made, stylish clothing. Toys were bright, clean, and stressed farming, construction, and auto-racing themes, not weaponry. Specially designed full-spectrum lighting cast a warm glow over the entire scene. And the air-conditioning, as predicted, was cool and satisfying. We had entered a little bit of nirvana, only a short drive from home.

This experience is the same in so many Wal-Marts in so many small towns: an almost upscale experience at discount prices. Wal-Mart does not succeed principally because it drives local stores out of business, but because it offers dramatically better value, so customers prefer it. Compared to what else is available, and to what customers expect, Wal-Mart occupies the premium role that a Nordstrom or Bloomingdale's might play in a wealthy suburb, and that traditional department stores played in larger cities for many years. The value proposition is almost irresistible.

Ironically, right next door to the Wal-Mart in Mattoon was a withered-looking Kmart about one-sixth the size. It seemed to specialize in tires and auto parts. Why would anyone want to go there rather than to Wal-Mart, thriving through its massive competitive advantages?

What amazes me most is how Wal-Mart's ecosystem in the early years completely evaded the leaders of other, similar ecosystems such as Kmart and Sears. Retailing in the United States has always been one of the most unprotected competitive sectors in business. Rivalry abounds. Kmart and Sears started with many times Wal-Mart's capital, expertise, and market coverage. So how, in such a merciless environment, did Wal-Mart avoid the fate of People Express? I contend that we can learn from the answer to this question. But to appreciate Wal-Mart's profound achievement, we really need to compare the lifelines of Wal-Mart's and Kmart's ecosystems.

A Major Move Off Main Street

Technological and societal shifts often open up new opportunity environments. In the early 1960s, the combination of cars, roads, and postwar affluence transformed retailing in the United States. That transformation led to the spreading of retail discount outlets and ultimately encouraged the rise of a vast array of high-volume general merchandise outlets like Wal-Mart, as well as retail category killers like Toys R Us and Staples. These megatrends changed retailing in this manner: To buy a wide range of goods at low prices, more and more customers would willingly hop in cars and drive a reasonable distance to malls or other non–Main Street locations. As cars and roads improved, people began to enjoy driving, and their estimate of a reasonable distance increased. Thus customers would gladly drive to a store, particularly if that store had a wide array of goods at low prices and saved a lot of time shopping around.

America's infatuation with cars triggered a vast change in the economics of retailing. Instead of the goods moving to small stores near the people—at the expense of the wholesalers and retailers—people began to move themselves to the goods. The resulting savings realized by the retailer—through less moving and breaking down of the goods into small lots, shared overhead of larger stores, and consolidated buying—could be passed on to the customers. Retailers recognized that the Main Street five-and-dime was yielding to the variety store. And variety stores, in turn, were threatened by the large discount store. By 1960, the total revenues of such discounters eclipsed a billion dollars in the United States. But no single player had deployed this idea as the basis for a large-scale retail and distribution ecosystem.

Here Come Kmart and Wal-Mart

In the early 1960s, many retailers began to move off Main Street and into the increasingly prosperous suburbs to capitalize on the discounting concept. One such company was S.S. Kresge, a large, successful, and publicly held firm founded on the five-and-dime store concept. With the slogan "Nothing over ten cents," Sebastian Kresge and John McCrow opened their first store in Detroit in 1899. By 1912, Kresge had 85 stores, expanding steadily to become one of America's leading general merchandise retailers in the 1950s. In 1958, the results of a company-sponsored market study prompted Kresge to try its hand as a discount retailer.

To test the concept first, the company renovated and reopened three of its unprofitable stores as Jupiter Discount Stores, followed by the first official Kmart in 1961. As these new discount stores began to dominate Kresge's revenues, Kresge recast its five-and-dime self completely into the discount mold and set up operations accordingly: large stores with large parking lots, placed to exploit the flow of traffic and easily accessible to the driving consumer. Kresge strategically positioned its big stores near existing strip malls and towns of more than 50,000 people, and carried large quantities of items aimed at the lower end of suburban taste. Fueled by ample capital, management talent, and corporate will, the Kmart ecosystem expanded rapidly in the early years. For a respectable while, it looked like a huge multibillion-dollar winner, the leader of mobile patronage and a darling of Wall Street with its strong financial performance and a thousand locations by the mid-1960s.

A second, much more improbable contender emerged at the same time, in rural Arkansas. Wal-Mart essentially cloned the discount model, borrowing brazenly from Kmart and grafting the best from other predecessors. Indeed, Sam Walton's genius manifested itself in his willingness to visit his competitors (as well as his own stores) and in his shrewd analysis of their components in the context of an ecosystem. He then experimented with these elements and models in his somewhat cloistered Arkansas laboratory.

By the late 1960s, Wal-Mart had worked out the basic structure of its own business ecosystem: Wal-Mart stores would stock a variety of well-known brands and sell them about 15 percent cheaper than those available in smaller "mom-and-pop" stores. But this structure differed from Kmart's and others in a significant way: rather than going to the suburbs where the money was, Wal-Mart stayed with rural and small-town markets, in towns of 5,000 people, especially in spots where one store might serve several of these towns. In these markets, established competitors often served customers quite poorly, so that Wal-Mart could slip easily into the role of the most important, best-stocked, least expensive store in the region—not as a second-rate retailer. The geography also enabled Wal-Mart to grow as a major non-farm employer in the area, which established it as a pillar of the community. Within its customer group, Wal-Mart developed extremely high perceived value and a great deal of day-to-day reliance and interdependence.

The rural markets had another important, perhaps hidden advantage to the Wal-Mart ecosystem: the natural boundary set by the customer's unwillingness to drive more than about ten miles to a general merchandise store. Within these ten miles, one Wal-Mart could saturate demand for many of these goods. The resulting Wal-Mart market definition was small enough for Wal-Mart to dominate, too small to attract rivals like Kmart, but large enough for Wal-Mart to consolidate buying power of people in several towns and to negotiate volume discounts.

Kmart, on the other hand, eyed the larger fish in the urban

areas. Rather than saturate its market, Kmart stimulated demand, a move that lured competitors as well as customers. Kmart relied upon its system of expansion rather than saturation, growing quickly in the early years but attracting fierce direct rivalry from discounters like Target and Venture, whose business models were nearly identical and who kept pace with new store openings. In later years, category killers like Toys "R" Us and Home Depot, which saturate a market with every conceivable product in a single category of goods, began hammering Kmart. Though Kmart's demise was less dramatic than that of People Express, the causes were eerily similar: expansion without establishing defended boundaries and edging out competitive weeds.

Squeeze Out the Weeds

While the original Wal-Mart locations could support one store, the customer population wasn't large enough to maintain two rival discounters. Once Wal-Mart had established a store in a particular area and had beaten back weak local retailers, it was seldom threatened with competition from other discounters, including Kmart.

One of the best ways to reinforce boundaries is to absorb all the carrying capacity of the bounded territory, leaving no nourishment for potential rivals. Economists call this notion "space packing." Its counterpart in biology is "species packing," where a set of existing species substantially utilize the available nutrients in a particular territory so that additional species cannot squeeze in. There's simply no room. Every year, I see my own miniature version of this concept in a tiny plot of land, my backyard. Each spring, if I succeed in getting bluegrass to grow dense enough, no crabgrass will blemish my lawn once summer weather rolls around. In effect, I have space-packed the lawn. But if the grass is a little too thin, the crabgrass takes root and I have an aesthetically unpleasant ecosystem war on my hands.

For Wal-Mart, space packing had an important but often

unappreciated consequence: it reduced the uncertainty to which Wal-Mart was subjected during expansion, and thereby lowered the company's implementation costs and risk. Wal-Mart could build its capabilities in the initial stages without the additional capital costs and planning complexities that would have been unavoidable with competition. Overall, the expansion did not face much risk of a larger competitor ambushing Wal-Mart at some vulnerable point, such as when the company might be short on capital or when management attention was absorbed by adding new capacity in another region.

Learn to Manage Remotely

Once its business strategy was up and running in a number of discount stores in the American South and Midwest, Wal-Mart's top executives concentrated on developing organizational capabilities that would let them replicate the bounded markets strategy over many markets rapidly. They had three obsessions, all of which boiled down to being able to manage remotely, rather than with Sam Walton's personal touch alone. These were:

- Building a set of incentives and measures that would ensure the commitment of employees and managers to local stores, which led to a complex system of training, oversight, bonuses, and stock-purchase plans for employees.
- Managing communication and control of a network of remotely located stores, which required close monitoring of a carefully drawn set of measures that were transmitted daily to Wal-Mart headquarters in Bentonville.
- Setting up an efficient distribution system that allowed for joint purchasing, shared facilities, systematic ordering, and store-level distribution of a large number of different goods. (This third "obsession" ultimately became Wal-Mart's trademark hub-and-spoke distribution system:

warehouses served constellations of stores located no more than a day's drive from the center.)[3]

Wal-Mart was essentially tying together its local ecosystem—each established in a bounded market that Wal-Mart dominated—into a broader ecosystem with economies of scope and scale. Wal-Mart's strategy has a fascinating parallel in the restoration of biological forests in Costa Rica. Santa Rosa National Park was created in 1971 and allowed for the restoration of the dry forest. Guanacaste National park, created in 1989, linked the dry forest to higher, wetter areas—including cloud forests on Orosi and Cacao volcanoes. The recently established Guanacaste Conservation Area joins together these areas plus several others. The result is a linked ecological system of much greater diversity and potential stability than any of the smaller communities alone.

Similarly, Wal-Mart's network of local community stores and regional distribution established the foundation for a broader, richer business ecosystem. The number of Wal-Mart stores grew rapidly, from 32 in 1970 to 195 in 1978, when the first fully automated distribution center opened, to 551 in 1983, when Wal-Mart employed its own satellite at the center of a communications network that kept its officers in daily touch with its now far-flung empire.[4]

Overall, these efforts achieved a number of economic advantages for Wal-Mart. The store systems and communications network allowed Wal-Mart to expand without adding excessive overhead. The distribution system provided economies of scope and scale that increased as the ecosystem grew.

In contrast, Kmart used its buying power to fund internal inefficiencies and made jumbled investments resulting in unpredictable inventory and precarious performance. For example, Kmart focused its strategy in 1980 on creating a more contemporary image—by cleaning floors, replacing burned-out light bulbs, and giving each store a fresh coat of paint. Remarkably, the new Kmart stores closely resembled the old Jupiter Discounts. In 1980 and 1983, Kmart added Furr's Cafeterias and Bishop Buffets to its business, only to sell them off in 1986. In 1984, the company's attempt to reposition itself as a major merchandiser resulted in an exceedingly large heap of discontinued items and a consequent 17.8 percent drop in fourth-quarter earnings. Its logistics disintegrated, it effectively achieved diseconomies of scale, its financing became more expensive, and its ecosystem became more chaotic and unwieldy as it grew.[5]

Use Stage II Dominance as a Foundation for Success in Stage III

By the early 1980s, the Wal-Mart ecosystem covered vast territory. The temptation might have been to seize some rewards through higher prices and higher margins. This would have fostered rivalry, however, and with it, a threat to the stability of the ecosystem. Fearing this, Wal-Mart resisted the temptation to charge higher prices in the markets and regions it dominated. Instead, top managers still viewed each market as "contestable"—as a potential opening for rivals if Wal-Mart ceased to give the maximum possible value to customers. Continued customer leadership, in turn, enhanced the Wal-Mart brand and further cemented the company's place in the minds and buying habits of consumers. Wal-Mart's system of "everyday low prices," in which there's no need for weekly sales or special promotions, has now become a standard in retailing.

In Stage II, as pointed out, the major competitive objective is to be the preferred ecosystem in a given market territory. This Wal-Mart plainly achieved. As a result, Wal-Mart was in a powerful position to enact Stage III dominance, which evolves from maintaining leadership and bargaining power *within* the networks of activities and organizations that constitute the ecosystem.

By the early 1980s Wal-Mart was becoming architecturally mature and heading into Stage III. The fundamental offer, process, and organizational arrangements were well established. Across the ecosystem, Wal-Mart focused on customer-perceived value and on strengthening bonds with other members. As the leaders of a highly successful and visible business ecosystem, Wal-Mart managers worked on continuing to assert the company's vision over other community members.

First, Wal-Mart reinforced its own direct value contribution to the ecosystem, by continuing to invest in and enhance its own fundamental economies of scale and scope in distribution. By the leadership stage, low-cost, highly automated, precisely targeted distribution had become a crucial ecological component of the Wal-Mart ecosystem.

Second, Wal-Mart created unprecedented involvement and entanglement in the affairs of its suppliers.[6] By 1984 (a point at which Wal-Mart was a very large and powerful channel to customers), it started exerting heavy pressure on suppliers to keep their prices down. Moreover, Wal-Mart compelled its suppliers to set up cross-company information systems to attain maximum manufacturing and distribution efficiency. For example, in 1987, Wal-Mart and Procter & Gamble reached an unprecedented partnership that involved extensive electronic ordering and information sharing between the companies. These sorts of relationships make it almost impossible for large suppliers to go to war with Wal-Mart, because their operations and processes are so intimately intertwined. This supplier vulnerability gives Wal-Mart, in turn, better bargaining power when terms and conditions of supply are negotiated. In return, Wal-Mart places very large orders and gives better payment terms than the rest of the retailing industry: on average, Wal-Mart pays suppliers within 29 days, compared with 45 days at Kmart.[7]

Once Wal-Mart had achieved this scale and bargaining power, it possessed economic advantages far beyond those that initially resulted from boundary-making. It was then ready to cautiously enter more contested markets, relying now on its other advantages to prevail. Starting in the 1980s and accelerating in the 1990s, Wal-Mart extended its reach into adjacent territories and ecosystems. In 1983, Wal-Mart entered the membership discount market with Sam's Club, which by 1992 included 208 clubs that contributed more than $21 billion in revenue. In 1990, Wal-Mart incorporated another ecosystem by acquiring McLane Company, the nation's largest distributor to the convenience store industry. McLane, under Wal-Mart's control, now serves about 30,000 convenience stores. In 1992, Wal-Mart also acquired the distribution and food-processing divisions of Southland Corporation. Southland operates a large chain of 7-Eleven convenience stores; the acquisition added 6,000 7-Elevens to the McLane–Wal-Mart customer base. By 1995 all of this activity added up to North America's dominant distribution and retail ecosystem.[8]

In stark contrast, the Kmart Corporation in 1995 mantained only 2,163 Kmart stores and 171 Builders Square retail outlets in the United States. The company sold most of its specialty operations in 1994. After selling off the cafeterias and buffet businesses in 1986 and acquiring a discount warehouse club business called PACE Club in 1988, Kmart gave up its struggle against Sam's Clubs in the Midwest and sold the PACE stores to Wal-Mart in 1994. Though Kmart plans to open about 60 stores in 1996, it closed 121 stores in 1994 and another 207 in 1995, with another 70 slated for 1996.[9]

The corporation continues shedding millions of dollars of old inventory, an impossible eventuality in the Wal-Mart ecosystem, and it has realigned itself simply to increase accountability and discipline rather than to link effectively with members of its ecosystem. According to the latest chairman and chief executive officer, Floyd Hall, Kmart's 1996 list of priorities includes improving merchandise mixes, becoming more competitive on pricing, controlling gross margins, improving availability of inventory, developing customer service—and keeping its stores clean.

The Scorecard

What makes the Wal-Mart story so relevant is that it is a saga of the creation of a well-managed ecosystem, not just a company. It contrasts sharply with Kmart, where the same basic paradigm—discount retailing—was at first wildly successful, but eventually collapsed under the pressures of unmanaged ecosystem effects. The following chart captures the critical points of comparison, so that you can better appreciate Wal-Mart's strategic growth and ecosystem management in contrast with Kmart's.[10]

	WAL-MART	KMART
INITIAL COMPONENTS	• 5 Ben Franklin stores • Rural locations • Limited funds	• Many locations, both new and converted five-and-dimes • Publicly held company • Multibillion-dollar firm
STAGE II **Population area of each store**	• Less than 5,000 • Bounded by geography	• More than 50,000 • Contiguous to other populated areas
Presence of store in market	• Saturates demand • Precludes rivals	• Stimulates demand • Attracts rivals
Overall system	• Links stores	• Expands stores
Results	• Stable store-level performance • Simple inventory and logistics • Cheaper financing • Well-planned and managed growth	• Unstable store-level performance • Disintegrated logistics • More expensive financing • More chaotic growth
STAGE III **Buying power** **Results**	Used to keep prices low and dominate markets • Integrated logistics • Economies of scale and scope in distribution • Predictable performance	Used to fund internal inefficiencies in system • Scattered logistics • Misapplications of scale • Chaotic performance
CURRENT STATUS	Information-based retailer, on top of all current competitive advantages and poised to move quickly on new opportunities	Logically challenged retailer, with troubled financing, market reputation, performance, and morale

Table 8.1

What is perhaps more compelling is a visual comparison of the financial performance of the companies, depicted in Figures 8.1 and 8.2.

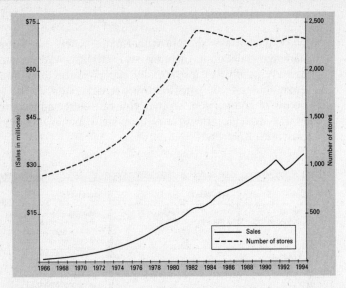

Figure 8.1. Kmart's stores and revenues: the ebb of an ecosystem.

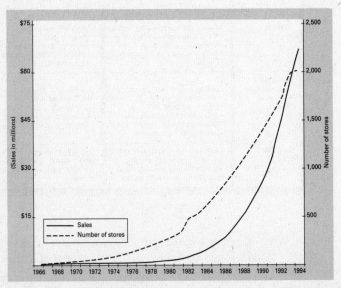

Figure 8.2. Wal-Mart's stores and revenues: the exponential expansion of an ecosystem.

First we look at numbers of stores and total sales. What we note is that Kmart starts off with a stronger base, grows rapidly, but in the 1980s growth in stores levels off, as the ecosystem becomes unwieldy and inefficient. Sales continue to rise, but at a slow rate. By contrast, Wal-Mart's growth curve in stores starts off slowly, but follows a very steady geometric progression as the ecosystem establishes itself across ever wider territory. Similarly, Wal-Mart's sales curve follows a strikingly orderly progression. Though it takes Wal-Mart more than a decade to surpass Kmart, when it does, it is by building on a very sound foundation.[11]

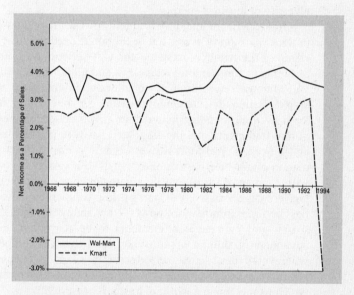

Figure 8.3. Net income as a percentage of sales for Kmart and Wal-Mart: Wal-Mart becomes more stable as Kmart becomes unstable.

The really interesting comparisons are with net income expressed as a percentage of sales. Here we see the rockiness of Kmart's earnings—indicating a company, and by implication an ecosystem, out of control. Wal-Mart, by contrast, holds rock steady at around 4 percent of sales for more than twenty years. The combination of steady net income and orderly growth is remarkable—suggesting a company in control of its destiny, and its ecosystem.

The Power of Thinking About Whole Systems

The overall power of Wal-Mart is that its executives think about the whole ecosystem in which they are nested. Over the years, they have created a very effective framework for coevolution, choreographing the expanding contributions of a wide diversity of business species.

Interestingly, the major investment in Wal-Mart today is not in the expansion of assets, but in the sophistication of the leadership of the whole ecosystem—the vast network of thousands of suppliers, thousands of endpoints, and millions of customers. Wal-Mart perceives itself as an information company. Sitting atop a continually changing framework for coevolution, it now leads by understanding better than anyone else the operation of that framework and the associated network of organizations and processes. Wal-Mart thrives because it has the best information about meeting customer needs in a variety of markets with a range of stores, fed by a vast network of suppliers and logistics capabilities.[12] Wal-Mart's prime competitive advantage has become information power—the ability to intelligently spawn and manage new elements of its ecosystem, to take advantage of shifting opportunities, and to meet competition wherever it lies. As we will discuss in detail in chapter 10, information power provides the ultimate point of strength from which to succeed in a world of business ecosystems.

Applying Boundary-Making to Your Business

The IBM case that we examined in the previous chapter shows what can happen when otherwise excellent managers focus only on the growth of their firm and allow the ecosystem to evolve without conscious direction. IBM had the might to spread its ecosystem across the broad territory of the market but, like Kmart, allowed a variety of players to establish themselves in more bounded, defensible territories. Moreover, IBM, again like Kmart, did not focus on turning its early gains into additional advantages—either in dominating markets or in achieving economies of scale and scope in the back office. The result in Kmart's case is that an alternative ecosystem thrived, ultimately at its expense. In the IBM case, as we will discuss in more detail, its ecosystem triumphed but it lost its lead role in the community.

During its highly successful expansion, Wal-Mart made two right moves. First, it wove as dense a mat of interlacing synergistic ecological relationships as possible, so that there was no space for crabgrass to enter. Second, it did this in isolation and behind geographic protections, at least until it could link its efforts and create shared economies that would allow its frontend ecosystems to thrive in more open, rival environments.

As illustrated in Table 8.2, boundary-making is a form of competitive advantage that requires moves in at least three aspects of the business ecosystem. You need to create close connections to customers so they will be resistant to the incentives your competitors may offer. You must identify submarkets that have some level of natural boundedness—that is, limits on market entry, as well as limits of customer willingness to go beyond their borders. For Wal-Mart, this entailed focusing on small towns rather than urban areas. Within these comparatively small submarkets, you need to satisfy as much of the demand as possible—both quantitatively, in terms of market share, and qualitatively, in terms of providing as much as you can of the total value that customers desire. In this way, you make a market that hopefully looks very unattractive to new entrants, and encourages them to look elsewhere to expand. Meanwhile, you put in processes to link bounded markets, expanding your total territory and developing economies of scale and scope where practical.

So the general notion of creating a defensible ecosystem during expansion has a four-fold focus: Find submarkets and hold on to them. Link together the ecosystems that you establish in these markets. Create economies of process, organiza-

DIMENSION OF COMPETITIVE ADVANTAGE	DEFENSIVE STRATEGY	RELEVANT BUSINESS GOAL	EFFECTS ON COMPETING ECOSYSTEMS
Customers	Create linkages to customers so they are reluctant to switch to the offers of other ecosystems.	Seek to become so dependable and rich as a source that customers reorient their lives and habits around you.	A competing ecosystem will be forced to present a value proposition that is strong enough to justify the high switching cost. This is a very stiff challenge.
Markets	Identify natural market boundaries and seek to dominate demand within their borders.	Seek to achieve 100 percent of bounded submarkets, rather than a smaller share of a larger market.	An alternative ecosystem will find market entry very expensive, with a long payback period, because in the early stages there will be little trade to provide revenues and margin to offset the costs of market entry.
Offers	Design offers that meet all or the most important related needs that a customer experiences.	Seek to provide 100 percent of the products and services that the customer experiences as complementary and related.	The new ecosystem will have to match the full line in order to be a credible supplier— which is a very expensive way to enter the market.
Overall aim	Create such a rich ecosystem, with customers so deeply enmeshed within it, that the available "carrying capacity" of the market is fully put to use by your ecosystem.	Overall, seek to drive up the cost and risk of competitive market entry, and lengthen the payback even if the opponent is successful.	Your hope is that these effects will cause the competitor to seek other markets —and leave yours relatively uncontested.

Table 8.2

tion, and stakeholder support, and use these to colonize more markets. Concentrate on customer bonding, on space packing in bounded markets, and on shared economies across customers and markets. These focuses support and reinforce each other in a powerful cycle.

Figure 8.4

For managers, these ideas raise a number of important questions:

- How can I define submarkets for my ecosystem to colonize?

  Once I do, I may be able to better start my colonization efforts and more effectively develop and defend my efforts.
- Are there some market definitions or selections that would allow us to escape head-to-head rivalry while we expand, provide a unique level of service, and dominate the available demand?

  These tests will help me prioritize my efforts, so that I do not become another People Express.
- What do I need to do as I build my ecosystem in these markets to dominate them—bonding with customers, filling the channels, saturating demand, providing such complete solutions that customers will not seek out alternatives?

  This will help me flesh out the plan for enriching the ecosystem within the market. The basic idea is not to race to cover the entire addressable space in the larger market, but to win the race in some smaller territories.
- What do I need to do to facilitate the efficient linkage of the colonizations I am making?

  This question focuses me on the systematization, incentives and methods, and training that is required for replication.
- What needs to be done to create shared economies among these colonizations?

  This will help me construct a plan for achieving scale, scope, cumulative learning, and radical innovation advantages.
- Given a continuing, accelerating set of advantages, what sequence of markets are addressable, and what is my program for entering, linking, and consolidating my gains?

The beauty of boundary-making is that its use is not limited to those who already have established strengths. Wal-Mart started out with no real advantages over Kmart. What it shrewdly did was use boundary-making to pick its competitive battles and to avoid confrontations it could not win. In any opportunity environment there are a multitude of opportunities to exploit similar microclimates. Silicon Graphics has thrived in the computer systems business by focusing on large niches, such as entertainment graphics. Successful financial services firms have adapted to meet the needs of specific customers and work to dominate particular local areas.

Microclimates can become even more important when a new market is booming. At those times, even large companies can seldom fill all the available territory in advance of demand, so there is almost always room for an ecosystem based on capturing territory left unoccupied by the players with the initial advantages. The race for territory usually has room for a grassroots-based ecosystem. Instead of going after 10 percent of a big market, successful players can go for 100 percent of many nontraditionally bounded markets. If these niche players can bond deeply enough with customers, they can secure what territory they gain and can sometimes triumph, as Wal-Mart did. Therefore boundary-making is a critical focus for expansion, and it provides real hope for small players with large ambitions.

Epilogue on Wal-Mart

In my view, Wal-Mart is a notable business success, a rich case study from which much can be learned. Wal-Mart adds a great deal of value to people in many of the towns it serves by providing a wide range of goods, employment, and investment opportunity. On the other hand, there are those who view the company quite differently. People who own or work in competing Main Street shops often experience Wal-Mart as an unfair bully, bent on destroying their livelihoods.

In Wal-Mart's defense, many argue that it simply conducts its business as any other business would, and that it should not bear any special responsibility for its economic impact. I take issue with this position. Wal-Mart, as it edges toward $100 billion in sales, is undergoing an identity crisis that may prove disastrous if the company fails to embrace a new role. Wal-Mart faces an important challenge, as do all firms when grappling with issues of value and policy. Wal-Mart is becoming a keystone species in many locales, as much of a fixture of the community as the local electric utility, the gas company, the major banks, or the local hospital. Wal-Mart's leadership must acknowledge and appreciate the extent to which others depend on it or feel vulnerable to it, as they do toward any greater establishment figure.

In truth, a Wal-Mart on the outskirts of town can weaken Main Street, not simply by pulling trade from a few shops, but by spurring the decline of entire town centers. Where a town is already economically marginal, a Wal-Mart can wield the final blow; civic groups may join with local merchants to fight Wal-Mart's arrival in such instances. But what about the recent widely discussed case, where Wal-Mart moved into a small town in Oklahoma, only to close its doors several years later, leaving a gaping hole in the local economy?

Such situations raise a more fundamental question: When a business ecosystem is powerful enough to reshape the social ecology of a local community, what responsibilities does it have? This question is by no means new to business leaders, but it is particularly relevant where companies pursue strategies based on boundary-making. Though Wal-Mart has moved into urban and suburban areas, it based its traditional business model in large measure on dominating rural regions—that is, on space packing (or, in biological terms, on species packing) and the competitive exclusion of others. The stability celebrated in this chapter is the result of Wal-Mart's pricing low enough and performing well enough to eliminate or at least debilitate its local rivals.

Ultimately, Wal-Mart's intent is to be the sole significant retailer wherever it does business, and it has the scale and efficiencies to do so. Companies that take this position in effect become the opportunity environment for many others, as well as operating in their own ecosystem. And because of their position, they find themselves under the intense scrutiny of governments and activists who tend to apply much higher behavioral standards to these firms. Wal-Mart's constituency will ask the giant retailer to contribute more to local charities, support local government services, and work carefully with local officials to mitigate the impact of any changes in hiring patterns at the site.

In short, Wal-Mart is not just another business within its environment, and it should not expect to be treated as one. Perhaps the largest managerial challenge facing Wal-Mart today is how to invest in the relationship building, the public campaigning, and the substantive policy studies to assume its role as a leader of local communities. From the perspective of business ecology, Wal-Mart hardly has a choice about taking up this mantle. It has become a keystone species—and the center of one of the most important ecosystems on its continent.[13]

9

Stage III: The Red Queen Effect

Once its niches become solidified and its species entrenched, a biological ecosystem reaches structural maturity. The amalgamation of the ecosystem has largely taken place and the species have developed a sustainable framework within which to live and coevolve. The prevailing species have made clear their dominance. The lesser species have accepted the smaller scale that will be their lot. With the cavalcade of colonists in place, the prey and the predators ensconced in their bargains of codependence, the ecosystem presents a gorgeous pattern across the landscape. This often heralds a long period of relative ecological stability.

Not that it will be without excitement. The species never pause in their coadaptation and coevolution one to another. Symbiotic relationships may expand or contract. Predators refine their attacks—and their prey respond with new defenses. At the same time, a new wave of participants begins to thread its way into the mature ecosystem by taking advantage of the fixed structure, and adds vastly to its complexity. To understand this, we need look no further than the intricate relationship between the tiny mite and the hummingbird.

In rain forests in Costa Rica, hummingbirds and Hamelia

flowers have developed a neat symbiotic arrangement. They have straightforward relationships that may be thought of as analogous to those woven together in Stage II of a business ecosystem. Hummingbirds alight on the red lips of the flowers and shed a dusting of pollen in exchange for a drink of nectar. Once this ritual became sufficiently fixed, it allowed the introduction of a third species: the mite. No bigger than a pinhead, the mite can't get very far on its eight miniature feet, and so, in pursuit of flowers to feed on, it has learned to ride the beaks of hummingbirds. When one of the birds settles on a flower, the mite scampers into its nostrils and then, when the hummingbird lands again on the same species of flower, the mite races off. The tiny creature feasts on the pollen in the flower and drinks some nectar, all the while finding the energy to do some mating.

Since the hummingbirds don't operate like scheduled airlines, but rather arrive and depart rather unpredictably, the mite needs an exquisite sense of timing. Also, a fine sense of smell. Each species of mite is quite particular about which flower it will dine on. Among other things, if a mite disembarks on the wrong flower, it will be killed by other mites residing there. Yet mites rarely make a mistake, since they are extraordinarily proficient at picking out a plant by the bouquet of the nectar.

There is a curious upshot to this evolutionary pattern. The tiny mite happens to boast a hearty appetite. It consumes almost half of a flower's nectar and about a third of the pollen. So the gratitude the mite shows its winged transportation amounts to rather ferocious and unwelcome competition for the available food.

Stage III Sets Off Intra-Ecosystem Rivalry

The coevolution that drives change in business ecosystems, like that in the biological world, also eventually stabilizes according to certain conventions. This stability then creates ample opportunities for new players—the business equivalents of the mites—to join the ecosystem. As they do, the ecosystem increases in richness and vigor, but internal competition for leadership and margins among the members also intensifies. I call this increasingly rivalrous period Stage III.

What becomes stable in Stage III is the design and structure of the ecosystem, but not necessarily its size. In fact, quantitative growth usually continues or accelerates in Stage III. Only qualitative, structural change slows down.

The way this happens is that an economic community, like its biological counterpart, comes to organize itself around a rich substructure of partly explicit, partly tacit agreements about how business will be conducted. The niches of the business ecosystem become clear. Products and services, business processes, and organizational arrangements become established. This lets the business species and populations become settled into their respective roles and range. What I like to call the "architecture" of the community emerges as something distinct from the species and interactions themselves. This new level of stability within the coevolutionary dance has profound consequences for leadership and strategy-making.

In a business ecosystem, the attainment of a stable architecture for the ecosystem is followed by a new wave of entrants jostling for position. A striking difference between biological and business ecosystems is that the agitation from late arrivals is far more pronounced in business. The reason is that economic entities are guided by consciousness, not instinct. Economic creatures are capable of choosing the environment and ecosystems in which they want to participate.

Consequently, when the structure of the ecosystem stabilizes, many new entrants and customers envision their own possibilities and are able to muster power they are eager to test. Tempted by the promise of joining an ecosystem overflowing with excitement, expansion, and potential profits, they are entirely comfortable exploiting the strategic architecture that another set of firms has built, and they often find a surprising receptivity among customers. As fresh participants join the ecosystem, rancorous leadership struggles may erupt when the interests of the traditional leaders and the new combatants drift apart. When this upheaval occurs, we know for sure we have entered Stage III.

Different Roles in Stage III

To understand fully the bursts of activity in Stage III, we should consider the different perspectives of its participants. Stage III has very different implications for an ecosystem's players, depending on their roles.

From the standpoint of the leaders, or potential leaders, competition within the ecosystem becomes as important as the competition at a higher level. Parties vie with each other for both leadership and bargaining power. Two factors start to frustrate the leaders: the increasing stability and resistance to change of the ecosystem's architecture, and the squeeze on margins touched off by hip customers and new entrants. This is when leaders feel an itching at their fingertips. Increasingly, they turn on one another in an all-out battle to wrest more of the ecosystem's margins and win the privilege of shaping the future.

Cooperation becomes ever more important in these intramural squabbles. The rivals struggle to hold adherents and keep the community rationalizing and improving while also supporting their black hole—their valued innovation pathway.

For the companies that merrily ruled as leaders in Stage II, the transformation to Stage III can come as a rude shock. In Stage III, the rules of competition and cooperation change markedly from the previous stages. The onset of intra-ecosystem competition becomes a predominant issue between allies that had been and must continue working together to make the whole ecosystem a success. If the leader stops driving innovation in the ecosytem, its power will erode.

Some longtime incumbent contributors to the ecosystem may spend time in denial of these brutal realities, and waste time propping up their declining businesses. But eventually they, too, will start looking for ways to reduce their cost structure, lopping off Stage II superstructures, outsourcing some functions, and generally moving from vertically integrated to deintegrated companies.

The strategic questions for leaders and potential leaders revolve around keeping expansion and innovation percolating, by moving hard against the sclerosis that otherwise grips the community. There is no way to immunize totally an ecosystem against conflict, but there are ways to soften the blow. The role of a leader in Stage III must be to reverse any rigidity. Leaders must keep the whole ecosystem innovating, as well as ensure their own protected role within the ecosystem.

From the standpoint of followers, their own incumbency diminishes in value if they can't coevolve with a leader. Why? Because new entrants are flooding the ecosystem and, in many cases, prying away what the followers do by doing it cheaper and sometimes better. So followers need to be exceedingly sharp in adapting to the leaders. Moreover, they must seek to participate in information power projects, and anything else that will give them a sense of the whole. That is the only sure route to achieving leverage in the leadership group.

From the standpoint of outsiders, they weasel their way into the ecosystem by settling for skimpier margins. They offset this by forgoing investments in research and development and by not having to shoulder the risks of the entrepreneurial activity that gave birth to the ecosystem in the first place.

What new entrants must do is meticulously examine the entire ecosystem for inefficiencies—niches where the incumbents perform poorly or reap excessive margins. By attacking these openings, they can enter the ecosystem. In some instances, they can actually dislodge the incumbents, and in others they can stimulate better performance and cause prices and supplier margins to drop.

There is also the special perspective of end customers. Through all this parrying and thrusting, customers are constantly learning. Their deepening knowledge allows them to better understand and discriminate among the various ingredients that make up the offers they are so dependent upon. Steadily, they begin to reduce this reliance—and the prices they are paying—by moving some of the functionality in-house, by purchasing from alternative off-brand suppliers, and by using the growing presence of alternatives to drive down prices.

Moreover, since the architecture of the community is relatively fixed and customers have learned how it works, they are often unwilling to pay for market development activities that would have seemed plausible in Stage II—things like customer education, sales support, and so forth.

The challenges facing the different players during Stage III are summed up in the following chart:

	COOPERATIVE CHALLENGES	COMPETITIVE CHALLENGES
Leader	Provide a compelling vision that draws allies to your leadership and provides a continued central place for your own innovative initiatives.	Block the leadership challenges from within the ecosystem, countering visions that run along different paths than your own and reinforce innovative contributions that would diminish the value of your own initiatives.
Follower	Align yourself with a winning direction, so that you can coevolve rapidly enough to avoid being cloned, while at the same time avoiding lost investments by moving toward futures that do not materialize.	Block other companies' attempts to clone your contributions and/or to join with opposing leadership and visions for the whole, that may render your contributions less valuable.
Outsider	Align with a winning direction to provide value that will be enduringly important, and for which the returns received will more than repay the cost of entry into the ecosystem.	Fight against insider attempts to exclude you from the ecosystem; fight others seeking to provide the same or similar value to the ecosystem.
Customer	Help work with key players to shape the value created by the ecosystem.	Become a savvy buyer, resisting excessive dependence upon other members of the system—and insist that the overall ecosystem structure reflect substantial consumer interests.

Table 9.1

Boom Times for the Community; Tighter Margins for Most Contributors

When ecosystems first become architecturally stable, and enter Stage III, they often experience veritable boom times. After all, you now have an eclectic swirl of companies and capital that was previously outside the ecosystem hankering for ways to enter. Companies study the ecosystem and identify activities where increased efficiency and effectiveness might be duly rewarded. They then join the ecosystem by trying to provide these very activities. In large and profitable ecosystems, literally hundreds or thousands of ventures may be launched.

Leaders should not confuse the concept of an architecturally stable business ecosystem with the notion of "market maturity" when growth in a business reaches its peak and companies must struggle with the implications of overcapacity. The beginning of Stage III is nothing like this. It is usually a time of explosive capital investment, as the new entrants gear up to compete. Once they do, the aggregate price/performance of the ecosystem benefits from the introduction of many different improvements in efficiency and effectiveness that spur further market expansion as prices drop, performance improves, and customers notice they have more choices.

As the rivalries heat up, though, margins begin to crash. Members of the ecosystem feverishly ask themselves: Where is the value now in the value chain? Ultimately, major contributions to the ecosystem turn into fungible commodities—traded by price, with no premium for distinctiveness. Only new innovation that substantially improves the performance of the ecosystem will reverse this cycle—distinguishing particular contributions, as well as restoring the vitality of the whole.

In biological ecosystems, too, there is an endless struggle among the members. As Jim Wetterer, a biologist who consulted on this book, puts it, "Because all of a creature's natural enemies—its competitors, its predators, and its parasites—are evolving to better compete, prey, and parasitize, creatures who slow or stop evolving may be driven extinct." Biologist Leigh Van Valen has written extensively on how species in biological ecosystems must continually innovate.[1] He came up with his "Red Queen Hypothesis," which maintains that many of the most important biological adaptations—such as sexual reproduction—originate during times of particularly intense coevolutionary pressure.

The Red Queen, you may recall, is a character in Lewis

Carroll's *Through the Looking Glass,* and takes Alice's hand and leads her on a run in the woods. Even though Alice and the Queen run very fast, they never leave the place where they are standing. Finally, Alice asks the Queen why they never seem to get anywhere. The Queen looks queerly at Alice and explains, "It takes all the running you can do to stay in the same place. If you want to get somewhere else, you must run at least twice as fast as that." In the case of biology, by mingling genetic material from two distinct mates, sexual reproduction allows more radical genetic experiments, enabling adaptive characteristics to emerge quicker. The species "runs twice as fast" in inventing possible ways to outstrip its enemies.

In business, simply running fast is often equated with lowering prices—and then struggling to get costs under control. In Stage III, most firms must come to terms with continuing declines in prices. Success requires at least accepting the trend toward commoditization, and in some instances moving aggressively to lower costs in advance of falling prices. High-volume producers that can thrive on low margins often temporarily become the stars of the ecosystem.

In Stage III, never doing better than running fast presents something of a long day of reckoning for leaders of an ecosystem. It forces the large firms that have been instrumental in the Stage II ecosystem expansion—like an IBM or an Apple in personal computers, or a Sony in consumer electronics—to take a new and candid look at shedding the burdensome cost structure associated with market development and expansion. Companies must aggressively trim their sales, administrative, and general costs. Outsourcing and rightsizing become key considerations. Companies retreat into their core competencies as new entrants outdo the leaders in certain functions and market segments.

As we will see, running "twice as fast" requires a new order of thinking. The winners in Stage III are the firms that go beyond rationalizing their own core contributions, and learn how to influence the structure and evolution of their business ecosystems and opportunity environments.

Winners and Losers

To be sure, even in the fast-moving, modular Stage III conditions, some species extract more margin from the ecosystem than others do. Some become better students of the Red Queen. Perhaps the most important single insight for strategy-making in Stage III is this: Clear-cut winners and losers will emerge across the same ecosystem. Certain players will realize a notably larger share of the returns of the ecosystem than others. The key to becoming a winner and a leader is bargaining power. You must be absolutely vital to the community, especially to customers. Contributors whose inputs are seen as necessities can gain an above-average share of the margins available within the ecosystem from their fellow community members. Savvy members should then reinvest a portion of these margins in further reinforcing their bargaining power and in establishing powerful leadership positions within the community.

Earlier I noted that the personal computer business affords a clear window into business evolution. This issue of uneven margins is especially evident in the rise of Intel and Microsoft and the decline of IBM, as the personal computer business embarked on Stage III of its evolution. By the mid-1980s, the IBM PC technical architecture defined the business structure for the personal computer business as a whole. The business was well into Stage III. Virtually any company could figure out how to make components and services that would dovetail effectively with other elements of the PC ecosystem. Compaq, Intel, Microsoft, and other suppliers were working together to determine common standards for hardware and software, with and without IBM's involvement.

In Stage III, comparatively high margins come from strong bargaining power, which in turn derives from having something the ecosystem needs and from being the only practical source. Sometimes this sole-source status can be established contractually or through patent protection. But in a dynamic world, it depends most of all on constant innovation, on creating value that is critical to the whole ecosystem's continued price/performance improvement. As the Red Queen might advise a management team in Stage III, "If you run as fast as you can, you can perhaps make average margins. If you want high margins, you'll have to run twice as fast as that." That is, you will have to lead the ongoing improvement of business ecosystems in addition to your specific contributions.

IBM barely picked up to a jog. As its personal computer ecosystem moved into Stage III, IBM didn't find a way to keep innovating, or even to achieve economies of scale. For most of the period IBM was the largest manufacturer and shipper of personal computers on the planet—for many years the only vendor doing multibillion-dollar years. Yet it never achieved substantial economies of scale in relation to its smaller competitors.

Instead, IBM continued to spend money on promoting and developing the ecosystem itself—that is, spending on Stage II–relevant activities because it could afford it, because it was in IBM mainframe tradition, and because it wrongly assumed it would benefit most from such a campaign. For example, IBM spent millions of dollars on television campaigns—including its celebrated "Charlie Chaplin's Little Tramp" ads—to promote ease of use and stimulate demand. These campaigns did almost nothing to differentiate IBM products from others—or to increase IBM's bargaining power across the ecosystem. Equally lavish were the conferences for special interest groups, such as educators, manufacturers, and financial services professionals—held at expensive resorts in Florida—to promote applications of computing. No one else in the ecosystem could afford these activities at this time. They invested in their core capabilities, innovation trajectories, and economies of scale.

To a large extent, Intel and Microsoft achieved their initial central position in the ecosystem by being in the right place at the right time—in short, by serving IBM. But Intel and Microsoft became students of the Red Queen. Both became intent on improving their core contributions, expanding the functionality of their contributions, and working with partners across the computer business to set standards that reinforced their incumbency. Andy Grove of Intel became famous for referring to the microprocessor as a "black hole" that would eventually take over the functions of the rest of the computer hardware—and thereby capture all of the value. Similarly, Microsoft under Bill Gates struggled mightily to incorporate more and more software features into the PC operating system, or into one of the company's software application products.

During this period, Microsoft in particular focused on gaining a superior position within the organizational architecture of the ecosystem, learning how to build and manage relationships with thousands of other businesses—mostly software developers—but also end users. Bill Gates's appearances at trade shows and user organizations became memorable lovefests, nothing like IBM's stuffy presentations and stiff spokespersons. All the while, Microsoft and Intel had an IBM-supplied safety net to support them if they exhausted their capital or expertise.

By the 1990s, the "IBM personal computer" community had become the "Microsoft-Intel" ecosystem. Margins had collapsed for innumerable players, including IBM. IBM's PC business made do with margins of about 30 percent, a far cry from the 70- to 90-percent margins of its mainframe business. IBM failed to wake up to the main Stage III challenge of maintaining authority and bargaining power. It had left undeveloped the three major potential sources of bargaining power in Stage III:

- **Innovation.** Developing an "innovation trajectory" and economies of scale that are vital to the ecosystem. Instead, IBM helped Microsoft and Intel develop the most powerful and central of such trajectories in the business.
- **Criticality.** Making sure that your contribution is valued by end customers as well as other members of the ecosystem. IBM's specific contributions became much less distinctive over time, and customers discovered that they

could achieve satisfactory results even if IBM was not directly involved in products and services they purchased.

- **Embeddedness.** Deeply marrying your own products, business processes, and formal and informal organizations with those of the rest of the ecosystem.[2] This is accomplished by working with other member firms to advance the structure and conventions of the ecosystem, and thus to continue to improve the framework of cooperation and coevolution. Rather than follow this strategy, IBM increasingly withdrew into itself and sought to impose its own products on the ecosystem—the most notable being the failed MCA bus architecture and OS/2 operating system. Hence, IBM gradually became divorced from the rest of the ecosystem and lost its leadership, influence, and bargaining power.

Develop an Innovation Trajectory

In Stage III, central companies reinforce their roles by making innovative contributions to the performance of the entire ecosystem. Successful firms establish a continuing "innovation trajectory" so that their offerings keep improving over time. The innovation trajectory can result in performance improvements in many different dimensions—from customer service and customer segmentation to hard-core technology advances. A sustainable innovation trajectory requires the orchestration of many individual and organizational capabilities. Companies will vary widely in the innovation trajectory on which they concentrate their energies.

For example, a key to Intel's value to what is now often called the "Wintel" (Microsoft, Windows, and Intel) personal computer ecosystem has been its ability to continually improve its microprocessors—giving them more functions and faster operations at less cost per unit of processing power. This trajectory is illustrated in the following figure.[3]

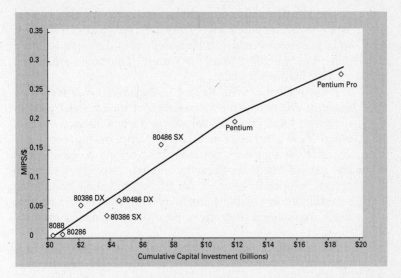

Figure 9.1. Intel's microprocessor innovation trajectory (1980–1995) as measured in millions of instructions per second (MIPS) per dollar.

This does not, of course, mean that the chips cost less. On the contrary, Intel microprocessors have gotten more expensive. The Intel 386 chip was introduced at $299. The first Pentiums debuted at around $900, but the Pentium provided roughly twenty times the computational capability.

Intel spends a staggering amount each year on capital investment and R&D to build capabilities and sustain this trajectory. That's the price of its leadership. Continuously improving capabilities range from chip design to manufacturing—or what semiconductor companies call fabrication, or "fab" for short. For example, Intel spent $2.9 billion in capital in 1993, and another $3.5 billion in 1994.[4] This is a hefty roll of the dice for a company grossing roughly $16 billion in 1995. It was these sorts of investments, however, that enabled it in 1995 to be the first to introduce the latest generation of chip fabrication capabilities, with circuits of 0.35 microns. Probably more important, as the Wintel ecosystem continues to boom and the demand for personal computers soars, Intel is the only plausible supplier to large-system vendors. It is the only chip company with not only new, branded designs, but with the fabrication capacity to feed the market's appetite.

Companies that wish to lead in dynamic, Costa Rica–style Stage III ecosystems must carefully plot similar trajectories of their own—and invest to make them happen. In an ecosystem where new entrants can hive off particular functions, any organization that does not maintain a strong trajectory runs the risk of being replaced by another. Executives need to reflect on their company's capabilities and their continuing investments in capability improvement, and make sure that these are driving the strongest possible performance improvement.

Maintaining a successful trajectory requires intense management focus and dedication of resources. This requirement often tends to favor specialist organizations—and results in an ecosystem of deintegrated players, some with a single focus and others with a portfolio of specializations—rather than old-line vertically integrated firms. But organization per se is not the most important condition of success. Rather, what is needed is an organization, a strategy, and an executive mind-set that can maintain the necessary level of commitment to stay ahead of an increasing pack of rivals.

Commitment is not enough. This core innovation trajectory must be supported and protected by an ability to shape the ecosystem to assure that its results continue to be valued. How Intel accomplishes this is the primary topic of the rest of this chapter, because it requires an extraordinary investment in maintaining criticality and embeddedness.

To appreciate what I mean, consider the situation from the traditional industry point of view. Intel is a conventional strategic planner's nightmare. From an industry perspective, semiconductor design and manufacturing has traditionally been thought of as a capital-intensive, cyclical business plagued with low gross margins. Intel has a single, largely undiversified core business, making microprocessors for personal computers. Research and capital-investment must be dedicated years in advance of the market, and their trajectories, once they are set, are relatively inflexible. Finally, the opportunity environment—the information space of computers, communications, and media—is rife with changing consumer preferences, technologies, business models, and lead companies. A planner must commit years in advance in a business of dramatically uncertain futures.

In the early days of Intel, the general mind-set was to mitigate these risks by conserving capital and maximizing the return on net assets. Intel's senior executives still recall the day in 1989 when Craig Barrett, head of the microprocessor operation, shocked the group by predicting that by 1991 the company would have to invest at least $2 billion of capital per year to maintain its innovation trajectory and stay ahead of clone chip companies. At the time, Intel was anticipating that total 1989 revenues would be just over $3 billion. In such circumstances, a $2 billion annual bet was a potentially staggering burden. Yet the alternative was worse: to be eaten alive by the collective innovation and investment of an increasingly strong collection of competitors. All in all, a classic Stage III problem.

The only way Intel could mitigate this risk was by finding ways to insure that the Intel-centered personal computer ecosystem continued to grow, and that its own contributions stayed central to the community. This brings us to our next topic. Intel has indeed adapted, and the numbers speak for themselves. Since 1990, Intel has consistently achieved among the highest gross margins and return on sales of any company in the world. It is instructive to explore both the ecological pressures on the company and the creative strategic and organizational inventions that have allowed the company to prosper. In short, we want to better understand the Intel inside Intel, and in the process consider the two additional principles of winning in Stage III: criticality and embeddedness.

Criticality: Reinforce Your Value to End Customers

Maintaining your innovation trajectory is not enough. Others in the ecosystem, and especially the end customers, must value this trajectory. The saddest cases are those who work hard on their capabilities, only to find their contributions no longer needed. The Sure Microphone Company, for instance, led the industry in producing magnetic cartridges for vinyl phonograph records. Each year it introduced new and better products. Unfortunately for Sure, tapes and compact discs made its contribution nearly irrelevant, except to a small cult of audiophiles. As we shall see, even contributions such as Intel's run the risk of missing the point, sometimes simply because they outstrip the needs of the rest of the ecosystem. How often have you heard that familiar refrain: "Who needs a faster computer? Mine does everything I want."

So you must work to make your innovation trajectory an important driver of the overall product and service improvements desired by customers and others in the ecosystem. This is what I call "criticality." Intel's success is predicated not just on making faster chips, but on making sure there is a demand for them within the ecosystem, and that it is the preferred supplier. When the criticality of its contribution began to shrink in the early 1990s, Intel had to take concerted action—not in terms of its innovation trajectory, which was never in doubt, but in terms of improving the appetite for its contributions across the rest of the ecosystem. Among other things, this involved stimulating demand for multimedia personal computers that required powerful microprocessors, and working with others across the ecosystem to bring such machines to market.

Establish Embeddedness in the Products, Processes, and Organizations of the Ecosystem

Investments made by others to follow or to ally with you reinforce and maintain your central contributor status. The reason

I call this attribute embeddedness is to suggest the degree to which the central contributor is enmeshed and bonded to others in the community. Embedding starts with branding one's contributions. Intel found great benefits in a campaign to promote its central attributes: hot chips, fastest to market, compatibility with earlier chips, and the software that users had invested in, as well as its own design choices and technical reliability. "Intel Inside" became a flag this campaign flew.

Embedding can also be accomplished by intertwining elements of the product architecture—for example, the mutual dependence of an advanced software product and a particular microprocessor capability.

You can also link business processes, for example, by using electronic data exchange to fuse inventory and manufacturing operations. Other examples include joint development and comarketing—any activity that creates an improvement in the total business process, from beginning to end, while also more closely marrying activities owned by two or more firms.

Finally, you can accomplish close bonding between organizations through formal mechanisms like joint ventures and shared or reciprocal investments. What's more, organizations can be linked by being located together, so that the informal cultures and communications of the people involved flow from one to the other.

Establish a Permanent Campaign to Reinforce Criticality and Embeddedness

Most executives recognize the need for investment in a continuing innovation trajectory. What can sometimes be missed is the need for a more comprehensive management campaign aimed at reinforcing criticality and embeddedness. In highly rivalrous Red Queen–type environments, your importance to others in the ecosystem cannot be taken for granted—irrelevance and interchangeability can occur with frightening suddenness.

Even snugly ensconced, dominant companies like Intel and

Microsoft cannot escape the hot breath of commoditization. Why? Because literally all other players who share the ecosystem with Intel and Microsoft are working to extend and expand their value, often at the expense of Intel's or Microsoft's centrality. As Andy Grove says, "Only the paranoid survive." This is an apt motto in a Stage III ecosystem, where all members coevolve simultaneously as fast as they can.

The challenge, then, is how to act on the Red Queen's imperative—how to reinforce systematically and comprehensively your status and contributions within an ecosystem. The following formula neatly summarizes the overall objective.

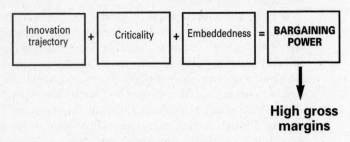

Figure 9.2

One convenient way to think about this sort of initiative is as a "permanent campaign" running across all seven dimensions of the ecosystem. The elements of the campaign, which also can be expressed as a sort of equation for producing value and bargaining power, are listed in Table 9.2.

The essence of the permanent campaign is to influence the structure of the ecosystem as a whole so that it expresses your core contributions. A link is established between your competencies and the value—and value improvement trajectory— desired by customers. The campaign starts with customers and with selling your value, and it starts with promoting visions of the future to which you can maximally contribute. The campaign seeks to reinforce this vision—and your importance—by dominating markets and channels.

The permanent campaign goes even further, however, by

DIMENSION	THE EQUATION	DIMENSIONS OF THE PERMANENT CAMPAIGN
Customers	Perceived value to end customers	Increase the perceived value of your contributions, in the eyes of the end customers.
Markets	Market and channel domination	Increase your domination of bounded markets and channels to those markets.
Offers	Criticality and embeddedness in the total offer	Increase your criticality and embeddedness in the total offer, as experienced by the end user.
Processes	Criticality and embeddedness in the business process architecture	Increase your criticality and embeddedness in the total business process architecture of the ecosystem.
Organizations	Criticality and embeddedness in the organizational network	Increase your criticality and embeddedness in the organizational network that is central to the ecosystem.
Stakeholders	Availability of resources on preferred terms	Increase the resources available to sustain your core contributions and leadership in the ecosystem.
Values and policy	Alignment with society	Increase the alignment with your contributions and leadership, and those of the societies and governments that are relevant to your markets.

Table 9.2

seeking to influence the evolution of the architecture of the product—that is, how it is offered to customers, what modules and subcomponents are used, and what functions they provide. It involves how business processes are conceived and, if necessary, transformed. It affects organizational relationships, helping to determine what is outsourced and what held dear. The campaign seeks to shape what is produced in large volumes and with economies of scale and scope. And it helps to determine what multiple suppliers provide, taking advantage of diversity and Darwinian selection across a broad population. Finally, the campaign seeks to secure preferred access to resources of all types and a close alignment to the values and policy apparatus of the society.

Such campaigns are increasingly at the center of business strategy. Their influence is much broader than that of conventional business plans, and they require skills that have seldom been bundled together in corporations—from marketing and product development to process engineering, organizational design, finance, and government relations. Probably the best way to get a feel for them is to examine one in detail.

Through an Ecosystem Lens: Intel's Challenge

As noted previously, for most of the early years in the personal computer revolution, Intel's business model depended on a powerful virtuous cycle involving customers, systems manufacturers, and the company itself. Customers demanded ever greater computer performance, and Intel microprocessors made it possible for systems vendors like IBM and Compaq to supply it.

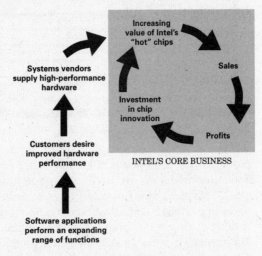

Figure 9.3

The key to the model was that many customers would pay a premium for early access to higher performance machines. Intel captured this premium, not only providing steady increases in processing power—its innovation trajectory—but accomplishing it better and faster than its competition. Until the early 1990s, the increased computational intensity of programs like Microsoft Windows boded well for Intel. Continual introduction of more and more elaborate software forced customers to keep upgrading to the latest Intel chips. Historically, Intel simply took advantage of the trend toward software complexity, rather than needing to make it happen. Intel's trajectory was critical to the value that customers wanted:

faster machines, brought to market faster. Intel's core business boomed.

Between 1990 and 1993, some worrisome ecological tendencies ran wild through the personal computer jungle. CEO Andy Grove, the Intel board of directors, and the top management team came to believe—putting the picture together—that these trends threatened Intel's leadership in the personal computer ecosystem and required concerted action. On the following pages, we will examine some of these trends. For clarity they are presented using the seven dimensions of the ecosystem.

CUSTOMERS DIDN'T NEED MORE PROCESSING POWER, UNLESS IT WAS FOR COMMUNICATIONS AND MEDIA

By 1990, trend spotters could see that the demand for more and more processing power would taper off. For many applications like word processing, users didn't need more powerful chips. Corporate customers, in particular, were resistant to upgrading and changing hundreds if not thousands of machines.

Almost any application that Intel managers could envision requiring lots of processing power would be based on multimedia video and communications. Unfortunately, the IBM personal computer architecture presented numerous barriers to these capabilities—with or without advanced microprocessors.

Finally, consumers increasingly would be buying computers as mass market items through chains like the discounter CompUSA, and they would want easy-to-use machines closer to the (non-Intel ecosystem) Apple Macintosh than the IBM PC. Either of these latter trends could render obsolete and irrelevant not only Intel chips but the whole IBM/Intel/ Microsoft ecosystem.

INTEL COULD SEE ITS LOCK ON THE MARKET UNRAVELING

Even in the 1980s, Intel's competitors could theoretically supply the same innovation trajectory. But Intel was largely insulated from competition at the high end of the market by its unique ability to set microprocessor standards for much of the personal computer industry, as well as by patent and copyright protection. Competitors had to helplessly wait for each round of Intel performance improvements. Then they scrambled feverishly to clone these improvements, while being careful to avoid violating Intel's property rights.

By the early 1990s, the continuing diffusion of technical knowledge was allowing other chip makers to clone Intel chips without infringing on Intel patents. The likes of Advanced Micro Devices and Cyrix were becoming quite proficient at being fast Intel studies, though they still had to labor in Intel's shadow. It was a portentous event when AMD introduced a clone of the popular 386 chip in mid-1992. This trend, were it to continue, appeared likely to enable companies to stampede into Intel's business at a dizzying rate, driving down margins and threatening to commoditize Intel's products.

Moreover, the worldwide personal computer market was growing explosively, outstripping Intel's ability to satisfy demand for its microprocessors and forcing it to put the systems vendors on unpopular "allocation" programs, under which each of them received a limited ration of chips. The allocation programs represented a chronic supply problem for systems vendors like Compaq and Dell, and made them receptive to buying from other suppliers who might enter the market. The allocation programs also undermined Intel arguments about the benefits of loyalty to its offers.

THE STANDARD PERSONAL COMPUTER ARCHITECTURE WAS BECOMING OBSOLETE

A third unfavorable development was that aspects of the personal computer architecture were creating a bottleneck to system-wide performance—a classic Stage III legacy problem. The architecture had become the organizing principle for thousands of suppliers, but also fixed a number of relationships in ways that restricted performance. For example, the capacity of the pathway between the microprocessor and the video controller card was not fast enough to keep up with either current generation processors or video video cards; Intel's innovations in processor performance were not fully reflected in system performance, and in important ways, were not of maximum value to customers. As Frank Gill, the senior executive who oversees much of Intel's ecosystem-shaping efforts, explained, "More and more, putting our processors in the existing system designs was like bolting a high performance car engine onto the suspension of a Volkswagen Beetle."

BUSINESS PROCESS PROBLEMS WERE SLOWING INNOVATION

Ecosystem-wide business processes were organized in ways that were starting to block rapid innovation. For example, each new generation of microprocessor requires computer systems vendors to upgrade their overall computer designs. Getting each new design right was becoming increasingly difficult and expensive for the computer manufacturers. As a result, some of the manufacturers started to resist adopting ever more powerful chips, hoping instead to slow down the rate of system redesign and lower their development costs. Had it gotten established, this movement had the potential to cut into Intel's sales of high-performance, high-margin microprocessors. One obvious answer to the problem might be for Intel to do system design and development, and provide the results to the manufacturers.

THE ORGANIZATION AND LEADERSHIP OF THE ECOSYSTEM WAS NOT EFFECTIVE

Perhaps the most threatening developments were at the organizational level. Intel executives did not believe that IBM could continue to exert the leadership needed to move the personal computer architecture forward.

Microsoft was assuming more community leadership, but its image of a desirable future was diverging from Intel's. Microsoft was investing to make itself and others less dependent on Intel. Microsoft was making its software work with other chips and systems that were arguably better designed than Intel processors and IBM-legacy systems. The most credible alternative was the MIPS consortium, which at its outset involved Digital Equipment, Compaq, and several Japanese firms. This group hoped to establish an alternative ecosystem, with Microsoft as a dominant player in each and benefiting from the hardware rivalry between the two ecosystems.

Some of the most interesting and, from Intel's standpoint, disturbing visionary leadership was springing up in parts of the opportunity environment outside of the IBM/Intel/Microsoft ecosystem. The previous year, Steve Jobs had introduced his NeXT machine, an easy-to-use, multimedia-ready device with advanced capabilities, powered by chips from Intel's semiconductor rival Motorola.

Andy Grove, in particular, believed he could see the future in this machine, and he was not happy about what it would mean if an alternative ecosystem took off around Jobs's offer. Something had to be done to restore both the criticality of the PC ecosystem and Intel's role within it.

OVERALL, INTEL NEEDED TO STRENGTHEN ITS ECOSYSTEM LEADERSHIP POSITION

Further analysis of the situation identified additional worries— or perhaps opportunities—at the stakeholders and values and policy dimensions. Intel realized that it could work better to solidify organizational links to other members of the community. The early success of the Microsoft/MIPS consortium provided a strong warning signal. Intel realized that it had not directed its management creativity or its enormous cash flows toward becoming more than a powerful stakeholder but an actual shaper of the future.

Finally, Intel executives concluded that they could do a better job of getting the message out about Intel's overall contribution to society. In this way, the world at large would more widely recognize Intel's value as a firm, its brand names would be made more resonant and defendable, and Intel might find itself in a stronger position to help develop government policy.

The overall conclusion was that these trends had the potential to drive a fundamental—and unpleasant—transformation in Intel's relationship to the personal computer ecosystem. From a conventional product/market point of view, Intel was doing enormously well. It was expanding, making lots of money, enjoying high margins, and had a great deal of market share. On the other hand, if it didn't make some aggressive moves it might well end up like IBM, forced into a lower margin role of reduced influence in an ecosystem it created.

These observations—both the obvious threats and the more subtle opportunities—appear in the following seven-dimension chart.

DIMENSIONS OF THE ECOSYSTEM	The situation in 1991–1993 (-) means conditions tending toward commoditization of Intel (+) means conditions that reinforce criticality and embeddedness (o) means no change in conditions
Customers	(-) Increasingly satisfied with the processor power of their machines; corporate customers were slow in upgrading to new processors.
Markets	(-) Clone processor vendors, such as AMD, were becoming more able. Intel was leaving a price umbrella under which clone processor makers could live—and was not meeting the volume requirements of the market. Some systems vendors were resisting paying Intel prices, slowing adoption of new generation processors, and flirting with clone processor suppliers.
Offers	(-) The standard personal computer architecture was becoming obsolete.
Processes	(-) Systems vendors were having increasing difficulty in designing machines that used the most advanced microprocessors. Intel business processes were largely independent of others.
Organizations	(-) IBM's leadership was faltering. Microsoft was becoming a stronger leader, but pushing out Intel. Microsoft NT was being made portable across processors—and RISC chips began to look viable in mainstream products. Intel had mostly traditional customer/supplier relationships with other members of the ecosystem.
Stakeholders	(-) Direct investors still regarded Intel as a cyclical, commodity supplier of chips—and Intel stock often carried a p/e (price-earnings ratio) in the low teens.
Values and policy	(+/-) Intel did have good relations with the U.S. Department of Defense and major politicians, but was relatively unknown in wider business circles. Intel was in general free of antitrust problems. But its patent defenses were eroding.

Figure 9.3

These insights became the basis for a very creative, multi-level campaign by Intel to restore criticality and embeddedness. I encourage any organization to conduct a similar seven-dimension audit of the commoditization trends in its situation. Questions to ask include: Are there particular dimensions of the ecosystem where your competitors, predators, and parasites appear to be evolving faster than you are? Perhaps more disturbing, do you have allies, partners, customers, or suppliers who are evolving more aggressively, and are becoming "value predators," i.e., reducing your criticality or embeddedness?

Such trends are symptoms of the Red Queen effect of a constant arms race of coevolution among the members of the ecosystem. Because these trends can be subtle and can occur even as a company's core business is booming, managers often miss these developments until they have gone too far to be addressed without great difficulty. In many cases, considering the issues earlier can sound a warning and stimulate a variety of potent ideas and actions to restore your position.

Creating a Permanent Campaign: Intel's Response

Intel's response to its predicament was to marshal its resources to buck the unfavorable trends. On one level, Intel executives recognized they had to accept some level of commoditization. In fact, they embraced the inevitable and went ahead and lowered prices on chips that were becoming competitive to maintain share. Intel's low-cost 386 chips settled into a price range below $200, and by 1992 were around $100. By working effectively to keep costs low, Intel made sure it would become the dominant supplier of chips that had become commoditized.

The price for Pentium processors, also introduced in 1992 in the $900 range, contrasted dramatically with that for the chips subject to direct competition and commoditization. On the hot, fast, new generation Pentium processors, Intel realized that it could do much more to protect prices and margins. It needed to take an active role in stimulating customer demand and in shaping the future of the personal computer ecosystem. Intel executives had to mount a comprehensive campaign to enhance the criticality and embeddedness of their hot processors.

Andy Grove is widely considered to be the company's top

environmental scanner and trend interpreter. As one executive put it, "Andy has sensors spotted all over the environment. Better than any of the rest of us, he can see trends coming and grasp their potential impact on the company." By the late 1980s, Grove was concerned about the commoditization of Intel microprocessors. Intel's skills were being copied, and its patents could not hold forever. The company had begun to fight for criticality and embeddedness through advertising campaigns targeted at consumers. The 1989 "Red X" campaign for the Intel 386SX processor was the first experiment. Its success was encouraging and eventually led to the celebrated "Intel Inside" campaign.

But Grove could see that this would not be enough. At Intel's annual Strategic Long Range Planning meeting (known as SLRP, pronounced "slurp") in April 1991, he reviewed many of the commoditization-promoting trends and gave his executives a challenge: "Give us an Intel-powered, NeXT-like computer that can be sold at mass market price points at CompUSA." By this he meant a machine with high performance and low cost, equipped for video and communications, and easy to use. He recognized that this was not technically a hardware problem, but what we would now call an ecosystem-level challenge. Intel would have to help stimulate and coordinate the contributions of many other companies, in areas as diverse as entertainment and telecommunications, software applications, and system software, as well as the manufacturers and distributors of hardware systems, electronic components, and peripherals like printers and video monitors.

The heart of the challenge seemed to be in software. Grove appointed Ron Whittier, one of his top executives, to learn more about software and, by implication, all aspects of the personal computer that Intel had not hitherto considered part of its charter. In addition, Craig Kinnie, a leading engineer, was given the job of developing a new personal computer architecture that would fulfill the vision of a NeXT multimedia machine at consumer prices.

Ultimately, these initiatives flowed into a comprehensive strategy to create a wider leadership position for Intel and to pluck it from its narrow role as a member of the semiconductor industry. Ron Whittier's oversight expanded, and he began working with other companies and visionaries to anticipate new uses and applications of the personal computer that would require advanced capabilities in what came to be called the "base platform," or fundamental personal computer architecture. Today Whittier's job is to attract content—especially entertainment offerings—to the Intel platform.

Craig Kinnie's appointment led to the formation of an organization called the Architecture Development Lab.[5] His charter was to evolve the base platform architecture to improve performance, communications and multimedia capabilities, and ease of use. To address performance, he asked himself, "What are the top five limitations of the personal computer architecture in terms of utilizing advances in Intel microprocessors?" In other words, how does the product architecture need to be revamped in order to be most hospitable to Intel's continuing innovation trajectory? Similarly, he and his engineers asked, Where and how will the base personal computer fail to support multimedia and communications? What limitations does it have in achieving the ease of use of the Macintosh or the NeXT?

This emphasis on identifying break points, and engineering beyond them, became characteristic of the lab's mode of operation. As a way of thinking about product and service evolution, it has much to recommend itself to companies seeking to provide leadership to Stage III ecosystems. Over the past five years, Whittier's and Kinnie's efforts have grown into what is now called the Intel Architecture Labs, with a mission of serving the entire ecosystem with architectural research and development—and with open processes for establishing standards.

During the same period, Frank Gill was asked to head the Intel Products Group. In the early 1990s, the Products Group was a somewhat eclectic array of businesses. The most promising was the systems business, which wholesaled computer systems in various levels of completion beyond the bare microprocessor. For example, a company like Compaq or IBM might buy chip sets in addition to microprocessors. Or a firm that wanted to concentrate mainly on distribution could buy complete motherboards, or even fully assembled computers.

Intel's systems business and its relationship to the microprocessor business had traditionally been seen in industry, not ecosystem, terms. Microprocessor prices fluctuated cyclically. The systems business was seen as mildly countercyclical, and thus presented a way for Intel to recoup some of its losses when chip prices plunged. The systems business would benefit from cheaper supplies when the microprocessor business suffered. In reality, such gains were not great. Moreover, other systems vendors found Intel's systems business confusing and threatening, for it seemed a first step in the direction of vertically integrating them out of business.

Gill saw the potential to use the systems business in a very different way: to drive new ideas and innovation into the ecosystem. He refocused it on doing fast-to-market implementations of designs featuring the hottest Intel chips and the most important of the Architecture Labs' ideas. Gill worked with distribution companies—such as Gateway 2000, the South Dakota–based mail-order champion—to seed the marketplace with hot boxes, in order to stimulate demand for new generation processors. The seeding has the effect of setting a benchmark that is picked up by the PC magazines and by leading customers. Other major manufacturers find themselves forced to match these performance levels or risk looking dowdy and behind the times.

Of course, in order to offer high-performance machines, manufacturers must buy the newest Intel processors. In many cases, manufacturers also choose to buy chip sets, motherboards, or complete systems from Intel. This is particularly true in the first few months of a new generation system. Intel supplies an extremely high share of the early machines, and then allows its contribution to decline as a percentage of the ecosystem's total production, when the other companies ramp up. The reoriented Intel systems business makes a powerful contribution to the ecosystem and has grown dramatically, becoming a multibillion-dollar revenue source.

There are other product shops that help bring new ideas into the market and the ecosystem. For example, Pat Gelsinger oversees the development of personal communications products. This includes the Proshare line of collaboration software and PC-based video conferencing. You can often tell how serious a company is about ecosystem-shaping efforts by who they put in charge. In Intel's case, the evidence speaks for itself. In the chip world, designers are close to God. Gelsinger was the designer of the 386 chip, and the design team leader for the 486 chip. Now, instead of chips, Gelsinger designs and implements technology for new uses of personal computers and works with other members of the ecosystem to establish frameworks of participation within which many can thrive. As Gelsinger says, "I used to design circuits. Now I worry more about the nature of 'industrial democracy' and the design of the interactions among companies, organizations, and individuals who will shape the new markets."

Thus, Intel has evolved a comprehensive system for bringing ideas into its ecosystem and for supporting its own innovation trajectory, criticality, and embeddedness. Simply put, new ideas and requirements are identified by Ron Whittier as he works with partners to encourage fresh uses of personal computers. Insights from his program and many other sources feed into the Intel Architecture Labs. The labs in turn develop designs for new generation personal computer architectures. These designs are refined and adopted through standards-setting processes supported by the lab. The early implementations of these designs are brought to market by the systems business and other Intel product shops.

What has been developed at Intel is a powerful new organizational mechanism for encouraging ecosystemwide innovation, and maintaining Intel's preeminence. The emergence of this mechanism is consistent with a business version of the Red Queen Hypothesis: intense intra-ecosystem pressure will stimulate the creation of new forms of organization that enable members of the community to retain their leadership positions. The particular approach taken by Intel represents an adaptation to the intense requirements of coevolution within information space. Intel's approach may not be as revolutionary to business as sexual reproduction was to biology. However, it is important and interesting, and I would commend it for study by other companies facing Stage III pressures.

Intel invests around $100 million per year directly in the Architecture Labs. This research in turn guides the Intel systems business—a multibillion-dollar operation—as well as the activities of other Intel product lines. But the greatest impact on the future comes as the standards fostered by the Architecture Labs are adopted widely across the total Wintel ecosystem—influencing billions of dollars of collective research and development, as well as products and services worth over a hundred billion dollars in 1995. As Craig Kinnie puts it, "The Architecture Labs are promoting an open framework for investment—a framework that invites others to bring their innovation to the personal computer platform. The framework is particularly valuable in making a place for smaller, highly creative companies. Our aim is to help coordinate the investments of others, rather than try to make these investments by ourselves." Intel has created a remarkable campaign for shaping the future. Overall, Intel has added dramatic ecosystemwide scope to its leadership activities, as illustrated below.

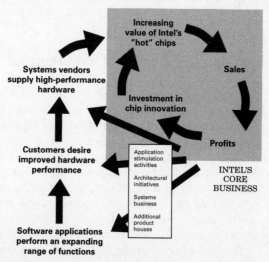

Figure 9.4. Intel's ecosystem-shaping campaign.

Let's review the major elements of the campaign, again using the seven dimensions.

Make Your Contribution Known to Customers, and Encourage Activities That Require Your Contribution

First, in terms of customers, Intel has been spending tens of millions of dollars a year on the Intel Inside and Intel Technology Briefing campaigns. These programs intend to teach customers that Intel microprocessors really are better than the competition, and to help customers understand how the value in a microprocessor translates into value for customers.

Second, the company has been working on stimulating new uses of personal computers that require a lot of processor speed and power—such as videoconferencing, voice processing, and other applications. Again, this is to get the customer to realize that there are many other things you can do with your PC besides spreadsheets and word processing, but those other things require more powerful machines.

Invest in Capacity, Saturate Market Demand

In terms of the markets, Intel has not only lowered its prices for its commodity chips so that it dominates that segment of the market, but it has also continued to expand its investment in fabrication capacity. The investment in capacity allows it to fill future demand for both hot chips and commodity chips. Its business planning for fab capacity expansions is based on trying to leave little or no demand unmet in the market. Intel has invested its way out of the situation where it had to allocate scarce capacity to sell to suppliers to one where it has enough capacity to supply almost the entire ecosystem.

The idea here is simple. In the end, only Intel can invest in capacity to match the immense growth of the industry.

Therefore, as the industry grows and Intel continues to match that growth, other smaller vendors like AMD, even though they're investing heavily in capacity, can't come close to mimicking the scale of Intel. As time passes, the other contenders for Intel's niche in the ecosystem will continue to drop further behind in terms of market share. The dramatic difference in absolute level of investment between Intel and AMD is seen in the following chart:[6]

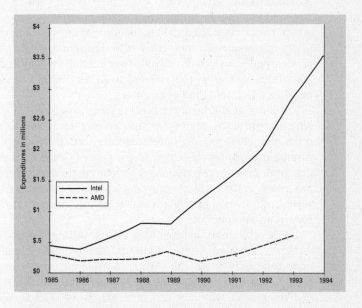

Figure 9.5. Annual capital expenditures of Intel *vs.* AMD: the cost of innovation.

Intel's investment strategy places a substantial bet on a particular future scenario—continued growth in demand for processors. Intel's conviction is seen in the consistency of its investment in new plant and equipment, which has remained in the range of 30 percent of sales for many years. So far Intel appears to be winning its bet: the market does appear to be

continuing to expand—the Wintel ecosystem is clearly dominant and preferred worldwide and Intel has the financial
resources to ride out substantial temporary slowdowns.

Encourage Favorable Product, Process, and Organizational Architectures

At the product architecture level, Intel established the Intel
Architecture Labs to support complementary standards, all of
which either favor the Intel architecture or are very supportive
of the processor advances that Intel brought forward. These
acts extended Intel's direct influence into the system part of
the business, and in the end led to systems that are clearly
optimized to Intel's kind of advances.

Similarly, at the business process level, Intel used the Intel
Architecture Labs and other related organizations to align
other suppliers' product development efforts with Intel's continuing innovation trajectory. In the case of Gateway and others, Intel has almost completely replaced their development
processes, again with systems development organizations that
were built around taking advantage of the innovation trajectory in microprocessors.

The revolutionary nature of the change at Intel was felt most
at the organizational level. Many managers began identifying
opportunities to work with partners outside the firm to improve
the personal computer ecosystem and elaborate the framework
of participation within which Intel was woven. As Frank Gill
put it, "Once the concept caught on, ideas sprang up all over the
place. We talked about ourselves as 'chip heads willing to
learn'—that is, as managers starting out with a semiconductor-
industry orientation learning to become ambassadors to a larger,
more diverse community of companies around us."

This perspective became embodied in a vast tangle of relationships between Intel and other firms. A central paradox
soon became evident. The standards that succeeded were the
ones that were seen by others as most fair, most open, and least

biased toward Intel. Thus, the standards themselves seldom served to directly increase Intel's embeddedness in the product architecture. On the other hand, the process and interorganizational relationships required to establish and implement the standards required very close collaboration among many participants in dozens of companies. Intel was at the center of these activities. Therefore, Intel became profoundly embedded in and critical to the processes and organization of the ecosystem even as it promoted open product architectures. Table 9.4 describes some of these efforts and illustrates the comprehensive and multifaceted nature of the overall effort.

Invest in Building Understanding and Appreciation Among Members of the Wider Business and Political Environment

Intel also invested in senior officer relationships with other VIPs in the industry that solidified the bond between Intel's organizations and others. These included not only system vendors but software developers, telephone companies, entertainment companies, and others across the entire extended information landscape.

Investor relations personnel got Wall Street to recognize that Intel is not simply a capital-intensive producer of a commodity but rather an important member of the fabric of the information industries. They portrayed Intel as a kind of a core pillar of the community, one expected to equal or surpass the growth rate of the information business and not easily substituted. Wall Street should regard it as a system company central to shaping the destiny of the industry and to capturing the best margins from it. I argue that even today a multiple of twenty is low for a company with this kind of grip on the whole business.

Finally, Andy Grove and other senior officers of the company made a great effort to promote the overall Intel story. Grove delivered the keynote address at Telecom, a meeting that takes place every four years of all the world's telephone

ASPECT OF THE PRODUCT ARCHITECTURE BEING IMPROVED	NAME OF THE STANDARD PROTOTYPE OR PRODUCT	BENEFIT
Performance	PCI Bus standard	Faster connection between the microprocessor and video cards and other peripheral capabilities
Media and communications	TAPI standard	Lets the personal computer work with telephone systems
	CablePort product prototype	A standard hardware architecture to which service and content providers can write cable modem applications to deliver Internet and online service via cable telephony.
	Personal Conferencing Specification/Proshare product line	A standard interface for data and video collaboration and conferencing/a product line seeding the market.
	3DR library	A software library for writing 3D graphics applications for personal computers
	Intercast standard	An approach for sending data alongside broadcast television signals
	Winsock II standard	Allows applications to invoke advanced communications capabilities without regard to the actual method of network transport of information
Ease of use	Plug and Play standard	Components of the personal computer can electronically identify each other, and configure their interactions accordingly
	Desktop Management Interface standard	Interface standard to foster local and remote management of personal computer software and hardware elements.
	Universal Serial Bus standard	A single connection for a broad base of personal computer peripherals, ranging from digital joysticks to ISDN communications.
Total system package	New Baseline Target Platform	Proposed minimum combinations of multimedia capabilities built into the basic personal computer as provided to end users, based on native signal processing.

Table 9.4

companies and everyone associated with telecommunications. Telecom was held in Geneva in October 1995, and Intel presented itself as one of the leaders of the new converging information space. Through this and many other efforts Intel intends to position itself as a world leader in this extended business fabric transforming the world. The Intel campaign elements are as follows:

DIMENSIONS OF THE ECOSYSTEM	ELEMENTS OF INTEL'S PERMANENT CAMPAIGN
Customers	**1.** Hot box campaigns: "Intel Inside" and "Intel Technology Briefing" **2.** Application stimulation: "ProShare" **3.** Use Gateway to stimulate hot box competition.
Markets	**1.** Sharpen price drop-off on aging processors just as clones reach the market. **2.** Invest in fab capacity so as to be able to fill all high-margin demand. **3.** Offer "Intel Inside" cobranding.
Offers	**1.** Use the Intel Architecture Labs to support complementary standards, favoring the Intel processor innovation trajectory. Provide R&D to complementary suppliers. **2.** Rationalize other Intel systems-level research to support the X86 architecture (and not the I860).
Processes	**1.** Use the Intel Architecture Labs to support and become embedded in other companies' product development processes. **2.** In the case of Gateway and others, replace these development processes. **3.** Provide chip sets, motherboards, and complete systems that embody cutting-edge designs and processors. **4.** Use Intel sales representatives to help sell complementary products.
Organizations	**1.** Create standards setting consortia among complementary suppliers. **2.** Develop a mind-set that favors open product architectures—and that creates embeddedness and criticality in terms of entwined processes and organizations.
Stakeholders	**1.** Invest in senior officer relationships with other major firms in the ecosystem—and in customer ecosystems. **2.** Encourage an understanding that Intel chips are not so much a cyclical commodity—as a critical element of the information revolution.
Values and policy	**1.** Promote the story of Intel as a contributor to the information revolution and the global economy. **2.** Continue to defend patents.

Table 9.5

Through this campaign, Intel provided substantive leadership to the ecosystem, and that has been both beneficial and necessary. In Stage III, a major problem is that ecosystems become crippled by product architectures, business processes, and locked-in yet suboptimal organizational arrangements. Intel helped immensely by using its leverage with the other players to get the entire community to move forward in product architectures, process architectures, and to some extent organizational architectures.

On the other hand, this leadership has not been without challenge. Other companies are itching to orchestrate a future very different from the one that Intel is creating. So many mites, so little time!

Competing Visions of the Future

The celebration of Independence Day is one of the high points of my summer. I have always loved fireworks, the successive booms and the searing brilliance of the red, white, and blue floating stars. I even like the smoke drifting through the crowds, their necks craned upward. In Boston, the annual fireworks display is launched from a barge bobbing on the Charles River, and up to half a million people assemble for the noisy display.

The Boston fireworks have become a reasonably precise metaphor for what is going on in the opportunity environment we called "information space" early in this book. Intel is just one of thousands of firms playing in this jungle space. Most of the players are attempting, with varying success, to make themselves centers of criticality and embeddedness, and to shape the overall evolution of the community to buttress their centrality.

Competition in open, Costa Rica–type, Red Queen–informed Stage III ecosystems plays out in several dimensions: products and services, value and margins, and ultimately for what vision of the future will prevail. Sometimes alternative visions of the future collide, leading to intense leadership conflicts. For example, we have seen that Intel wants to sell hot boxes. Compaq in the mid-1990s has a different vision for itself and the Wintel personal computer ecosystem.

Compaq does not want to pay upwards of $600 to $800 for a leading-edge hot microprocessor for each of its computers. It believes that many users would be just as happy with the performance of processors costing less than $200, if only Intel didn't stir up these customers and convince them that they need hot chips. Compaq wants to sell not-so-hot-boxes, with less expensive microprocessors, that are differentiated by how they are sold (marketing channels and promotion), how they physically look, what peripherals they include, and what software is loaded in them. Even at the high end of the market—both business and consumer—Compaq would like to expand its margins by saving on microprocessor costs. Compaq's innovation trajectory is to understand variation in the customer base, to identify market subsegments, and to target distribution and configuration of machines for small sets of users.

These two alternative visions hit their peak of conflict in the 1994 Christmas buying season, as Compaq came roaring on the airwaves telling consumers, "Don't think about it as a computer." Intel countered with its massive Pentium-promoting, "Intel Technical Briefing" campaigns. That fall and winter, both companies prevailed because the total computer market expanded and absorbed both hot and cheap machines.

But in the fall of 1995 the conflict emerged again. Consumer multimedia and video were all the rage. Compaq, along with IBM, introduced inexpensive computers with special, dedicated chips that enabled full-motion, full-screen video. Compaq set up displays in stores featuring their machine called Presario playing the feature film *Top Gun* from a CD. The chips that made such high-quality video possible were inexpensive "digital signal processors"—and they enabled Compaq and IBM to use the least expensive versions of Intel Pentiums in the machines. IBM even went so far as to advertise its Aptiva machine as having two processors—an Intel Pentium and an "IBM Multimedia processor." These campaigns clashed with an Intel-sponsored drive to create a new standard for multimedia personal computers based on "Native Signal Processing"— meaning, of course, doing video "native" with only a single, high-end Pentium processor.

These sorts of conflicts are inherent and continuous in life in business ecosystems, and are only likely to increase as company executives become more aware of the stakes involved in shaping the future. In information space—as in other major opportunity environments—there is a multitude of members seeking to gain influence over particular issues in order to benefit themselves and their own innovation trajectories. Microsoft wants computer networking to be controlled by smart servers and personal computers, and it wants the role of the telephone companies reduced to providing electronic bandwidth pipes. IBM and AT&T, conversely, want to put software and services in their networks—and shrink the contribution of Microsoft-powered servers. Larry Ellison at Oracle is promoting $500 Internet-access devices as substitutes for personal computers, hoping to steal the future from Intel and Microsoft.

Whatever the resolution of these or any other particular conflicts, campaigns to shape the future are the new center of action in business, and not just in computers. To some extent, the vision-to-vision competition exists in all stages of business ecosystem development, but becomes a central and pressing managerial challenge in Stage III. Conflicts among campaigns are often accentuated if and when the ecosystem drops into Stage IV and must contend with alternative visions of renewal. As we will see in the next chapter, there are a number of competing visions of the future of health care, and these alternative visions have dramatic consequences for the margins, and the power, of the respective players.

The Intel Inside All of Us

You may be asking whether this discussion applies only to big, powerful companies. What about companies that must follow? Regardless of whether we lead or follow, the opportunity environments in which most of us operate are populated by centers of intense coevolution. Business ecosystems are a reality in all sectors of the economy—and not just the information space of Intel and Microsoft. For executives, there are several implications to this. First, we need to understand the dynamics. For any given sector of the environment, we need to ask: What are the organizing paradigms for products and services in this sector? What constitutes a "total offer"? What roles do various companies and individuals play? Who are the thought leaders, and what are their interests? What assets and capabilities do these leaders possess, and what do these qualities tell me about how they will seek to shape the future products and services, processes, and organizational arrangments in this environment?

To find our role, we must focus on our own capacity to contribute. What core capabilities for continuing innovation do we have that might help this ecosystem and its members attain their goals? How unique is my potential contribution? At what rate can I improve it over time? What sorts of competitors and substitutes will I face striving to take my role? From the answers, we can begin to design a role for ourselves, either as a member—or a leader—of a specific business community. That is, we can find a role as a species within a particular ecosystem.

We do not necessarily need to be shapers of the business ecosystem community we join, especially if we trust and respect its leadership. But we must find a valued contribution to make—one that allows us to develop our innovation trajectory. Most of all, we need to make our contribution enduringly critical to the ecosystem, and embed it in the fabric of the community. If we do this, perhaps we will be able to create a sustainable subecosystem of our own, something of a defended microterritory. We will be able to contribute real benefit to ourselves and our neighbors—and to achieve a good return on our investments in continuing innovation.

10

Stage IV: Renewal or Death

Early in this book, I pointed out that biological communities erupt in fits and starts rather than unfolding in an entirely orderly and incremental fashion. After protracted periods of stability during which species and their relative populations remain basically the same, sudden bursts of massive biological change can result in the radical transformation or even wholesale collapse of an ecosystem. Often physical developments, like earthquakes, fires, floods, droughts, or volcanic eruptions, can trigger this change. The arrival of exotic species, or the precipitous decline of one or more of the community's central keystone species, can also bring about collapse.

Examples of such transformations in nature abound. In Nevada, guppies dumped by aquarium enthusiasts into the thermal springs near the Elko River have flourished, but have pushed native species like the white river spring fish to the brink of extinction. Inevitably, these ecosystem disruptions instigate a domino effect. The Montana shrimp is a piquant example. Back in the 1960s and 1970s, Montana stocked the tributaries of Flathead Lake with exotic freshwater shrimp to increase the amount of food for game fish. Alas, the shrimp infiltrated the lake itself and eradicated the native zooplankton. Consequently, the kokanee salmon that ate the zooplankton greatly dwindled. Then a bald eagle population that preyed on the salmon faded. Suddenly, an entirely new order prevailed.

On the other hand, biological ecosystems can often heal themselves or be restored with the help of conservationists. Along the Pacific Coast of North America, human hunting of otters has been largely stopped. Otters eat sea urchins. Urchin populations have been reduced, and a variety of species have returned to the ocean floor. Similarly, the dry forests of Costa Rica are making a strong recovery—aided by initiatives to purchase land, dedicate it to conservation, and tie parcels together to establish regional forest ecosystems of critical size and richness.

Finally, biological ecosystems are being transformed constantly in positive ways that enhance capability and/or diversity. Means by which this happens include coevolution among members, the introduction of new species, and geographically splitting and evolving in parallel but distinct directions. Most profoundly, new biological species continue to evolve—and their capabilities in turn can stimulate the reorientation of ecosystems.

The same sort of changes—declines and restorations—beset business ecosystems. A business ecosystem threatened by obsolescence slips into Stage IV. But its destiny is not set. It faces renewal or death—not death alone. And even if it slips into irredeemable decline, it will usually provide species and feedstock for its successors.

Simply put, Stage IV of a business ecosystem most often occurs when rising new ecosystems and innovations imperil mature business communities. Alternately, a community might reel from the business equivalent of an earthquake, of abrupt new environmental conditions like changes in government regulations, customer buying patterns, or macroeconomic circumstances. Deregulation of the phone business, for instance, registered high on the business Richter scale.

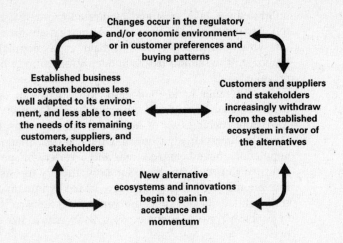

Figure 10.1

As the preceding illustration shows, these factors reinforce each other. An altered environment, certainly one ruptured by an earthquake, is often more hospitable to new or formerly marginal business ecosystems. And as new business ecosystems become established, they siphon trade and other forms of support away from the established ecosystem, rendering it even less competitive.

The Ultimate Challenge

Stage IV is perhaps the most underrated of the four stages. It lacks the glamour of Stage I beginnings, Stage II market races, and Stage III power struggles. Who can get too interested in something that might involve death? But Stage IV often deals with extending the useful life of business ecosystems of massive scale, sometimes containing billions of dollars of assets, serving millions of customers, and employing hundreds of thousands of people. It is both important and inevitable.

In fact, coping well with the threat of obsolescence is the ultimate challenge for a dominant company. Just because

Microsoft and Intel seem impregnable leaders now does not guarantee their current ecosystem immortality. Leading successive generations of innovation is crucial to an ecosystem's long-term success and its ability to renew itself.

As the pace of business change accelerates—and all of us begin to feel like Alice running with the Red Queen—we tend to celebrate the entrepreneurs and the industry creators, the wide-eyed thinkers who bring primary colonization to an uncharted landscape. Yet we often undervalue industry converters, those sleeves-to-the-elbows troopers who march into a complex business ecosystem facing decline and deftly turn it around. In nature, however, continuous renewal is the order of the day and primary colonization the rarity.

Certainly, isolated instances have captured the public imagination. The stunning deathbed turnarounds of the Ford and Chrysler automobile ecosystems in the late 1970s and early 1980s were romanticized by industry analysts and the popular press alike. In general, however, the conversion of existing assets, no matter on how large a scale, is heralded only in isolated instances. With the rate of new business ecosystem development on the rise—and with existing business models therefore becoming obsolete more rapidly—the ability to recognize assets in a dying ecosystem and reuse them will be an increasingly vital talent in the twenty-first century.

Some business ecosystems pose especially daunting recycling and reuse challenges by leaving unwieldy or poisonous assets for future generations. Many of the nuclear power plants built in the 1950s and 1960s during the heyday of nuclear energy will reach the end of their useful lives within the next decade. The vast drilling platforms in the North Sea, spidery superstructures forty feet tall, rust in the icy winds, laden with toxic wastes and unreclaimable. Mining activities around the world conclude once all the minerals are extracted, leaving peelings and pollutants.

In ecosystems of computers and communications, where the state of the art moves more quickly, there are often several generations of older products that work well enough but do not match the very highest levels of performance. Quite often, powerful end-to-end microecosystems, of genuine value to at least some customers, can be fashioned from these war-horses. Even as telephone companies install fiber networks, potent solutions can run over the old twisted-copper wire.

In some cases, leaders can slow and stabilize the decline of an ecosystem before all is lost. The ecosystem shrinks back to the economic microclimates and territories to which it is still well adapted. For example, tech watchers have predicted the demise of the mainframe computer for many years, but mainframes endure for applications to store and manipulate extremely large data sets, accessed in centralized locations with high security and reliability. Enduring microenvironments for mainframes include banks, government agencies, and large national retailers.

To avoid a Stage IV collapse requires moving rapidly and aggressively to refocus an organization on those markets and economic microenvironments that best suit it. This move usually warrants shifting some resources into new ecosystems, better frameworks of cooperation, and more robust economic orders likely to succeed across wider market terrains in the future. By reducing overheads, by focusing resources, by targeting the appropriate niches, ecosystems that may no longer be best for large portions of the opportunity environment may still survive and even thrive for long periods in appropriate subsegments of the overall environment.

Management of a Stage IV ecosystem conversion must actively focus its effort and creativity. Before proceeding, let me set some expectations. My purpose in this chapter is to demonstrate that the managerial and strategic challenges of Stage IV are distinct and worthy of close attention. I introduce some principles and concepts proven helpful in Stage IV situations, so that you can explore, apply, and I hope extend these and related ideas.

One of the best ways to sensitize yourself to Stage IV management challenges is to examine a particular case in more detail. I propose to explore Stage IV issues in one of the wildest and most imposing opportunity environments that exists: health care. For our limited purpose of exploring Stage

IV issues, and given health care's complexity, I have concentrated on changes under way in the U.S. health care system. Obviously, a comprehensive examination of health issues would address the challenges and innovations encountered in other parts of the globe. But meaningful analysis of the global issues would make an already tall order overwhelming.

I use the rich example of health care because it is our most critical Stage IV situation, one of life and death to all of us. Health care issues are explosive and difficult; they try many of our deepest values and pose immensely complicated problems. This chapter will neither say all about Stage IV, nor solve all in health care. What it will do, I hope, is throw out some ideas you will find relevant and suggest some ways in which Stage IV situations can be constructively addressed.

Health Care as an Opportunity Environment in Crisis

Health care is not itself an ecosystem but an opportunity environment—similar to "information space"—in which myriad ecosystems play and compete and rub up against one another. For all its problems, its observers would still argue that significant subsystems work quite effectively, and I emphatically agree. Medical professionals are extraordinarily dedicated, caring, and well trained. Around the world, dramatic advances have been made in this century both in medical treatment and in public health. Numerous medical procedures are unquestionably state of the art. Medical knowledge, technology, and infrastructure represent substantial asset value. Nevertheless, the sector as a whole is clearly rife with business ecosystems in search of their successors.[1]

Perhaps the most wrenching admission about Stage IV ecosystems is that in most cases the individuals are usually competent and dedicated in their specific contributions. What tends to become obsolete is not the individual but the framework of cooperation that bonds the talent together. The problem of health care is not with patients or doctors or nurses. It is not with pharmaceutical executives or hospital administrators. It is not even with policymakers. It is with the underlying assumptions that govern their work together. The ecosystem as a whole is underperforming, not the species. The best parallel in nature might be an Ice Age where temperature changes render entire ecosystems nonadaptive.

There is probably no reason to spend a lot of time demonstrating that health care is a Stage IV environment. Obviously, the current paradigms of practice crumble all around us. Patients are confused and worried. For many individuals, particularly middle-income employees within major organizations, there is a real probability that their health care benefits will decline under almost any future scenario.

Hospitals and other health care institutions fail and close all over America. In San Diego, competition among managed care networks is so ferocious that the current price of membership is less than $100 per person per month, even though no one delivers quality care for this bargain price. In New York, an effort to consign Medicaid patients to health maintenance organizations has spawned so-called look-alikes—HMOs that spend vast sums on slick marketing and promotion, but precious little on making people better. Now they must somehow be roped in and regulated before they quite literally threaten their members' health.

Physicians, frustrated by paperwork and what they consider to be inane cost cutting, are deserting medicine. The system cannot accommodate major surpluses of trained talent. Of the nation's some 650,000 doctors, an estimated 100,000 to 200,000 will be downsized from the profession within the next few years.[2] Matchless training programs close because their graduates cannot expect to find jobs. For example, Stanford University's prestigious anesthesiology resident program took on not one new student in 1995. The bigger picture is no brighter. The cost per citizen for care in the United States is among the highest in the world, but in public health measures like infant mortality, the nation fares poorly against other developed nations.

In the short term, the gardeners of the ecosystem are frustrated and cutting off its funds. Imagine if Phoenix, Arizona—a blooming tropical oasis in the desert, artificially supported by irrigation from the waters of the Colorado River—had to rely again only on its local watershed. Desert blooms would wither. Suburban lawns would revert to sand and sagebrush. Residents desperate for water would clash. Medical care in the United States has bloomed for more than four decades by drinking the generous waters of major company-and labor union–supported benefit plans, private and public insurance plans like Blue Cross/Blue Shield, and the Medicare and Medicaid programs that protect the nation's elderly and poor.

Now these stakeholders that provide the water to the ecosystem have become deeply frustrated by the ecosystem and band together to turn off the spigot. In terms of cost, the system is reaching the point where government and, to some extent, society won't let it continue to expand unchecked. Moreover, everyone from major corporations to the smallest companies find health care costs an unbearable burden, and actively search for ways to cap the costs.

Hence the species in the ecosystem have been thrust into competition with each other for declining resources. Unfortunately, there is no grand Solomon character to adjudicate resource allocation. Rather, the members of the ecosystem gravitate toward a wide array of partial solutions. Physicians, insurance companies and other payers, drug companies and equipment suppliers, and hospital administrators and health systems executives all trumpet their alternative visions of crisis resolution. At worst, each vision attempts to address some of the needs of the whole system, while also assuring its authors of a continuing commanding role. At best, the alternative visions promise some progress, but their implementations are rife with unanticipated consequences and unmanaged risks.

Obscured by all the partisanship and partial solutions are issues of value and delicate societal tradeoffs. What are we willing to pay for universal access to care? When it is easy to measure cost and difficult to define quality, how do we control costs without destroying quality? Must we sacrifice innovation in treatments to achieve system-wide cost reductions?

To what extent will we ration care, and how will we do so?

What makes the United States health care system a Stage IV case is not that it is incompetent in its specific tasks. Rather, it is because as a total ecosystem it does not appear able to address effectively the overall issues that confront it. The governing architecture of the ecosystem is far from adequate, not the performance of its members. In this condition—when the overall framework of cooperation that an ecosystem depends upon becomes inadequate—the ecosystem risks death and invites renewal.

Create a Basis for Action

My own work with Stage IV business ecosystems has included a number of ecosystems in high technology and heavy industries, and a limited exposure to health care. Without a doubt, I have found that Stage IV situations are among the hardest to influence. These ecosystems have vital ongoing responsibilities to customers. In health care, the customers are patients whose physical well-being depends on the system. You cannot simply shut down operations—tell the heart attacks and the cancers to wait a year or two—while everything gets retooled. What's more, these ecosystems are replete with suppliers and other associated organizations, and all of them have their own vital interests and points of view about what sort of future they prefer.

The Stage IV community as a whole—and especially its larger organization—is often subject to marked financial instability. One manager put it like this: "Large organizational systems are kept alive by the relationship of two very big numbers—revenues and costs. It doesn't take much of a movement in either number to throw you dramatically into the red, into losses you won't be able to contain and that your stakeholders won't tolerate. And when your stakeholders start to walk away, collapse may not be far off."

I have learned that managers must bring several elements together for reform and renewal to have a chance:

- You must survey the opportunity landscape and understand the current power players and their interests and assets. You must assess their alternative visions for the future, and consider whether they might converge these visions into a meaningful whole. You must also anticipate which visions will lead to unacceptable outcomes and risks—and be prepared to block or transform them.
- You must develop valid information about the performance of the whole business ecosystem. Questions that must be answered include: What does it mean for this ecosystem to succeed? How can this be measured? What factors are required for success? How might these factors be influenced to improve performance? Such information is often hard to gather. In health care, for example, you would want comparative information on the overall performance of alternative paradigms for organizing and delivering care. Such information is simply not available, except the gross calculations for cost per capita. Indeed, the outcome of the 1995 meeting of the revered Jackson Hole Group was a call for better information that focuses on quality of care and "functional" outcomes, such as how well the patients are doing, to be able to draw such comparisons. Without comprehensive measures, there is no practical way to determine whether renewal is in fact occurring—in health care or in any other Stage IV business ecosystem.
- You must organize yourself and your campaign so that you can affect the aspects of the business ecosystem that require transformation. You will experience great difficulty if you are organized only to address part of the problem. You need a charter to take responsibility for the most important sets of coevolving factors and actors. The lack of a charter and a sufficiently powerful platform of influence is of course a major problem in health care reform. There are many organizations from which reform efforts are being launched, but none is widely recognized as combining a high sense of public interest with comprehensive information and a sound platform from which to intervene.

In Stage IV situations, it is a challenge to gain the right organizational platform from which to effect change. Suffice it to say that most government agencies—and indeed many corporate business units—have aging charters suited to earlier eras. Seldom do they match up well with the centers of coevolution that need to be addressed.

Survey the Landscape

Every business ecosystem can be said to embody an underlying set of assumptions. These include environmental conditions—for example, the regulatory situation, or the conditions of the overall economy. Also involved are assumptions about customers, about the nature of the offer and how to pay for it, and about who creates it and how. In very old and established business ecosystems, managers take many of these assumptions for granted to the extent that they seldom consider them seriously. In fact, participants may consider them literally "unthinkable."

On the other hand, in new ecosystems—and in opportunity environments in flux—these assumptions become the central questions of strategy-making. Executives construct alternative scenarios to express different assumptions and spend prodigious amounts of time attempting to determine what business models will work in their futures. Such of course is the state of affairs in health care.

Some call the sets of assumptions expressed by an ecosystem a business model or a paradigm—or simply an "approach" to conceptualizing and organizing activities. Whatever name you use, your assessment of a business ecosystem begins with identifying those core assumptions.

A survey of the landscape usually starts by examining the approaches that are breaking down. To make the health care example somewhat manageable, I will refer to the established health care order as a single ecosystem, embodying a central set of assumptions. While I think this way is best to explore both health care and Stage IV situations in general, I should add that there is significant variation even within the current established order—variation from one region of the country to another, and among different approaches to organizing practice. A more comprehensive survey, beyond the scope of this book, would obviously deal in more depth with these differences and their implications.

"Fee-for-Service": The Established Ecosystem in American Health Care

For many decades, the implicit assumptions governing the health care ecosystem in the United States remained essentially the same. One of the most important features was the primacy of individual physicians in making medical decisions. Doctors took on patients, managed their care over their lifetimes, and were the gateway to other services. Their judgment was largely unquestioned.

Physicians were paid by the service—that is, for their time, and for their procedure, intervention, or treatment. For this reason, many observers prefer to refer to the traditional ecosystem as "fee-for-service." In the middle of the century, the nation had what amounted to two levels of service. For affluent patients or those with private insurance, physician decisions attempted to maximize the individual patient's well-being, without systematic concern for the cost of treatment. For other patients, doctors did what they could within the confines of what the patient could afford, and what could be covered by a reasonable amount of pro bono and charity-supported care.

Over the past twenty years, access to full service medical treatment has broadened dramatically. In 1950, about half of the United States population had basic hospitalization insurance, and only about 15 percent had what we would today consider comprehensive coverage. Medicare and Medicaid brought the government in as payers in the 1960s, widening the coverage to elderly and low-income patients. In addition, health care as a benefit of employment spread rapidly, so that by 1995 about 85 percent of the country had health insurance, and there was a widespread social expectation that everyone should be covered.[3] The "waters" that fed the landscape of health care were deep and plentiful.

Until the 1980s, the various contributors to the medical ecosystem had evolved with little global oversight or intervention on the part of policymakers. This had two results. First, within the specialties, there was much innovation in focused treatment methods and technologies, bolstered by steadily increasing numbers of insured patients who would pay for them. Second, in many cases, the effective integration of the specialties became increasingly complex and hard to manage, such that "continuity of care" became an often-repeated rallying cry and challenge for providers.

The government played a generally passive oversight role, concentrating its energies on becoming the major payer. There were some exceptions to this rule. For example, government was active in regulating narrowly defined quality standards, such as in Food and Drug Administration testing of the efficacy of drugs. It also worked with the leaders of the various professional sub-specialties to certify professional standards, as well as to limit entry into the field and reduce rivalry among the players. But it did not develop a comprehensive understanding of the performance of the health care ecosystem as a whole. Nor did it systematically develop effective means for influencing the evolution of the system.

The traditional health care system is, of course, in steep decline. Absent comprehensive information and effective evolutionary oversight, the ecosystem spawns or engenders largely unmanaged change. As I mentioned above, obsolete ecosystems often shrink back to smaller niches rather than vanishing completely. Fee-for-service health care is already in steep decline, but unlikely to go away. Wealthy customers may still prefer it, and therefore be able to support viable niche systems for many years. Fee-for-service may also persist in the most rural areas of the country, where sparse populations cannot underwrite much more than a lone local doctor. If the law allows them, fee-for-service models continue in other parts of the world where national health programs are the dominant system.

The most likely scenario is that fee-for-service will be joined by a number of other ecosystems—each with appealing benefits, as well as important limitations. No single form of ecosystem is likely to prevail completely unless backed by the force of law, an unlikely outcome in the current charged U.S. political climate. On the following pages I examine several of the prototypical ecosystems that are forming on the landscape—to get a sense of how the future may play out, as well as to explore in more depth the issues raised by Stage IV conditions.

Three Emerging Approaches, Many New Ecosystems

Let us run through the three new approaches that predominated in the health care opportunity environment at the time this book was being written. Obviously, in any fast-paced environment the paradigms are constantly morphing, coalescing, and reinventing themselves, just as their encompassing ecosystems grow or shrink. What follows is my snapshot of reality, so that we can make some interesting comparisons.

1. Self-help, self-healing.

The most radical form of transformation focuses on the patient. It envisions a much smaller role for the major health care institutions and an expansion of individual responsibility aided by tools and techniques, education, and health-promoting investments of time and energy by people like you and me.[4] New ecosystems embodying these ideas aim to bypass the traditional system almost entirely and empower the patient to take charge. We see this occurrence in the "wellness" movements, the rapid growth of "alternative healing" activities, and the increasing availability of medical supplies and equipment to consumers.

I can give you some sense of the value of this paradigm by relating an experience in my own family. My wife and I have two young sons. When our youngest was a little over a year old, he began to suffer respiratory problems accompanied by fevers of over 105 degrees at night. The first time fever hit, we called our doctor, who simply did not believe the reading or the thermometer, a new infrared scanning ear type. The doctor trusted neither the technology nor our ability to use it.

After some negotiation and a second reading with a mercury thermometer—and, believe me, three-minute glass thermometers and a sick infant in the middle of the night are a volatile mix—we agreed that we had two options: (1) take our son to a local hospital and have them confirm the fever, after which they would probably refer us to Children's Hospital in Boston ("The local hospital won't have a pediatric specialist on hand," we were advised); or (2) go directly to Children's Hospital. Since Children's was not much farther than our local hospital, we packed the baby into the car and headed for Boston.

Children's Hospital in the middle of the night is an experience not to be repeated. Kids and parents converge from all over the city, with coughs, sneezes, broken bones, and afflictions not for the squeamish. Then there was the prolonged process. First the paperwork with the admissions nurse. Then a staff nurse took our boy's temperature—with a scanning thermometer, of course—and at last confirmed our own reading ("Hmm," she said, nodding, "it is pretty high"). Then blood tests ("We just need to rule out anything really serious"), followed by a strong dose of both Tylenol and Advil. We waited. We read ten-year-old *National Geographic*s. We waited for the test results, waited for an intern to interpret the test results. We watched day break and looked for our physician to drop in on time for his regular early hospital rounds. At last, the fever started to break. Of course, we waited to be released, we endured more paperwork. Finally, after six hours, they let us go home.

Contrast this episode with how it could be: When we first began visiting with the doctor, he could have prescribed a home monitoring system—temperature scanner, heart and blood pressure monitor, and video telephone—to use whenever we needed emergency consultation. My wife and I would take a certification course to be certified in using the technology, which might itself give us the knowledge to tackle a wider range of conditions ourselves.

In event of an emergency, we would have a much more meaningful phone conversation, including agreement on something as simple as whether there is a fever or not, because my wife and I would be certified to take measurements and save on hospital and doctor visits. But the kit could also contain a small medicine cabinet with drawers to be unlocked, by remote, over the phone by the doctor—and only the doctor—so that we would not have to go searching for commonplace drugs at two in the morning. Since in many cases the diagnosis would be clear via telephone, the doctor could make the right drugs instantly available.

There are any number of companies working on systems like this—particularly for serving diabetics, the elderly, and the bedridden. These tools, plus books and workshops, and neighborhood support groups—including virtual communities on the Internet—respond to the strong desire for people to take responsibility for their health. Generally speaking, these ecosystems are in the pioneering stage. A lot of experimentation is under way. Of course they are consistent with, and to some extent reinforced by, long traditions of self-care, both within Western medicine as well as other ancient healing traditions.

To be sure, there remains a danger that these systems will lead to a much more fragmented approach to health care, with no one helping the client coordinate and integrate his treatment. On the other hand, plenty of people, most notably civil libertarians, believe that we ought to have more of that freedom in our health care system, that there should be more access to treatment directly. Indeed, this notion helps to fuel the movement to make prescription drugs available over the counter. In essence, proponents make the case that educated consumers can in fact do their own integration.

The prospects for this paradigm seem excellent. It is driven by a growing resource—the educated consumer. When it works, it saves time and money. There are plenty of species of businesses too happy to participate by producing books, tapes, and other tools of liberation. Measurement and diagnostic capabilities, sold directly to consumers, promise to have a particularly liberating effect.

An interesting model comes from an unlikely source. AIDS testing in the United States costs about $125 for what is known as the confirming test. Most of the cost is for factors like labor and administration of the testing labs and documentation. In West Africa that kind of cost is not affordable. International AIDS activists realized that the actual chemicals used in the test cost a few pennies. So they made kits that allowed local Africans to assemble and administer their own tests, using local labor, often for free or next to nothing.

There is a great deal of unnerving talk about the need to "surplus" more than 150,000 physicians in the United States during 1996–1997, as the traditional medical sector downsizes. From an ecological standpoint, the question that comes to mind is: Where will they go, and what will they do?[5]

In my Stage I discussion, I described how new ecosystems come about through value chaining—that is, by cobbling together previously fragmented resources with unmet needs. It is fascinating to imagine what may happen once thousands of underemployed—but still licensed and trained—physicians are set loose on the landscape. Quite interesting ecosystems might emerge from a combination of radicalized, inexpensive physicians, liberated technology, and consumers willing to take additional responsibility for their health. It is another reason why this paradigm is so flush with provocative possibilities.

2. Managed care.

The dominant new approach in health care—spawning both Stage II expansions and even Stage III unbundling—is managed care, also known as the HMO concept. Managed care is billed on a capitated per-person basis with statistically based reimbursement. Bricks and mortar are distinct obstacles in this system. Medical specialists are used only when their contributions can be clearly justified in the short term. And the locus of the treatment, rather than being the hospital, is really the outpatient center that provides services as part of an integrated system that bundles health insurance, management, and the provision of primary care through the hospital.

At least in its initial form, this model is really a cost-centered paradigm. It ultimately hopes to make quality process improvements as well, but such achievements take longer and require measurement and control over the behavior of the participants in the system—patients and providers—which are difficult to establish.

There is little question that managed care exemplifies the most dramatic change in American health care. For it signals that physicians, insurance companies, and hospitals are restructuring into vertically integrated units. On the positive side, the actors in all three sectors are participating to figure out how they can build new systems of managed care. This involvement is fueling profound restructuring of the health care system. It is also leading to integrated process units, possible breeding grounds for progress in primary care. By synthesizing all the interests—access, cost, and quality—these new end-to-end systems have an opportunity to truly improve the processes of medicine.

On the other hand, even if it fulfills the needs of payers and society to reduce expenditures, managed care also subjects patients to rationing and cost controls that can militate against their best interests. From the patient's perspective, there is almost no effective way to compare and contrast health care ecosystems. No consumer rating organization has yet emerged to review the programs, and few consumers are qualified to make their own judgments. Without proper measures, we cannot know the extent to which managed care contains costs at the expense of quality.

Another potentially disastrous consequence is that the level of insurance borne by the smaller HMOs may be inadequate to defend the system against unexpected catastrophic illnesses, which might financially dismember it. Comprehensive regulation of the risk indemnification side of these new units does not yet exist, nor is there a sector to provide these units with reinsurance for their most devastating future scenarios.

In late 1995, many markets were experiencing overcapacity in managed care systems, as well as overcapacity in various classes of physicians and other professionals. In locales like the San Diego metropolitan area, cutthroat competition between managed care operators led companies to slash their prices—most notably to employers—to well below not only their current costs but below any responsible cost projection. No matter how efficient the organization, prices like that require too many people to stay healthy.

This sort of wildly unmanaged and ruthless competition among managed care ecosystems virtually assures the economic implosion of some of these networks, or else deplorable skimping on care. As I've said, skimping is hard for the patient to detect without detailed, objective outcome and performance measures. The absence of system measurements is one of the glaring flaws of the health care system. The results of runaway competition in managed care may, at least in the short term, lead to tragic results.

Through the lens of this book, I find myself both respectful of and concerned about managed care. Many of its leaders are deeply committed to quality process improvement in health care. But the potential for unintended negative consequences seems high in the absence of meaningful regulation and oversight of the evolution of these ecosystems. The pressure on people to join an HMO has led to a large universe of individuals who have entrusted their most precious treasure—their family's health—to a custodian still too amorphous and free-wheeling to be trusted.

Where will the funding for the continuing creation of managed care ecosystems, and for the transformation of behavior across these ecosystems, come from? As we have seen in previous stages, ecosystem leadership is expensive. The successful leaders usually draw on economies of scale to fund their campaigns, to establish the by-now-familiar double-looped cycle of investment in core innovation and in the ecosystem. The managed care companies do not demonstrate economies of scale sufficient to fund the large-scale, sustained campaigns necessary to realize true process improvements. Rather, many of these companies seem destined for cash deprivation, limping along on the thinnest of margins.

3. Disease-state-focused health care ecosystems.

Still another alternative is for powerful actors previously at the periphery of the system to create other kinds of comprehensive systems of value, similar to that of telecommunications. To a large extent now, other actors—particularly the government and insurance companies that pay the bills—view pharmaceuticals and technology firms as problematic high-cost suppliers, and not as the major contributors to progress as in the old system. These players, especially the drug companies, have been among the most threatened, yet the most creative in restructuring themselves and initiating new paradigms. They are instructive examples of how one positions oneself relative to an ecosystem going through massive change in Stage IV. They well illustrate the general approaches to both self-protection (trying to slow the coming of change) and self-renewal.

During the past few decades, pharmaceutical companies have operated under a relatively consistent, if largely implicit, social compact with government regulators. In exchange for investing heavily in product and process innovation, drug companies have enjoyed comparatively high margins and protection from competition through patent laws and lengthy approval processes. But that social compact is disintegrating. The public, government, and corporations all want health care costs reduced. Drug company leaders see lean times ahead, as they confront the possibility of price and profit caps, as well as consolidated purchasing of drugs by HMOs and government agencies.

Responding to this environmental shift will force changes

across all major functions. In the short term, the drug companies are switching from selling the drug to a primary physician (usually through a very large sales force of "detailers," who offer both education and selling relationships to physicians) to a situation where many prescription drugs are sold to HMOs or other large combines. In these organizations, the gatekeeper is a board that rules on whether the drugs are in an approved formula area, a much more sophisticated type of salesmanship demanding considerably more strategic thinking.[6]

In a variety of ways, suppliers are trying to slide down the value chain toward the consumer to provide new innovative benefits, as well as to bond more closely to customers. To that end, they are forging different relationships with both the end user and the HMOs and pharmacies. In terms of the end user, suppliers are aggressively seeking ways to reach through the various market intermediaries: the physicians, the hospitals, the HMOs, and other buying bodies directed to the end user. Drug companies are collaborating with the FDA to convert drugs from prescription status to over-the-counter status, treated as consumer products. The companies are investing in consumer advertising, using newspapers, magazines, and television to stimulate demand for branded, new generation, on-patent products. And in many cases, companies are consolidating so that those that principally had prescription drugs can also develop a strong consumer products distribution position.

In terms of changing relationships with large organizations, drug makers have purchased pharmacy benefit management companies so that the drug companies take over the relationships, the administrative management, and sometimes the indemnification for the pharmacy. Sometimes manufacturers sell individual drugs to an intermediary like an HMO, with nursing consultation and telephone follow-up included as part of the price of the drug. The management of diabetes is an excellent example. The nursing staff from the drug company calls the patients directly, builds a relationship with them, encourages compliance with treatment protocol, and gets data quickly on side effects and the general reaction of the patient to the drug and the treatment, a feedback loop for research and development. In this way, the drug company can develop a close relationship with customers.

However, such ties are just the beginning. In the longer term, the drug companies are investing heavily to create end-to-end microecosystems where they can dominate markets and assure themselves of a central position. They are, in fact, working to increase their criticality and embeddedness. Their approach to restructuring health care is two-pronged: to influence managed care and government policy, and to pursue their own vision of a more desirable future for themselves.

Eli Lilly & Company serves us here. Lilly is betting its future on an approach called "disease management." The company is targeting five major categories of disease: diabetes, heart disease, central nervous system disorders, cancer, and infectious diseases. Lilly will seek ways to take responsibility for (1) end-to-end treatment of the disease state, not only the drugs but all other aspects of care; and (2) management of the disease within a population—for example, through prevention, slowing of contagion, and systematic reduction of secondary effects.[7]

This is a very different concept for the company. No longer is its main role limited to providing one element of care. Instead, it is taking overall responsibility for the care of certain diseases.

Lilly believes that disease management is the best way to keep from being shoved to the end of the value chain and treated as a commodity. Lilly and other suppliers can sell their new value proposition to managed care organizations by arguing that by assuming total responsibility the supplier can increase patient compliance, reduce complications, and ultimately save the HMO money and produce satisfied customers.

The real plus for Lilly is its belief that it is taking a critical and embedded role in these small ecosystems for its innovation trajectory. Moreover, Lilly enjoys vast economies of scale when one of its drugs becomes a "hit." Lilly can plow these profits into further core innovation as well as ecosystem development. In terms of our double-looped cycle of investment, the key in Stage IV is gaining information and insight used to lead change. The drug companies are ideally positioned to fund and benefit from such efforts.

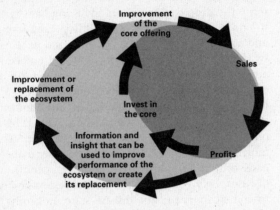

Figure 10.2

This insight suggests that the leaders of the drug companies and others with economies of scale wield more power in setting standards than most of the managed care leaders. Like IBM before Wintel, the drug interests will have more money and people to throw at the problem.

If you scan the health care landscape, you see other agents sprouting with miniature economic systems like those of the drug companies. You see surgery centers advertising to end users in elective areas like plastic surgery. You see the specialty clinics that provide so-called "life extension," essentially physical examinations and follow-ups for middle-aged people concerned about heart disease and stress. You see the development of wellness centers and health spas of one sort or another that build relationships with wellness specialists. You see the medical device manufacturers not only designing devices for physicians but thinking comprehensively about how to build the end-user market for a given device and how to assemble whole systems of value, taking innovation public. A good example is the corrective surgery for nearsightedness, introduced comprehensively by a division of Lenscrafters.

*   *   *

In my survey of alternative approaches to shaping the future in health care, I have obviously oversimplified some very complex ideas. At this point, you may find several lines of thought worth your while.

First, you may want to review and compare these three emerging paradigms and fee-for-service, and then reflect on your own experience with health care. What are your personal values for the care you and your family receive? Which of these approaches—or what combination of approaches—seems most aligned with your values? We all have a great stake in this particular renewal, which directly involves our health and the health of loved ones.

Second, you may want to ask yourself, how confident am I in the current developments in health care? What would I want to know—or want policymakers to know—to increase my confidence that change will be real progress?[8]

Finally, you may want to ask: What can I learn from health care that applies to my own business situation? Some of us are embroiled in one or more Stage IV situations. Many of us are actually in Stage I, II, or III, but with symptoms of Stage IV business. What aspects of my situation are entering Stage IV obsolescence and may need to be transformed? What current approaches seem most promising, and what are the essential features of these alternative visions? Characterizing alternatives always helps to launch analysis. In the next section, we will briefly walk through a method for comparing and contrasting points of view, and for making one or more of them come true.[9]

Develop Valid Information

A true leader always understands that no single approach is complete and no approach will be completely triumphant. In a Stage IV environment we must avoid becoming too attached to any single solution; instead we must transcend slightly above the terrain and seek the tools and insights for becoming the business equivalent of a gardener, or landscape architect, or forester.

While leaders must always understand the power players and paradigms at any given moment, the key to success is seldom found in any one of them. The true breakthroughs come through investing in the collection of information and the generation of knowledge and insight that sit conceptually above any of the paradigms. You must develop a strong analysis that helps you understand the available alternative ecosystems and their relative strengths and weaknesses. From this information, you may be able to glean ways to invest to improve gains for customers and foster the conditions for renewal.

When we try to evaluate the alternative approaches and ecosystems—as with the health care approaches—we are confronted with four problems:

1. How do you measure success?
2. How do you properly establish the scope or boundaries of the system being transformed?
3. How do you identify, understand, and affect the actual creation of value in each ecosystem?
4. How do you evaluate a portfolio of possible investments in ecosystems across this landscape?

The better you answer these questions, the more you can reconcile alternative interests and visions of reform—and the faster you can stimulate meaningful, lasting change. This grain of wisdom has been the seminal discovery of the "total quality" movement in manufacturing—that profound knowledge lets you lower costs and improve quality. Business ecosystems are far more complex than manufacturing processes, but in this respect, at least, the same principles apply.

1. Measurements of success.

In all Stage IV renewals, gaining an accurate measure of the performance of the ecosystem is a challenge. To the extent that we have statistics as a diagnostic, they tend to measure discrete activities rather than the value of the whole. On the other hand, the customer experiences the "total offer," and makes choices based on his or her overall experience of the business ecosystem. For a reasonable chance of accomplishing reform, we need to do what we can to measure performance as the customer experiences it.

This problem exists in spades in health care. Patient outcomes are difficult to document, much less measure in detail. In many cases the ultimate success of a procedure—such as a cancer treatment or heart surgery—is not known for years. The best available information tends to be cost-related, and even that primarily focuses on current costs, not on capital costs or any broader measures. Because stakeholders are principally interested in cost control, most of the paradigm struggles dwell explicitly on cost containment, not on high quality, innovation, or even gauges thereof.

Patient satisfaction is the easiest "quality" factor to measure, and a number of studies suggest that patient satisfaction correlates with short- and long-term quality outcomes. On the other hand, we can model a number of situations where perverse incentives tempt the patient and the health care provider to collude unwittingly in exchanging the patient's long-term welfare for a short-term positive experience.

Virtually no one has tried to measure the innovative progress of health care ecosystems as a whole. Yet if you compare what's happening in health care to the most advanced industries, you find that most have gone through a combination of cost-oriented, quality-oriented, and innovation-oriented improvement efforts, and they methodically continue to measure all three.

2. System boundaries: getting at cost-causers.

The second major issue in the transformation of large systems relates to ensuring that your model of the whole system includes all the important elements and all the important behaviors affecting total performance. In health care, it is blatantly obvious that all the cost-causing behavior is not in the system itself. Drug and alcohol use drive something like 20 percent of the cost of health care in the United States. Guns and the illegal use of weapons are another major factor, particularly in urban areas. Obesity, unmanaged high blood pressure, sedentary behavior, and smoking all add appreciably to cost, yet no system—whether nationalized, managed care, or fee for service—has found a way to address these behavioral issues effectively.

For many years, HMOs have argued that they have an incentive to address behavioral issues, but most studies have not shown that HMOs have any appreciable effect on the behavior of their members. Perhaps we need a health system, one that brings all cost-causers into line, potentially through strong incentives. Current insurance surcharges, like those for smokers, are one means of allocating the costs to those whose behavior generates them (as well as perhaps helping to deter people from smoking). The remaining questions are: How do we address the large number of cost-causing behaviors, and how do we reward people for acting in the long-term interests of not only themselves but of society?

The problem of boundary-defining crops up in almost every Stage IV situation. In many cases, problems precipitated by particular business ecosystems have been defined as outside the management boundary during the earlier stages, but then come back to haunt its owners. With ocean-based oil rigs, nuclear power plants, and metal ore mining operations, the Stage IV work involves addressing so-called externalities—massive and dangerous superstructures, nuclear waste, pools of toxic poisons—and finding ways to reclaim them or at least render them as harmless as possible.

In some cases, the original Stage I and II value proposition would not have been positive if the valuation model factored in these externalities. As a result, the net value of some of these business ecosystems turns out to be a destructive impact on society. One positive development in this regard is the movement to insist that industrial processes, and even consumer products, be defined from the beginning to include all of their byproducts and environmental impacts. In Europe, government regulations hold manufacturers to standards of clean manufacturing and totally recyclable products. The standards help steer business creativity toward activities that truly create wealth, rather than merely appear to do so in the early years of their business ecosystems.

3. Identifying locations of value creation.

Here we must return to the fundamental ideas stressed in the book so far. You are creating a business ecosystem—in this instance, one that is to be renewed. It must gain new sources of innovation and value creation, and they must enable the ecosystem to exceed the performance of the alternative ecosystems it will compete against. For example, the disease management approach to diabetes assumes that innovations in drugs and in patient use of drugs (compliance with the treatment plan) will make a dramatic difference in overall complications. This in turn should translate into improved quality of life for patients and reduced overall costs for the health care system. To turn this admittedly attractive idea into practice, its promoters must specify as clearly as possible how the relevant drugs and delivery methods will work, and with what consequences.

Thus leaders of ecosystems understand how continuous innovation trajectories will drive the transformation and renewal of this ecosystem. What are the central innovation trajectories—such as improvements in drug-based treatment—on which this approach to renewal is cast? What theoretical performance improvements are available? The answers will give a sense of whether or not the transformed ecosystem can truly hold its own against alternatives. In our drug example, the improvement must be great enough to justify the immense efforts that will be required to assure its adoption.

Once we assess the theoretical gains, then we can turn theory into practice. How long will we take to achieve these gains? Are there critical uncertainties that we must resolve in implementing the anticipated advances? Do we need major changes in consumer behavior or in supplier behavior, both tricky achievements? Or in some cases a critical technology may not be perfect yet, or its costs still too high for broad applicability. With these sorts of limitations, we must determine how to surmount them. When and how will we be sure the approach is likely to succeed? This is how you can set priorities for action and single out what issues need to be most carefully managed.

4. Evaluating alternative investments.

One of the most important questions is whether or not ecosystem reform is worth the effort—or whether the same money and creativity might better be invested in a new and alternative business ecosystem. This question is often put in terms of the well-known S-curve, originally developed to express how technologies create value over time.[10] The S-curve reminds us that continued investment in a particular idea has accelerating returns in the early period, as the idea is perfected and scaled up, and diminishing returns in later life, as the idea and its applications become fully exploited. This same general pattern of value creation over time holds for business ecosystems and their underlying frameworks of cooperation. The pattern is expressed in a similar manner in the four stages—and is illustrated below:

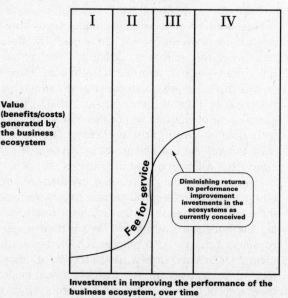

Figure 10.3

The first task of analysis in Stage IV is to determine whether we can turn up the value-improvement trajectory of the business ecosystem again, through either selective or wholesale insertion of new ideas and approaches, in combination with the current species, as seen below:

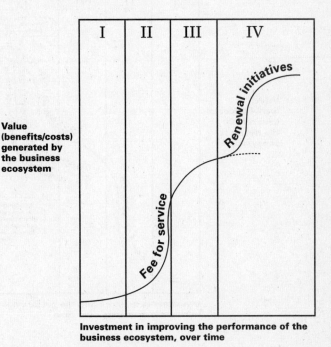

Figure 10.4.

For example, although politically unlikely at this point, we could retain fee-for-service health care on a widespread basis by adopting some reform and renewal efforts. Indeed, "preferred provider networks" represent such an effort. Disease management may also have some effect in extending the life of the fee-for-service paradigm.

The second task of analysis is to compare the costs and benefits of renewal with the costs and benefits of new and emerging business ecosystems based on dramatically different approaches. In essence, this overlays the anticipated S-curve of the new ecosystem on that of the old, and looks to determine where the crossover point in relative value creation lies.

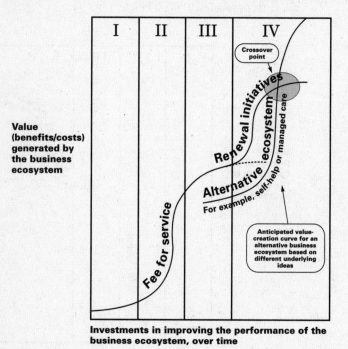

Figure 10.5

With more sophisticated versions of this analysis, we could understand the risks involved in establishing the new ecosystem and then adjust its curve of value creation accordingly. Similarly, we could adjust the curve of value-renewal generated for the existing ecosystem. We might notice variation in the shape and relative position of these curves according to market segment or other factors and incorporate this data in the analysis.

All in all, such analysis helps us determine the extent to

which we should invest in renewal, as well as in alternative ecosystems. It is indispensable as a foundation for the next step: organizing for action. In the real world, though, the advantage of one approach and its related S-curve over another is seldom as decisive as in theory. Existing ecosystems often persist in at least a reduced form for far longer than we tend to anticipate. On the other hand, new approaches and ecosystems often take longer to establish than their proponents imagine, and they almost always encounter unexpected challenges.

Reformers often spend a lot of energy trying to decide whether to invest in the new ecosystems—the "greenfield" starts—or to work on injecting new ideas and technologies into the old, what some call "brownfield" efforts. In fact, you usually need to create a portfolio of initiatives, balancing investments in old and new ecosystems, to maximize your chance of effective positioning for the future. In many instances, there may even be opportunities for old and new ecosystems to share resources or assets and support each other. In the best cases, we take advantage of the creative opportunities presented by the coexistence and coevolution of such multiple centers of synergy and vision—sharing ideas, stimulating constructive competition, and adapting to varying market segments and economic microclimates.

Put another way, in a classic Stage IV situation, fresh developments do not simply come along and colonize a new market territory as they do in Stage I. Instead, a secondary colonization of a landscape replete with species and deeply established relationships among the species takes place. In health care, for example, the very ground upon which entrepreneurs and visionaries will erect new health care systems will inevitably consist, in part, of the wreckage of the old—a landscape of health care ecosystems, interacting and penetrating one another and elements of the wider society.

In closing, what can we say about the state of understanding of value creation in health care? We are making progress, to be sure, but are far from drawing anything like S-curves for fee-for-service, self-help, managed care, or disease management. Much of the basic data is unavailable or kept under wraps by those who have it. To stimulate and guide reform, such information would need to be available to either consumers or perhaps to consolidated buying agents—including the government or well-intentioned employers—who could use it to channel trade to the most effective ecosystems.

Given that such information is not available anywhere in an integrated form, consumers remain befuddled. There exists no *Consumer Reports* or *J.D. Power* for health care.

And so hospital accreditation authorities have just started to make available comparative information about hospitals, and on a very limited basis. The drug companies conduct studies of drug effectiveness, and are starting to collect information on total disease incident costs and outcomes, but this information remains proprietary and reserved for their own marketing and drug development purposes. Cost information exists for comparing doctors, procedures, and even patients. But this information data is not currently or readily available to the consumer and is sometimes used against consumer interests by unscrupulous insurers or payers who use it to exclude the more expensive doctors, procedures, and even patients from coverage.

Perhaps one of the best possible investments in health care reform is in comprehensive measurement that both patients and their agents can use for making decisions. Empowering the consumer is fundamental to improving medical care quality and cost of any product or service, medical or otherwise.

Organize to Affect the Aspects of the Business Ecosystem Requiring Transformation

So how does management tackle big Stage IV change? First, I'd say, with respect. With respect for the magnitude of the task, with respect for the investments involved, with respect for the customers, and perhaps most important, with respect for the people inside the systems. It is easy to minimize the contribution to society and to the world of a large system whose theoretical base has become obsolete. But that system may still involve thousands or even millions of people with minds and emotions who are creating real ongoing value for society.

Perhaps the most significant aspect of Stage IV is the extent to which we must recognize that the talents required—while they incorporate some of the Stage I entrepreneurialism and thinking—involve skills particular to accomplishing large system change. These skills include the detailed financial and technical analysis of sunk investments and their conversion. The leader for Stage IV must boast the ability to direct large-scale organizations interested in implementing change, as in persuading customers and other individual members to embrace a new paradigm. The skills set is radically different from the market development and people development issues of a Stage I ecosystem, which, as it happens, are also almost always a part of a Stage IV system.

These skills can be sorely tested by the sheer numbers and sheer magnitude of the task of converting the old. The value of a Lee Iacocca is that ability to give both hope and structure to the mission. That is how one engages all the stakeholders and participants across the seven dimensions come together with a heartfelt devotion to doing something arduous. Society will need more leaders with this special gift as we experience accelerating rates of industrial change.

Second, would-be Stage IV leaders must find an organizational platform that lets them address the full dimensions of the ecosystem, as well as the wider opportunity environment. Again, I return to the seven dimensions of business ecosystems. To make effective change, you will likely have to modify consumer attitudes and behavior, and reshape markets, offers, processes, and organizations. You will need to address stakeholders and consider the relationship of the ecosystem to society's values.

In health care reform, it is hard to identify an institutional base from which to address all aspects of the situation, a major reason why renewal is so formidable a task. Managed care organizations cannot address individual behavior. Drug companies cannot treat the whole person. Government agencies are fragmented, lacking in information, and unable to intervene except in the broadest manner. The one role that addresses all aspects of the situation is that of customer and patient. The consumer can shape his or her behavior, and can integrate many different treatment modalities. Consumers today often tackle their own ills with over-the-counter medicines and alternative treatments like homeopathy. For this reason, I bet that the most powerful innovations in the long run will not flow from managed care or from broad policy interventions, but from the self-help paradigm. I envision educated individuals supported by advanced consumer medical technologies. When consumers need professional help, consumer-oriented information and referral will be readily available. The roles of both physicians and managed care organizations—while not vacated—will decline dramatically in importance and in the percentage of health care money spent on them.

The good news is that, every day, I see more attention to issues of Stage IV conversion. After all, only in the past few years has health care reform become a topic of general concern. While much remains to be done, at least a lot of smart people are thinking about it. Similarly, the environmental movement has done much to focus our attention on the potentially damaging side effects of many business ecosystems gasping their last breaths. Unfortunately, exploiting environmental and social "externalities" is still a vigorous way of life in many areas of the world, particularly in parts of Asia. Still, it is encouraging to see the progress being made by some businesses and governments in internalizing these costs into core business models and in applying innovation to reduce the costs and accomplish what we all would like, which is more true wealth for society.

11

The Paradox of Powerless Activism

Strategy is the art of bringing values and resources together to influence and shape the future. An essential message of this book is that we can indeed join together to affect our future. But this is easy to say, hard to do. We must grapple with a tension between our nearly unlimited ability to imagine alternative futures and our limited ability to influence it. Leadership, in this wider perspective, is a new challenge.

Every year for the past twenty years, Bo Ekman—currently chairman of SIFO, a leading European consulting organization—has held a seminar that amounts to an ongoing dialogue on organizational learning and large system change. The meetings are held at a small resort hotel in Tällberg in the lake country of North Central Sweden, an isolated setting where reindeer meat and potatoes appear on the menu. The air is clear and fresh—the village of Tällberg has only a few hundred residents—and the isolation fosters reflection and conversation. If the sessions are held midsummer, the sun is always up; if it's fall, the sun sets fast in the afternoon. You are well aware of your proximity to the Arctic Circle.

By design, the meeting brings together a few dozen leaders from business, government, and labor, most of them representing countries, unions, or multinational firms headquartered in Northern Europe, and a few from Japan and the United States. There is always a handful of consultants and pundits to leaven the loaf. I assume I am invited as some form of yeast.

The overt goal is to discuss problems that cross one another's boundaries—employment, technology and its impact on society, environmentalism, and education. Each year focuses on a different obscure topic, one both vague enough and ambitious enough to set people dreaming. The longer term goal is to appreciate one another's perspective and to forge deeper personal understandings of how to effect change.

The discussions are usually quite candid. By the last day of the sessions, the talk often gets personal and emotional. In 1995, one of the tenser moments occurred during a discussion of worldwide economic and social trends. One of the participants had presented a view that cyber-capitalism as it is currently playing out can probably bring comfortable lives—in a material and health care sense—to several billion people in Asia and India, but may have to write off the futures of Africa and much of Latin America, perhaps two billion people. On balance, he said, this tradeoff was not so bad—certainly better than what any other economic or political system had accomplished.

The leader of a major international labor union slowly raised his hand, was acknowledged, and turned to the first speaker. "You know, in my line of work we put faces on those two billion people," he said. "That is our job. And when you put faces on people—when you know them—you can't just write them off."

As we talked during the final session, it dawned on me what is so difficult about this holistic notion of shaping the future. At once, it invites you to be more ambitious than you have ever been, while at the same time reminding you, and humbling you, about your ability to manage these extended systems in any conventional manner. There wasn't a person at the Tällberg sessions who wasn't to some extent overwhelmed by the task before him. All of us felt the tension of living in an era of environmental and social challenge, combined with a powerful ability—aided immeasurably by new communications technologies—to imagine and empathize with people and other beings all over the world.

The old adage about never accepting a job where the authority doesn't match the responsibility simply doesn't fly in the new world. Every serious leadership position—whether working to restore your neighborhood, struggling to contribute to health care, or trying to reverse the fortunes of the United Nations or the European Community or the United States Government or the Japanese Diet—requires shouldering responsibility and then creating a campaign to achieve influence. None of these challenges offers up authority on the scale required. Such authority simply does not exist in a world of multiple independent players coevolving together in networks and communities.

But the issue runs deeper than that. We are coming to the end of the supremacy of the engineering point of view that has so dominated management thinking and that has been so successful in so many walks of life. There is a saying popular in high-technology circles, coined by Alan Kay when he was a leading scientist at Xerox's Palo Alto Research Labs: "The best way to predict the future is to invent it." Like many others, I have been inspired by this simple statement. In a sense, this slogan expresses the spirit that underlies our current technological revolutions, especially in information space and in biotechnology.

But as I sat among my fellow seminarians at Tällberg, it occurred to me that this slogan is obsolete. It asks an impossibility. It implies a goal of prediction. It invites us to believe that we can reliably invent the future. And yet we know from studying complex systems that prediction in any conventional sense is simply not possible. Not in biological ecology—and not in business and social ecology.

Certainly we can influence the future—but at heart it is wild and open, shaped by chance and fad and intersections of random events, as well as by what we hope to make it. In this sense, it is rather like our children. Thus, in the end, perhaps the only predictable thing about the future is that it will not be as we expect. And this is so even if we try our best to engineer a particular outcome.

Over the past few years, many of the business leaders that I find most effective have subtly begun to shift their stance toward leadership. Executives are letting go of prediction and invention, and embracing pattern recognition, anticipation, and campaigns of shared responsibility and influence. They need to take action on many dimensions—as we have seen throughout this book—and also be more responsive to their environment and the coevolving capabilities of other members of their ecosystems.

How do we balance our interest in shaping the future—indeed, an absolutely fundamental strategic imperative to shape the future—with a prudent respect for the limits of our abilities to do so? This requires new approaches to what we might think of as our "personal ecology" of leadership.

Evolving a Personal Ecosystem

It is obvious that the world of management gets more complex each year. We are hammered with new business models, changing business boundaries, technology discontinuities, and ecosystem-to-ecosystem competition. These features not only stretch and shake up our companies, they also challenge each of us as individuals. Several of the best executives I know—each working in different business sectors—have recently raised a very difficult question: Given that the environment is not going to slow down, how do I increase my personal capacity to cope with it? How do I stay in the center of the game and continually improve my abilities for judgment and action?

For a thought on this question I return to Jim Henson, creator of the Muppets, and a person who had enormous impact on several wider ecosystems. Jim taught me the importance of creating a personal ecosystem—of finding ways to take the spark of your own creativity and vision and gather others who can share your dreams. In a sense, Jim created a kind of "personal ecosystem of Jim Henson," an informal group of associates who extended his range of learning and impact.

The ecosystem of Jim Henson consisted of people playing three broad roles. There were those who formed what I call Jim's "kitchen cabinet"—trusted friends and allies with whom he could share dilemmas and challenges, bounce around ideas, and develop hypotheses about how to move forward. Members of the cabinet would come and go, but over the years a core group remained fairly constant. At the center of this group was David Lazer, who started his career at IBM but joined Jim in the early days. David acted as a kind of emotional center for Jim and for the company—balancing the ups and downs of successes and failures, gently suggesting alternative perspectives and options, and sometimes playing diplomat during conflicts. Also involved over the years were Jim's wife, Jane, Frank Oz (who became a successful film director in his own right while still playing Miss Piggy, Kermit the Frog's antithesis), and Bernie Brillstein, Jim's Hollywood manager.

Significantly, the only member with true operating duties in the company was Robert Beitcher, the managing director. The primary purpose of the kitchen cabinet was not to take action, but to promote perspective and reflection. It was a network for hypothesis formulation—for getting the questions right, and not necessarily for answering them.

The kitchen cabinet was complemented by a group that we might think of as the analysts. These included in-house and outside production planning, financial, and legal talent. These were people Jim relied upon for hypothesis testing—for precise, detailed answers. Interesting ideas originating in the kitchen cabinet needed to be tested in the bright light of day. Rigor, objectivity, and simultaneous attention to the whole picture—and to all the details—were the capabilities demanded for these roles.

Finally, there were the agents. I don't mean simply talent agents or public relations agents, although Jim used both and I put them in this category as well. I include all of Jim's most reliable and accomplished managers and individual talents—

actors, directors, artistic designers, musicians, composers, as well as business executives. These were the people who made plans come to life, who realized the visions of the company on magnetic tape and celluloid, and ultimately delighted audiences around the world.

Together, these three roles constituted a learning system that supported Jim's quest. The learning system joined idea exploration with rigorous analysis and connected both aspects to aggressive, feet-on-the-street action. At the center of this system was a fourth role, one which could not be delegated: the responsibility for making tough choices. In the final analysis, it was Jim alone who made the close calls, who selected the people, set the priorities, winnowed out the chaff.

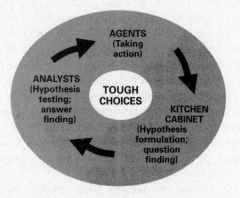

Figure 11.1

Over the years, I've found this model useful for strengthening my own leadership and that of others. As a diagnostic exercise, you might consider listing who you have in your "Personal Ecosystem." You may find areas that have become sparsely populated. We all know executives who are light on perspective but long on analysis—missing the forest for the trees. On the other hand, there are those who are weak on capability to act. And some have difficulty with detailed analysis or tough choices. Particularly as we rise in hierarchical organizations—and even new-style flat or networked organizations—we lose touch with many of the individuals who might have been in our kitchen cabinet. It can get lonely at the center if we don't continue to cultivate friends who know us, care about us, and are not afraid to tell us when we are off base.

The good news is that we can strengthen our personal ecosystem. Each of us is in effect a gardener of our own personal enterprise. In many cases, we can increase our effectiveness by recruiting even a few strong new members to our personal ecosystem. We can experiment with its composition and balance, and with how best to use our associates—individually and in relation to one another. A nice feature of this model is that it does not necessarily require that we change our personal style in order to be more effective. Instead, it focuses on the extended organization that we create around ourselves. We remain the fulcrum, but we extend our leverage.

The particular design is not what is most notable about what Jim Henson did. It is rather that he, and other leaders, are investing personal time in experimenting with ways to leverage themselves and their colleagues. In a sense they are being forced to do this, I believe, because the complexity of managing has outstripped the ability of any one person to carry on alone. Managers have trouble scanning enough, analyzing enough, and acting in a timely and forceful manner. On the other hand, adding more people to the conventional hierarchy is too unresponsive, too inflexible, and too impersonal.

We need new models that better extend our scope of action and learning. David Packard says he lives by the maxim: "More companies die from indigestion than from starvation." I would say the same is probably true for most companies—and most executives. In complex environments like Jim Henson's entertainment world, investing in our own personal ecosystem—in our own informal enterprise—can make a substantial difference in our effectiveness and longevity.

Putting Business Ecosystems in a Wider Context

As you invest in your own personal learning system and begin to experience problems more holistically, Tällberg-style, a shift occurs in your perspective. You find yourself slipping over boundaries more fundamental than those between industries or business models.

The first boundary you cross is between business and what might be thought of as society. Business is totally dependent on society—although we sometimes don't experience it that way. The two major factors that you don't control as a businessperson—but upon which you are critically dependent—are customers and the values and policy environment of your society. It is no accident that the seven dimensions used throughout this book start and finish with these two dimensions. Many of our stories—from health care to Wal-Mart to Intel—involve changing tides in society and the initiatives of companies as they strive to influence customer and societal reality. Wal-Mart starts out being a real boon to local towns, but in many cases is then seen as a pariah.

The second boundary you cross is between the ecological metaphor and the environment itself. All businesses, even in their most limited form, confront environmental issues, some more than others. Shell has its North Sea oil platforms, Intel its chemical byproducts of chip manufacture, and GM and Ford their depletion of fossil fuels.

So you find yourself moving from ecology as metaphor to ecology as reality. Economic systems are subsystems of the biological: if you eliminated all economic systems, you would still have the biological—as was true for hundreds of millions of years before modern history. But if you remove the biosphere, you could not sustain economic activity for very long, even in a space capsule launched from a dead Earth.

Ten years from now, I am firmly convinced, business leaders will be actively and daily addressing social and environmental issues. The world is becoming smaller. Faster innovation, global development, and environmental and social decline are forcing us to attend to problems as whole cloth. Business is just a subset, a distinctly human activity within the social and natural environments. The so-called externalities to which we alluded previously are in fact internal to the world system as a whole, and business leaders will increasingly have to address them. Clearly, as a world community, we must work together with the understanding that we do so within this single all-encompassing framework.

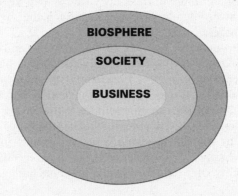

Figure 11.2

Seen broadly, we realize that there are different types of ecosystems, each with distinct purposes and governing values. Business concerns itself with forming economic ecosystems around innovative ideas. The fascinating interaction among the potentials of technology, the values of society, and the preferences of individual customers eventually develops into what I call business ecosystems—in the end, shaping a new future for all involved. Business ecosystems are the embodiment of values—values of customers, suppliers, and society and its agents—centered around economic activities and conforming to the laws of investment and return.

Some societal ecosystems are not primarily businesses and do not reflect business values as their overall concerns. Rather, they abide by the laws of social movements, communities, and human development. Churches, nonprofits, and neighborhoods all have their values, expressed through the aims of their common projects and the ways people relate to one another. Perhaps calling these "social ecosystems" would help us see them as collections of actors, working and coevolving together as businesses do, but with an underlying value set maximizing qualities like care, mutual support, and human development rather than profit and economic innovation. Neither of these sorts of ecosystems should be seen as more moral or more intrinsically virtuous than the other, but simply as two different systems dancing together in one wider environment.

In the same way, we all ultimately depend upon the overall biological environment. The values of the biological environment are diversity, complexity, richness, and competition within the frame of a wider coevolutionary tapestry.

Overall, we can represent these three types of ecosystems as interlacing, overlapping sets of mutually reinforcing relationships and activities with centers of gravity in biology, society, or business. That is, while they move in different spheres of reality, they influence each other immensely.

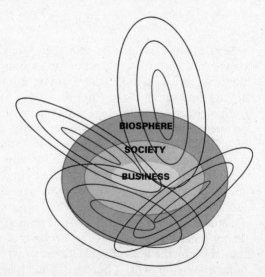

Figure 11.3

One of the major issues we face is how our business ecosystems will relate to our social and biological ones. The relationships will be especially critical when these ecosystems clash—that is, when one sort of ecosystem wreaks havoc on the others. These clashes are pressing and obvious in our discussion of the health care sector relative to society. These clashes also occur whenever companies like Wal-Mart become especially effective at organizing ecosystems in ways that greatly influence social communities. How do we resolve value conflicts going forward? Who will stand up for the noneconomic values? These are difficult questions.

This past fall, twenty or so physicians and their spouses who have been meeting monthly for ten years to hear the thoughts of various experts invited me to speak in their small "salon" forum. I was intrigued because I wondered what the process would be. The meeting was held in one of the members' homes, a rotating responsibility. There was a potluck dinner, followed by about an hour and a half of presentation and discussion, and the session finished with dessert. I had a great time, and I found it was very helpful to get their thoughts on the ideas I've shared with you in this book.

I was impressed by the fact that my host suggested that I focus on subjects other than health care, since the group was already intimately familiar with the topic and was looking for fresh ideas outside the sphere of their daily lives. And so I turned to other business sectors—computers and communications, oil, retail.

Overall, the notions of business ecosystems intrigued them. Reflecting on my account of the world, several members expressed measured concerns about the relative power of the business sector to shape the future—especially in a time when government still has not been reinvented, the environmental movement lacks great momentum in the United States, and citizens shy away from our most intractable social problems. They, too, wondered who will give voice to a wider range of values. If no one comes forward, then will we develop a culture with a narrower range of values and with more homogenous attributes and experiences? Can we expect business ecosystems to fulfill all our wants and needs?

It may not be fair to hold business leaders responsible for delivering these values. How can we expect the economy to provide for all of us any more than we can demand everything from government, nonprofits, environmentalists, or any other established group? We need a range of voices—a diversity of inputs—and the skills to listen, appreciate, and respect each of them. We need more "salons," if you will, more forums and policies in which the crossruffs among the three major categories of values—those of business, social, and biological ecosystems—can be wholly understood and debated, and tradeoffs and reciprocal adaptations made.

In one of his personal journals, Henry David Thoreau jotted a note to himself: "Obey the law which reveals, and not the law revealed." I've long loved this thought—that it is worthwhile to look behind ideas and ask where they came from. In the case of this book, the core concepts have emerged from the muck and mire of struggling with strategic and leadership challenges—my own and those of my clients—while being inspired by concepts drawn from the study of complex biological systems and relationships.

Ecology is particularly helpful in liberating our thinking from the narrow confines that the demands of daily life jam us into, and leading us into something broader, higher, and more intriguing. Better than any other means, it connects us with the multilevel, nested, constantly transforming nature of reality. Another favorite quotation is by a seventeenth-century biologist named Albrecht von Haller. He commented on both the richness of nature and the limitations of our minds:

> Nature connected her things in a net, not a chain: but humans can follow only by chains because their language can't handle several things at once.[1]

This is a particularly essential point today. Human beings have always separated themselves from other species by the degree to which they transform their environments to meet their needs. On the other hand, our minds have always had a limited ability to see the big picture and understand all the consequences of our actions. Today our power to change our world has grown to the point where we run the real risk of destroying it. Our capabilities still outrun our abilities to understand them. But there is no turning back from these capabilities. And so we must find ways to embrace our powers in a positive fashion. We must develop ways to augment our thinking. Studying ecology is one of the most promising ways to stretch our minds—and on occasion to help us succeed in reaching beyond chains.

Notes

CHAPTER 1

1. For more information on the ecological crisis in Hawaii see: Elizabeth Royte, "Hawaii's Vanishing Species," *National Geographic* (September 1995).

2. For more information on the ecology of Hawaii see: Bishop Museum, *Ecological Atlas of Hawaii* (Honolulu: Bishop Museum); and Steve Barth, *The Smithsonian Guides to Natural America, The Pacific: Hawaii and Alaska* (Washington, D.C.: Smithsonian Books; New York: Random House, 1995).

3. Interviews with ABB Asea Brown Boveri executives in Canada and at ABB headquarters in Switzerland, 1995–1996.

4. For a comprehensive discussion of adaptation and evolution in ecological systems see: Edward O. Wilson, *The Diversity of Life* (New York: W. W. Norton, 1992).

5. I introduced "business ecosystems" in my article "Predators and Prey: A New Ecology of Competition," *Harvard Business Review* (May–June 1993).

6. *Steps to an Ecology of the Mind* (New York: Ballantine Books, 1972) is Gregory Bateson's core work on human ecology. Bateson extends his analysis in *Mind and Nature* (New York: Dutton, 1979).

7. For an early Batesonian approach to leadership and strategy see: Karl E. Weick, *The Social Psychology of Organizing*, 2d ed. (New York: Addison-Wesley, 1979).

8. Alfred D. Chandler, *The Visible Hand: The Managerial Revolution in American Business* (Cambridge: Harvard University Press, Belknap Press, 1977).

CHAPTER 2

1. For background on the ecology of Costa Rica see: D. H. Janzen, *Costa Rican Natural History* (Chicago: University of Chicago Press, 1983); and J. C. Kricher, *A Neotropical Companion* (Princeton, N.J.: Princeton University Press, 1989).

2. For a definition of ecology see: M. Abercrombie, et al., *The New Penguin Dictionary of Biology* (London: Penguin Books, 1992).

3. Wilson, *Diversity of Life.*

4. Interviews with executives at Sun Microsystems and AT&T, 1992–1995.

5. Michael J. Piore and Charles F. Sabel's *The Second Industrial Divide* (New York: Basic Books, 1984) provides an excellent analysis of how the global market encourages specialization and network organization. Another work of interest in this area is Fumio Kodama's *Emerging Patterns of Innovation* (Cambridge: Harvard Business School Press, 1995).

6. Over the past several years, a number of analysts of social phenomena have drawn parallels to biological processes and evolution. Some of the more interesting works in this area include: Richard Nelson and Sidney Winter, *An Evolutionary Theory of Economic Change* (Cambridge: Harvard University Press, 1982); W. G. Astley and C. J. Fombrun, "Collective Strategy: Social Ecology of Organizational Environments," *Academy of Management Review* 8:4 (1983); W. G. Astley, "The Two Ecologies: Microevolutionary and Macroevolutionary," *Administrative Science Quarterly* 30 (1985), pp. 224–41; Glenn R. Carroll, *Ecological Models of Organizations* (Cambridge: Ballinger, 1988); Bruce Henderson, "The Origin of Strategy," *Harvard Business Review* (November–December 1989); and Michael Rothschild, *Bionomics* (New York: Henry Holt and Co., 1990).

CHAPTER 3

1. Background on the ecology of leaf-cutting ants: B. Hölldobler and Edward O. Wilson, *The Ants* (Cambridge:

Harvard University Press, 1990); and James K. Wetterer, "Nourishment and evolution in fungus-growing ants and their fungi," in *Nourishment and Evolution in Insect Societies*, J. H. Hunt and C. A. Nalepa, eds. (Boulder, Colo.: Westview Press, 1994), pp. 309–328.

2. For an in-depth study of antagonistic and mutualistic relationships see: H. F. Howe and L. C. Westerley, *Ecological Relationships of Plants and Animals* (New York: Oxford University Press, 1988).

CHAPTER 4

1. Donald A. Schön has had a tremendous influence on my approach to systems thinking and organizational behavior. His work includes: *The Reflective Practioner: How Professionals Think in Action* (New York: Basic Books, 1983); and Donald Schön and Chris Argyris, *Organizational Learning Part II* (New York: Addison Wesley, 1996).

2. For a definition of succession see: M. Abercrombie, et al., *New Penguin Dictionary of Biology.*

CHAPTER 5

1. James Moore and GeoPartners Research, Inc., analysis, 1995.

2. Richard Neustadt and Ernest May, *Thinking in Time: The Uses of History for Decision Makers* (Cambridge: Free Press, 1986).

3. For historical analysis of the automobile industry see: James P. Womack, Daniel T. Jones, and Daniel Roos, *The Machine That Changed the World: The Story of Lean Production* (New York: HarperPerennial, 1991).

4. Professor Charles H. Fine and other members of the faculty of the Massachusetts Institute of Technology International Motor Vehicle Program have done leading work on the automotive industry. See: Fine, "Technology Supply Chains and Business Cyclicality," Sloan School of Management, MIT, Cambridge, Mass., October 1994.

5. Alfred D. Chandler, *Scale and Scope: The Dynamics of Industrial Capitalism* (Cambridge: Harvard University Press, 1990), pp. 53–61.

6. Interviews with the faculty of the MIT International Motor Vehicle Program and the Office of the Study of Automotive Transportation at the University of Michigan, 1994–1995.

7. David Halberstam, *The Reckoning* (New York: Avon, 1987).

8. For an exhaustive study of the Japanese automobile giants Nissan and Toyota see: Michael Cusumano, *The Japanese Automobile Industry: Technology & Management at Nissan & Toyota* (Cambridge: Harvard University Press, Council on East Asian Studies, 1989).

9. For further discussion of Toyota see: Maryann Keller, *Toyota: Collision* (New York: Doubleday, 1993).

10. For a quantitative analysis of automobile manufacturer-supplier relationships see: Sean P. McAlinden and Brett C. Smith, *The Changing Structure of the U.S. Automotive Parts Industry*, Office of the Study of Automotive Transportation, University of Michigan Transportation Research Institute, February 1993.

11. For further discussion of Chrysler see: Gregory K. Scott, "IMVP New Product Development Series: The Chrysler Corporation," International Motor Vehicle Program, MIT, Cambridge, Mass., April 1994.

12. Alexander Trotman, chairman, Ford Motor Company, speech at press conference regarding Ford's World Car, Detroit, Mich., March 1994. Interviews with Ford Motor Company, 1994. Additional background on Trotman's World Car strategy obtained from Trotman briefing to analysts, Boston, Mass., September 8, 1995.

13. For firsthand insight into Toyota's research and development strategy see: Yoshiro Kimbara, senior managing director, Toyota, "Remarks by Mr. Kimbara at the 1991 New York Information Meetings: R&D at Toyota."

14. Amory B. Lovins and L. Hunter Lovins, "Reinventing the Wheels," *The Atlantic Monthly* (January 1995), p. 75.

CHAPTER 6

1. For the best chronicle on the early days of the personal computer business see: Paul Freiberger and Michael Swaine, *Fire in the Valley* (New York: Osborn-McGraw Hill, 1984).
2. Gifford Pinchot III, *Intrapreneuring* (New York: Harper & Row, 1985).
3. Interviews with executives from Starlight Telecommunications 1994–1996.

CHAPTER 7

1. Wilson, *Diversity of Life*.

CHAPTER 8

1. Discussion of Sam Walton's retail strategy covered in depth in: Sam Walton with John Huey, *Sam Walton: Made in America* (New York: Doubleday, 1992).
2. Wal-Mart financials from Wal-Mart Annual Reports 1970–1994 and quarterly reports 1995.
3. Walton with Huey, *Sam Walton*.
4. Pre-IPO Wal-Mart store history from: Sandra Stringer Vance, *Wal-Mart: A History of Sam Walton's Retail Phenomenon* (Old Tappan, N.J.: Twayne Publishing, 1994).
5. Kmart financials from Kmart Annual Reports 1970–1994 and quarterly reports 1995.
6. Ongoing studies on Wal-Mart's buyer-supplier relationships and the retail industry conducted by Kenneth E. Stone, extension economist, Iowa State University.
7. Additional information about the company's supplier relationships and inventory-management strategies gathered via interviews with Wal-Mart executives 1993–1995.
8. Wal-Mart Annual Reports 1980–1994, quarterly reports 1995.
9. Kmart Annual Reports 1970–1994, quarterly reports 1995.
10. Ibid.
11. Wal-Mart Annual Reports 1980–1994, quarterly reports 1995; pre-IPO Wal-Mart store history from: Sandra

Stringer Vance, *Wal-Mart: A History of Sam Walton's Retail Phenomenon.*

12. Randall Mott, chief information officer, Wal-Mart keynote address, CMP/Gartner Group Commercial Parallel Processing Conference, Chicago, Ill., September 1994. Mott discussed the company's strategic investments in information technology. Mott explained that Wal-Mart's sophisticated inventory tracking/distribution system saves the company 2 to 3 percent off the industry average cost of sales.

13. For a case study of Wal-Mart and its strategies for competing on capabilities see: George Stalk, P. Evans, and L. E. Shulman, "Competing on Capabilities: The New Rules on Corporate Strategy," *Harvard Business Review* (May 1992). For further discussion about Wal-Mart see: Professor Pankaj Ghemawat, Harvard Business School case, "Wal-Mart Stores' Discount Operations," May 1989.

CHAPTER 9

1. Professor Leigh Van Valen introduces his Red Queen hypothesis in the essay, "A New Evolutionary Law," *Evolutionary Theory* (University of Chicago) 1:1 (July 1973).

2. Over the past ten years, criticality and embeddedness have received increasing attention among academic economists. See: Michael Katz and Carl Shapiro, "Network Externalities: Competition and Compatibility," *American Economic Review* 75 (1985); Michael Katz and Carl Shapiro, "Technology Adoption in the Presence of Network Externalities," *Journal of Political Economics* 94 (1986); Brian Arthur, *Increasing Returns and Past Dependence in the Economy* (Ann Arbor, Mich.: University of Michigan Press, 1994); Robert Willig, "Contestable Market Theory and Regulatory Reform," chapter in *Telecommunications Deregulation Market Power and Cost Allocation* (Cambridge: Ballinger, 1990).

3. James Turley, senior analyst, Microprocessor Report, contributed to the MIPS/dollar analysis of Intel microprocessors, Mountain View, Calif.

4. Intel's research and development and capital expenditures from: Intel Corporation Annual Reports 1989–1994.

5. Background on Intel strategy and Intel's Architecture Labs (IAL) based in part on interviews with Intel executives, 1994–1996.

6. Data on Intel and AMD's capital expenditures from Intel Annual Reports 1985–1994 and AMD Annual Reports 1985–1994.

CHAPTER 10

1. James Moore, "Convergence and the Development of Business Ecosystems," in *Crossroads on the Information Highway: Convergence Diversity in Communications and Technology* (Queenstown, Md.: Aspen Institute, Institute for Information Studies, 1994), pp. 67–88.

2. U.S. Department of Commerce, Economics and Statistics Administration, Bureau of the Census, *The Statistical Abstract of the United States of 1994* and *The Statistical Abstract of the United States of 1995* (Washington, D.C.: U.S. Government Printing Office); interviews about health care policy with analysts from Institute for the Future, Menlo Park, Calif., 1994; interviews with executives and analysts in the health care industry 1993–1995.

3. Historical background on Americans covered by health insurance can be found in U.S. Department of Commerce, Bureau of the Census, *Historical Statistics of the United States: Colonial Times to 1970*; U.S. Department of Commerce, Economics and Statistics Administration, Bureau of the Census, *The Statistical Abstract of the United States of 1966*; U.S. Department of Commerce, Economics and Statistics Administration, Bureau of the Census, *The Statistical Abstract of the United States of 1995* (Washington, D.C.: U.S. Government Printing Office).

4. For an interesting example of the self-help paradigm see: Dr. Dean Ornish, *Dr. Dean Ornish's Program for Reversal of Heart Disease* (New York: Random House, 1990).

5. James Moore and GeoPartners Research, Inc., analysis, 1995.

6. Interviews with executives of Eli Lilly & Co., PCS Health Systems, and McKesson Corp., 1994–1995; PCS Health Systems company data.

7. Interviews with executives of Eli Lilly & Co., 1994–1995.

8. For a comprehensive historical perspective on the economics of health care see: Alain C. Enthoven, "The History and Principles of Managed Competition," *Health Affairs Supplement* (1993).

9. For further background on the managed care debate see: Stephen M. Shortell, Ellen M. Morrison, and Bernard Friedman, *Strategic Choices for America's Hospitals: Managed Change in Turgent Times* (San Francisco: Jossey-Bass, 1992); D. M. Berwich, "Continuous Improvement as an Ideal in Health Care," *New England Journal of Medicine* 34 (1989), pp. 349–68.

10. For a definitive summary of work on S-curves see: Richard Foster, *Innovation: The Attacker's Advantage* (New York: Summit Books, 1986).

CHAPTER 11

1. Latin verse by Albrecht von Haller adapted from a translation by Howard Nemerov, *The Western Approaches Poems 1973–75* (Chicago: University of Chicago Press, 1975), p. 43.

Index

About the Author

James F. Moore is one of the world's foremost advisers on leadership and strategy. His *Harvard Business Review* article "Predators and Prey: A New Ecology of Competition" won the prestigious McKinsey Award for best article of 1993. He earned his doctorate from Harvard and conducted research at Stanford and Harvard Business School. He is the founder and chairman of GeoPartners Research, Inc., a strategy-consulting and investment firm based in Cambridge, Massachusetts.